精品课程新形态教材

21世纪应用型人才培养系列教材

新时代创新型人才培养精品教材

U0730848

国际贸易单证操作实务

主 审　周莹

主 编　吴轶群　杨楚欣　黄芸

GUOJI MAOYI
DANZHENG CAOZUO
SHIWU

中国海洋大学出版社

CHINA OCEAN UNIVERSITY PRESS

图书在版编目（CIP）数据

国际贸易单证操作实务 / 吴轶群，杨楚欣，黄芸主编 . —青岛：中国海洋大学出版社，2018.7（2024.7 重印）
ISBN 978-7-5670-1893-8

Ⅰ.①国… Ⅱ.①吴… ②杨… ③黄… Ⅲ.①国际贸易—原始凭证—高等学校—教材 Ⅳ.①F740.44

中国版本图书馆 CIP 数据核字（2018）第 174336 号

出版发行	中国海洋大学出版社
社　　址	青岛市香港东路 23 号　　　　　邮政编码　266071
出 版 人	杨立敏
网　　址	http://pub.ouc.edu.cn
电子信箱	58327282@qq.com
订购电话	010-82477073（传真）　　　　　电　　话　010-82477073
责任编辑	由元春
印　　制	涿州汇美亿浓印刷有限公司
版　　次	2018 年 7 月第 1 版
印　　次	2024 年 7 月第 3 次印刷
成品尺寸	185 mm×260 mm
印　　张	15.5
字　　数	382 千
印　　数	13000—18000
定　　价	38.00 元

《国际贸易单证操作实务》
编写委员会

主　审：周　莹

主　编：吴轶群　杨楚欣　黄　芸

副主编：戴莹莹　凌　鸣　马　宇　刘　珊

　　　　汪鼎喜　曹银华　郑婷婷　张雅琼

　　　　彭　虹　魏雪莲　杨　阳　陈瑞清

　　　　吴静斐　郭　琳　肖　频　张丽莉

　　　　王艳萍

前　言

党的二十大报告中指出："加强基础学科、新兴学科、交叉学科建设，加快建设中国特色、世界一流的大学和优势学科。"

随着国际经济形势的回暖和互联网+时代的到来，我国的贸易规模稳居世界前列，因此需要大量创新型的外贸类人才。然而目前该类人才的培养不论是从培养规模还是培养质量上来看，与行业的发展速度都是不匹配的。另外，从教育教学改革的角度来看，课程改革则是人才培养的核心环节。根据业务流程的展开情况，模仿真实的贸易背景来编写专业教材是培养学生职业岗位能力的关键。

外贸单证操作技能是进出口业务进程中的一项核心职业技能，实操性强，必须结合基本的国贸实务知识和商务英语知识，在信息化时代还要求具有一定的计算机操作能力，再加上跨境电商这一新型贸易业态的迅速普及，使得传统的外贸单证教程已远不能适应新形势的发展。为此，《国际贸易单证操作实务》一书以项目化教学为编写理念，以进出口单证业务流程为导向，根据外贸单证员的几大典型岗位能力设置编写项目内容，将业务操作知识仿真化、项目化，将进出口单证操作业务分成十一个工作项目，引入真实的贸易背景和公司单据，并邀请外贸企业和银行国际结算部的业务骨干共同设计，力求打造成体现教育改革理念、校企深度融合、符合岗位需求，同时亦可供行业人士自学的高质量专业用书。

本教材作为国际贸易专业省级示范特色专业的重点建设成果之一，以一名外贸单证员应完成的一笔完整的单证业务为项目主线，特别加入了进口单证项目和跨境电子单证两大项目，突出时效、注重实用，将本书分为信用证审核与修改业务操作、商业单据业务操作、运输单据业务操作、保险单据业务操作、官方单据业务操作、金融单据业务操作、进口单据业务操作及跨境电商电子单据业务等十二个典型工作项目。每个工作项目都从一个典型的工作任务开始，分成项目预期目标、项目实施条件、开篇任务引入及多个子项目等四大板块，不论是典型任务中的业务讲解还是拓展任务中的模拟操作，均采用外贸公司的真实贸易背景、业务单据和图片、数据，充分体现了传统进出口业务及跨境电商业务的真实性。同时，为了尊重商业机密，部分核心信息如交易双方信息、商品参数等内容已做了技术替换，如不慎发生雷同，实属巧合，谨此声明。

由于编写时间紧、任务重，书中内容难免出现疏漏和错误，真诚欢迎各位批评指正，以便再版时予以修正。

编　者

目 录
Contents

项目一
单证员岗位及单证业务介绍

第一节　项目描述与目标

一、项目描述

◆ **开篇业务引入**

2020年5月，国际贸易专业毕业生李望应聘到长沙鹏兴进出口有限公司，成为一名外贸单证员。李望的主要职责是根据外销合同审核信用证及相关资料，并结合具体业务要求完成全套单据的制作，同时负责日常的单证归档及管理工作。

◆ **项目预期目标**

通过对外贸单证员这一岗位的描述以及国际商务单证工作的介绍，使国际贸易、国际商务类相关专业的同学对该岗位的基本职业素养、核心技能以及业务操作准则有基本的了解，为今后单证业务的展开奠定扎实的基础。

表1-1　项目预期目标

目标类型	单证员岗位及单证业务介绍
知识目标	熟悉外贸单证员的岗位要求
	掌握单证工作的基本要求和制单"三原则"
能力目标	能初步理解外贸单证员岗位
	能熟悉并整理基本的单据类型
职业素质目标	细心、谨慎的工作态度
	与国外客户和银行的沟通衔接能力
	风险控制意识

二、项目实施条件

1. 组织学生查看外贸公司各类单据，了解单证员岗位的基本要求
2. 学生能通过真实案例理解单证工作的重要性。
3. 教师必须具备外贸单证员培训师资格或具备外贸企业单证工作经验。

第二节 知识模块

一、外贸单证员岗位职责

（一）具备良好的职业道德

作为单证员应充分认识到单证工作的重要意义，应具有良好的职业道德、严谨的职业操守，责任心强，严格遵守外贸纪律和本企业的规章制度，在工作中能够不断努力学习，更新知识，充实自己。

（二）掌握必要的专业技能

作为单证员应知晓国家对外贸易的有关方针、政策及其最新变化，了解国际贸易发展现状和趋势以及相关国际法规和惯例，掌握进出口业务知识，熟悉进出口合同各项条款内容，特别是与单证相关的内容，能熟练审核信用证并缮制、审核各种单证，了解与国际贸易单证相关的国际标准和国家标准并能熟练使用各种制单专业软件和现代办公设备。

（三）打好扎实的外语基础

目前国际贸易单证工作中使用的语言以英语为主，只有少数国家要求某些进口单证或个别单证中的某些项目必须使用该本国语言，如俄罗斯等中亚国家一般使用俄语单证。所以单证员必须能够熟练使用英语缮制单证、阅读合同、信用证和相关单证。

（四）拥有丰富的实践经验

单证员必须在日常工作中不断丰富和积累经验，善于发现问题、处理问题、总结教训，对合同、信用证、相关国际法规和相关国际惯例要吃准吃透，对合同履行的各个环节要烂熟于心，对单证工作涉及的各个部门要了如指掌，经常研究讨论各种业务案例以增强解决问题的实际能力。

（五）坚持认真的工作态度

单证工作内容烦琐，工作量大，时间性强，所以要求单证员必须具有一丝不苟、踏实细致的工作作风和认真负责、严格细致的工作态度。否则，一单之错，甚至一字之差都可能给合同的履行造成障碍和困难，给企业造成经济损失。

二、外贸单证工作描述

（一）定义

即单据证书，"export documents"，简称单据，是指在出口业务中使用的单据与证书，凭此来处理货物的交付、运输、保险、商检、结汇、报关等工作。

（二）工作流程

审证→制单→审单→制单→交单→归档。

（三）地位

1. 国际贸易结算的基本工具。

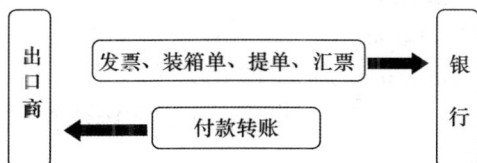

图1-1 出口结汇业务涉及的国际贸易结算工具示意图

国际间的商品买卖，由于买卖双方处在不同的国家、地区，商品与货币不能简单地直接交换，所以就出现了以单证作为交换的手段。尤其是按 CIF 成交，并以 L/C 为支付方式的合同，是典型的"单据买卖合同"，即所谓的"象征性交货"，当事人处理的是单据而不是实际的货物。因此，在国际贸易中，一套完整、正确的单据是买卖双方及时取得物权凭证的保证，单证的任何差错都会给双方带来不同程度的经济损失。

长沙鹏兴进出口贸易公司出口阿根廷布宜诺斯艾利斯货物一批，合同规定 2020 年 10月 10 日交货，因 10 月 10 日前无船去该国，立即与进口商联系延续 20 天。对方表示同意以后，我方在 10 月 25 日装船，30 日持全套单据向议付行进行议付。银行审单后，予以拒付。为什么？

2. 交易双方履约的凭证。

如在托运环节中：

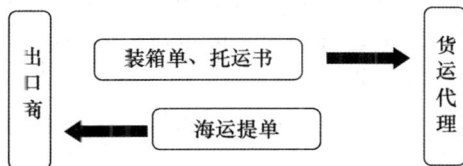

图1-2 货物装运环节涉及的国际贸易结算工具示意图

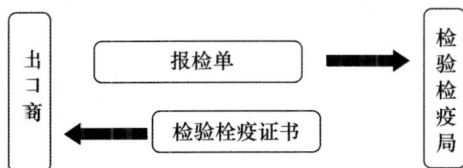

图1-3 货物报检业务涉及的国际贸易结算工具示意图

在外贸业务中，无论是使用信用证，还是托收、汇付等支付方式，按《联合国货物销售公约》的规定，出口商不仅有交付货物的义务，同时还必须移交单据。因此，单证是买卖双方履行合同的必然结果，也是完成外贸交易各环节工作的证明文件。

思考：长沙鹏兴进出口有限公司与日商签订一份出口合同。我方按合同规定的品质、数量、交货时间等条款履行后，持全套单据进行了议付。货到达目的地后，日商发现货物数量短缺，便直接向我方提出索赔。我方对此予以拒绝。为什么？

3. 经营管理的重要环节。

单证工作服务于国际贸易业务的整个过程，它不仅仅是单证的缮制和转递，而且必须妥善地处理各种问题，保证结汇的安全。

例如，单证工作能及时反映货、船、证等业务的管理现状，工作责任性强可及时解决、杜绝差错事故的发生，避免带来不必要的经济损失。

同时，单证工作能做到准确、完整、快速，不仅能保证收汇安全，又能加快收汇，加速资金周转，进而树立企业自身信誉。

思考：长沙鹏兴进出口有限公司与澳大利亚客商签订一份销售合同，目的港为悉尼。由于单证员疏忽，制单时误填为墨尔本，以至进口货物未能到达该地。你设想一下，会给该公司会带来什么后果？

三、国际商务单据的种类

外贸业务中涉及的单据种类繁多，且有不同的分类，主要有以下几种：

（一）跟单信用证统一规则（UCP600）对国际商务单据的分类

（1）运输单据：海运提单、非转让海运单、租船合约提单、多式联运单据、航空运单、公路铁路和内陆水运单据、快递收据、邮政收据或邮寄证明。

（2）保险单据：保险单、保险凭证、联合声明、预约保单等。

（3）商业发票及其他单据：装箱单、重量单、产地证明书、普惠制单据、检验检疫证书、受益人声明或受益人证明等。

（二）托收统一规则（URC522）对国际商务单据的分类

金融单据：汇票、本票、支票或其他用于取得付款资金的类似凭证。

商业单据：基本单据、附属单据。

其中，商业单据主要有商业发票、海运提单和保险单；附属单据主要有领事发票、海关发票、原产地证明等官方单证和装箱单、商检证书、受益人证明、装运通知、船公司证明等说明单据。

（三）UN/EDIFACT 标准对国际商务单证的分类：

生产单证

订购单证

销售单证

银行单证

保险单证

货运代理服务单证

运输单证

出口单证

进口和转口单证

四、制单的基本原则——"三一致，四要求"

（1）三一致：单证一致，单单一致，单货一致。

（2）四要求：正确、完整、及时、整洁。

第三节 任务拓展模块

项目任务：参观外贸单证员岗位，了解该岗位要求及基本的单证工作原则。

项目二
信用证的审核与修改

第一节　项目描述与目标

一、项目描述

◆开篇业务引入

2019 年 7 月 5 日，长沙鹏兴进出口有限公司与加拿大的 ELBY 实业有限公司签订了一份马克杯出口的销售合同，根据合同要求，双方以跟单信用证的方式来完成货款的收付。该业务具体由单证员李望负责，并按照合同条款认真审核操作信用证业务。

◆项目预期目标

通过对该出口销售合同条款的认真解读，结合出口方银行开来的信用证通知书内容，以及 UCP600 等国际惯例，使同学们了解信用证的基本业务操作流程，熟悉跟单信用证的基本结构和重要条款，根据受益人的立场掌握信用证条款的审核与修改。

在项目实施过程中，通过信用证审核与修改任务的分解，在分工与合作中逐渐培养翻译、审核、风险控制等国际商务单证基本职业能力，亦培养独立操作信用证业务和与国外客户或进出口双方银行有效沟通的能力。

表 2-1　项目预期目标

目标类型	信用证的审核与修改
知识目标	熟悉信用证业务操作流程
	理解跟单信用证的基本结构
	掌握信用证条款的审核与翻译
能力目标	能根据合同审核信用证条款
	能根据己方需要对信用证提出适当的修改意见
职业素质目标	独立业务操作能力
	与国外客户和银行的沟通衔接能力
	风险控制意识

二、项目实施条件

1. 组织学生参观中国银行或其他银行的国际结算部，参观外贸公司并收集业务资料。

2. 学生能够在网上同虚拟的国外客户或银行交流业务信息。

3. 学生可以在课程资源库中查阅信用证业务交易明细。

4. 指导教师掌握扎实的国际贸易政策，具备扎实的外贸业务操作能力。

第二节　知识模块

一、定义

信用证：（Letter of Credit，L/C）是银行开立的有条件承诺付款的书面文件。即：（开证行）根据买方（开证申请人）的请求，或自己主动向卖方（受益人）开立的一定金额的，并在一定期限内凭受益人提交符合信用证内所规定的单证，承诺付款的书面文件。

二、特点

1. 信用证业务是一种银行信用。

信用证一经开出，开证行承担第一性付款责任。只要出口商提交了信用证规定的单据，开证行就必须付款。

2. 信用证是独立于贸易合同之外的自足文件。

信用证一经开出就成为独立性的文件，所有当事人，特别是有关银行，只受信用证条款的约束，不受合同条款的约束。

3. 信用证业务处理的是单据而不是货物。

凭相符单据付款，"认单不认货"。想要安全、迅速结汇，就必须使单据在表面上与信用证条款规定的一致，同时各种单据之间也要一致，即"单证一致、单单一致"。

三、形式

1. 信开本（To open by airmail）：开证银行采用印就的信函格式的信用证，开证后以航空邮寄送通知行。

2. 电开本（To open by cable）：开证银行使用电传、传真、SWIFT 等各种电讯方法将信用证条款传达给通知行。

四、基本当事人及主要内容

（一）信用证的主要当事人

1. 开证申请人（applicant），又称开证人（opener），指向银行申请开立信用证的人。一般为进出口业务的买方。有时也可能由银行自己主动开证，即为其自身开证，此时则没有开证申请人。

2. 开证银行（opening bank，issuing bank），也称开证行，指接受开证人委托或为其自身开立信用证的银行，一般为进口地银行。开证银行开出信用证后，即承担保证付款的责任。

3. 受益人（beneficiary），指信用证上所指定的有权使用该证的人，一般为进出口业务的卖方。受益人通常也是信用证的收件人（addressee），他有按信用证规定签发汇票向指定的付款银行索取价款的权利，但也在法律上以汇票出票人的地位对其后的持票人负有担保该汇票必获承兑或付款的责任。

4. 通知行（advising bank，notifying bank），指接受开证行的委托，将信用证通知受益人的银行。一般为出口地银行，且通常是开证行的代理行或分行。通知行只证明信用证的真实性，无其他义务。

5. 议付行（negotiating bank），又称押汇银行，是指愿意买入或贴现受益人交来跟单汇票的银行。议付银行可以是由开证银行在信用证条款中指定的银行，也可以是非指定的银行。（议付行的付款有追索权）

6. 付款银行（paying bank，drawee bank），指信用证上指定的付款银行。一般为开证行，但有时也可能是受开证行委托代为付款的另一家银行。付款银行通常是汇票的受票人，故也称受票行（drawee bank）。（付款行如同一般的汇票受票人，一经付款，即使事后发现有误，对受款人也无追索权）

7. 偿付行（reimbursing bank），也称清算银行（clearing bank），是指受开证行的指示或授权，对有关代付行或议付行的索偿予以照付的银行。（此偿付不为终局性付款，因为偿付行并不审查单据、不负单证不符之责。开证行在见单后发现单证不符时，可直接向寄单的议付行、代付行追回已付讫的款项）

8. 保兑行（confirming bank），是指应开证行请求在信用证上加具保兑的银行，它具有与开证行相同的责任和地位。（付款或议付后无追索权）

9. 承兑行（accepting bank），对承兑信用证项下的单据，经审核确认与信用证规定相符时，在汇票正面签字承诺到期付款的银行。

10. 转让行（transferring bank），是应受益人的委托，将可转让信用证转让给信用证的受让人即第二受益人的银行。（转让行一般为通知行，也可是议付行、付款行或保兑行）

11. 受让人（transferee），也称第二受益人（second beneficiary），在可转让信用证条件下，受益人有权将信用证总金额的全部或一部分转让另一出口人使用，该出口人即为受让人。

（二）信用证的主要内容

1. 自身说明：如信用证的编号（letter of credit No.）、开证日期、到期日（This Credit is valid for payment/negotiation in China until 31st July 2003）、到期地点、交单期限等。

2. 兑付方式：即期付款（sight payment）、远期付款（after sight payment）、延期付款（deferred payment）、承兑（acceptance）、议付（negotiation）。

3. 信用证的种类：是否可撤销（可撤销 revocable，不可撤销 irrevocable）、是否经另一家银行保兑（保兑 confirmed，非保兑 unconfirmed）、可否转让（可转让 transferable，不可转让 untransferable）。

4. 信用证的当事人：开证人（applicant）、开证行（opening bank）、受益人（beneficiary）、通知行（advising bank，notifying bank）、付款行（paying bank，drawee bank）、偿付行（reimbursing bank）、承兑行（accepting bank）、议付行（negotiating bank）。

5. 汇票条款：包括汇票的种类、出票人、受票人、付款期限、出票条款及付款日期等。凡不需汇票的信用证无此内容。

6. 货物条款：包括货物的名称、规格、数量、包装、价格。

7. 支付货币和信用证金额：币别、总额。

8. 装运与保险条款：运输路线、运输方式、投保险种等。

9. 单据条款：该笔业务所需的单据种类、份数及制作要求。

10. 附属条款。

五、SWIFT 信用证格式简介

目前国际上使用最多的信用证为 SWIFT 格式的信用证，该类信用证的特点是格式简明统一，覆盖全球绝大多数银行，且文件传输速度快，费用较为低廉。其中 MT700 和 MT701 为信用证的开证格式，MT707 为信用证的改证格式，具体格式简介如下：

【MT700 和 MT701 开证格式】

代码 Tag	栏位名称（Field Name）
27	Sequence of Total 电文页次
20	Documentary Credit Number 信用证编号
40E	Applicable Rule 适用条文
45B	Description of Goods and/or Service 货物和/或服务的描述
46B	Documents Required 所需单据
47B	Additional Conditions 附加条款
50	Applicant 申请人
59	Beneficiary 受益人
32B	Currency Code，Amount 币种、金额
39A	Percentage Credit Amount 信用证金额上下浮动允许的最大范围
39B	Maximum Credit Amount 最高信用证金额
39C	Additional Amount Covered 附加金额
41A	Available with...by... 指定的有关银行及信用证兑付的方式
42C	Drafts at... 汇票付款日期
42A	Drawee 汇票付款人
42M	Mixed Payment Details 混合付款条款
42P	Deferred Payment Details 延期付款条款
43P	Partial Shipment 分批装运
43T	Transshipment 转运
44A	Loading on Board / Dispatch / Taking in Charge at / from... 装船、发运和接受监管地点
44B	For Transportation to... 货物发运的最终目的港（地）
44C	Latest Date of Shipment 最迟装船日
44D	Shipment Period 装期
45A	Description of Goods and / or Services 货物与/或服务描述

代码 Tag	栏位名称 (Field Name)
46A	Documents Required 所需单据
47A	Additional Conditions 附加条款
71B	Charges 费用情况
48	Period for Presentation 交单期限
49	Confirmation Instruction 保兑指示
53A	Reimbursement Bank 偿付银行
78	Instructions to the Paying / Accepting / Negotiating Bank 对付款/承兑/议付银行的指示
57A	Advising through 通知银行
72	Sender to Receiver Information 银行间的备注

（一）跟单信用证开证格式（MT700）简介

必选　20 DOCUMENTARY CREDIT NUMBER（信用证号码）

可选　23 REFERENCE TO PREADVICE（预先 通知 号码）

　　如果信用证是采取预先通知的方式，该项目内应该填入"PREADV/"，再加上预先通知的编号或日期。

必选　27 SEQUENCE OF TOTAL（电文页次）

可选　31C DATE OF ISSUE（开证日期）

　　如果这项没有填，则开证日期为电文的发送日期。

必选　31D DATE AND PLACE OF EXPIRY（信用证有效期和有效地点）

　　该日期为最后交单的日期。

必选　32B CURRENCY CODE，AMOUNT（信用证结算的货币和金额）

可选　39A PERCENTAGE CREDIT AMOUNT TOLERANCE（信用证金额上下浮动允许的最大范围）

　　该项目的表示方法较特殊，数值表示百分比的数值，如：5/5，表示上下浮动最多5%。

可选　39B MAXIMUM CREDIT AMOUNT（信用证最大限制金额）

　　注意：39B与39A不能同时出现。

可选　39C ADDITIONAL AMOUNTS COVERED（额外金额）

　　表示信用证所涉及的保险费、利息、运费等金额。

必选　40A FORM OF DOCUMENTARY CREDIT（跟单信用证形式）

　　跟单信用证有五种形式：

　　（1）IRREVOCABLE（不可撤销跟单信用证）

　　（2）IRREVOCABLE TRANSFERABLE（不可撤销可转让跟单信用证）

　　（3）REVOCABLE TRANSFERABLE（可撤销可转让跟单信用证）

　　（4）IRREVOCABLE STANDBY（不可撤销备用信用证）

（5）REVOCABLE STANDBY（可撤销备用信用证）

必选　41a AVAILABLE WITH... BY...（指定的有关银行及信用证兑付的方式）

（1）指定银行作为付款、承兑、议付。

（2）兑付的方式有 5 种：BY PAYMENT（即期付款）；BY ACCEPTANCE（远期承兑）；BY NEGOTIATION（议付）；BY DEF PAYMENT（迟期付款）；BY MIXED PAYMENT（混合付款）。

（3）如果是自由议付信用证，对该信用证的议付地点不做限制，该项目代号为：41D，内容为：ANY BANK IN。

可选　42a DRAWEE（汇票付款人）

必须与 42C 同时出现。

可选　42C DRAFTS AT.（汇票付款日期）

必须与 42a 同时出现。

可选　42M MIXED PAYMENT DETAILS（混合付款条款）

可选　42P DEFERRED PAYMENT DETAILS（迟期付款条款）

可选　43P PARTIAL SHIPMENTS（分装条款）

表示该信用证的货物是否可以分批装运。

可选　43T TRANSSHIPMENT（转运条款）

表示该信用证是直接到达，还是通过转运到达。

可选　44A LOADING ON BOARD/DISPATCH/TAKING IN CHARGE AT/FORM（装船、发运和接收监管的地点）

可选　44B FOR TRANSPORTATION TO...（货物发运的最终地）

可选　44C LATEST DATE OF SHIPMENT（最后装船期）

装船的最迟的日期。44C 与 44D 不能同时出现。

可选　44D SHIPMENT PERIOD（船期）

44C 与 44D 不能同时出现。

可选　45A DES CRIPTION OF GOODS AND/OR SERVICES（货物描述）

货物的情况、价格条款。

可选　46A DOCUMENTS REQUIRED（单据要求）

各种单据的要求。

可选　47A ADDITIONAL CONDITIONS（特别条款）

可选　48 PERIOD FOR PRESENTATION（交单期限）

表明开立运输单据后多少天内交单。

必选　49 CONFIRMATION INSTRUCTIONS（保兑指示）

其中，CONFIRM：要求保兑行保兑该信用证。

MAY ADD：收报行可以对该信用证加具保兑。

WITHOUT：不要求收报行保兑该信用证。

必选　50 APPLICANT（信用证开证申请人）

一般为进口商。

可选　51a APPLICANT BANK（信用证开证的银行）

可选　53A REIMBURSEMENT BANK（偿付行）

可选　57a "ADVISE THROUGH" BANK（通知行）

必选　59 BENEFICIARY（信用证的受益人）

　　　一般为出口商。

可选　71B CHARGES（费用情况）

　　　表明费用是否由受益人（出口商）出，如果没有这一条，表示除了议付费、转让费 以外，其他各种费用由开出信用证的申请人（进口商）出。

可选　72 SENDER TO RECEIVER INFORMATION（附言）

可选　78 INSTRUCTION TO THE PAYING/ACCEPTING/NEGOTIATING BANK（给付款行、承兑行、议付行的指示）

【MT707 信用证修改格式】

代码 Tag	栏位名称（Field Name）
20	Sender's Reference 送讯银行的编号
21	Receiver's Reference 受讯银行的编号
23	Issuing Bank's Reference 开证银行的编号
52a	Issuing Bank 开证银行
31c	Date of Issue 开证日期
30	Date of Amendment 修改日期
26E	Number of Amendment 修改序号
59	Beneficiary（before this amendment）受益人（修改以前的）
31E	New Date of Expiry 新的到期日
32B	Increase of Documentary Credit Amount 信用证金额的增加
33B	Decrease of Documentary Credit Amount 信用证金额的减少
34B	New Documentary Credit Amount After 修改后新的信用证金额
39A	Percentage Credit Amount Tolerance 信用证金额上下浮动允许的最大范围
39B	Maximum Credit Amount 最高信用证金额
39C	Additional Amount Covered 附加金额
44A	Loading on Board / Dispatch / Taking in Charge at / from... 装船、发运和接受监管地点
44B	For Transportation to...货物发运的最终目的港（地）
44C	Latest Date of Shipment 最迟装船日
44D	Shipment Period 装期
79	Narrative 说明
72	Sender to Receiver Information 银行间备注

（二）信用证修改（MT707）格式简介

必选　20 SENDER'S REFERENCE（信用证号码）

必选　21 RECEIVER'S REFERENCE（收报行编号）

　　　发电文的银行不知道收报行的编号，填写"NONREF"。

可选　23 ISSUING BANK'S REFERENCE（开证行的号码）

可选　26E NUMBER OF AMENDMENT（修改次数）

　　　该信用证修改的次数，要求按顺序排列。

可选　30 DATE OF AMENDMENT（修改日期）

　　　如果信用证修改没填这项，修改日期就是发报日期。

可选　31C DATE OF ISSUE（开证日期）

　　　如果这项没有填，则开证日期为电文的发送日期。

可选　31E NEW DATE OF EXPIRY（信用证新的有效期）

　　　信用证修改的有效期。

可选　32B INCREASE OF DOCUMENTARY CREDIT AMOUNT（信用证金额的增加）

可选　33B DECREASE OF DOCUMENTARY CREDIT AMOUNT（信用证金额的减少）

可选　34B NEW DOCUMENTARY CREDIT AMOUNT AFTER AMENDMENT（信用证修改后的金额）

可选　39A PERCENTAGE CREDIT AMOUNT TOLERANCE（信用证金额上下浮动允许的最大范围的修改）

　　　该项目的表示方法较为特殊，数值表示百分比的数值，如：5/5，表示上下浮动最大为5%。39B与39A不能同时出现。

可选　39B MAXIMUM CREDIT AMOUNT（信用证最大限制金额的修改）

　　　39B与39A不能同时出现。

可选　39C ADDITIONAL AMOUNTS COVERED（额外金额的修改）

　　　表示信用证所涉及的保险费、利息、运费等金额的修改。

可选　44A LOADING ON BOARD/DISPATCH/TAKING IN CHARGE AT/FORM（装船、发运和接收监管的地点的修改）

可选　44B FOR TRANSPORTATION TO...（货物发运的最终地的修改）

可选　44C LATEST DATE OF SHIPMENT（最后装船期的修改）

　　　修改装船的最迟的日期。44C与44D不能同时出现。

可选　44D SHIPMENT PERIOD（装船期的修改）

　　　44C与44D不能同时出现。

可选　52a APPLICANT BANK（信用证开证的银行）

必选　59 BENEFICIARY（BEFORE THIS AMENDMENT）（信用证的受益人）

　　　该项目为原信用证的受益人，如果要修改信用证的受益人，则需要在79 NARRATIVE 修改详述）中写明。

可选　72 SENDER TO RECEIVER INFORMATION（附言）

　　　/BENCON/：要求收报行通知发报行受益人是否接受该信用证的修改。/PHON-

BEN/：请电话通知受益人（列出受益人的电话号码）。/TELEBEN/：用快捷有效的电讯方式通知受益人。

可选　79 NARRATIVE（修改详述）

详细的修改内容。

六、信用证审核

受益人主要审核信用证的条款，信用证的真实性以及开证行的资信状况则由通知行来审核。审核内容如下：

1. 信用证通知书。

在审证之前，要仔细阅读信用证通知书的内容。若认为开证行资信状况差、信用等级低，可要求开证申请人找一家可靠的银行加以保兑，使该信用证成为保兑信用证（Confirmed L/C），获得开证行和保兑行的双重第一性付款保证；若收到的为预先通知信用证时，则需要谨慎处理，因为预先通知信用证在法律上是无效的。

2. 审证依据。

（1）外贸合同。信用证是依据外贸合同开立的，其条款应与外贸合同的条款相符。

（2）UCP600。审核信用证时，应遵循 UCP600 的规定来确定是否可以接受信用证的某些条款。

（3）业务实际情况。对于合同中未规定或无法根据 UCP600 来做出判断的信用证条款，应根据业务实际情况来审核。

3. 审证要点。

（1）开证申请人和受益人的名称。开证申请人和受益人的名称是出口单证中必不可少的，若信用证开错应及时修改，以免影响安全收汇。

（2）信用证金额。信用证金额必须与外贸合同相符。若外贸合同订有商品数量的"溢短装"条款，信用证金额也应规定相应的机动幅度。若所开的信用证金额已扣除佣金，则不能在信用证上再出现"议付行内扣佣金"词句。

（3）货物描述。信用证中货物的名称、货号、规格、包装等内容是否与外贸合同完全一致。

（4）信用证有效期。按 UCP600 第 6 条 d 款的规定，信用证必须规定一个交单的有效期。

（5）交单期。信用证还应规定一个运输单据出单日期后必须提交符合信用证条款的单据的特定期限，即"交单期"。

（6）装运期。卖方将货物装上运往目的地（港）的运输工具或交付给承运人的日期。若信用证中未规定装运期，则最迟装运期与信用证有效期为同一天，即通常所称的"双到期"。

（7）运输条款。信用证运输条款中的装运港（地）和目的港（地）应与外贸合同相符，交货地点也必须与价格条款相一致。

若来证指定运输方式、运输工具或运输路线以及要求承运人出具船龄或船籍证明，应及时与承运人联系。

（8）保险条款。若来证要求的投保险别或投保金额超出了外贸合同的规定，除非信用证上表明由此而产生的超保费用由开证申请人承担并允许在信用证项下支取，否则应予修改。若保险加成过高，还需征得保险公司同意，否则应予修改。

（9）单据条款。要仔细审核信用证中的单据条款，特别要注意一些软条款，如信用证暂不生效条款、商业发票经买方复签生效、1/3 正本提单直接寄给买方等。

（10）银行费用条款。一般情况下，出口方银行费用由受益人承担，进口方银行的费用由开证申请人承担。关于银行费用承担，进出口双方应在谈判时加以明确。

七、信用证的修改

（一）修改原则

在既不影响开证申请人正常利益又维护受益人自己的合法利益的前提下，有如下 5 种常见的处理原则：

（1）对我方有利又不影响对方利益的问题条款，一般不改。

（2）对我方有利但会严重影响对方利益的问题条款，一定要改。

（3）对我方不利但在不增加或基本不增加成本的情况下可以完成的问题条款，可以不改。

（4）对我方不利又要在增加较大成本的情况下可以完成的问题条款，若对方愿意承担成本，则不改；否则，要改。

（5）对我方不利若不改会严重影响安全收汇的问题条款，则坚决要改。

（二）修改流程

（1）受益人给开证申请人发改证函，协商改证事宜。

（2）协商一致后，开证申请人填写改证申请书，向开证行提出改证申请。

（3）开证行同意后，向信用证的原通知行发信用证修改，即 MT707。

（4）原通知行给受益人信用证修改通知和信用证修改，进行信用证修改通知。

（三）UCP600 中对信用证修改的规定

（1）UCP600 第 9 条 d 款规定，经由通知行或第二通知行通知信用证的银行必须经由同一通知行通知信用证的修改。

（2）UCP600 第 10 条 b 款规定，开证行发出修改之时起，即不可撤销地受其约束。保兑行可将其保兑扩展至修改，并自通知该修改之时，即不可撤销地受其约束。但是，保兑行可以选择将修改通知受益人而不对其加具保兑。若然如此，其必须毫不延误地将此告知开证行，并在其给受益人的通知中告知受益人。

（3）UCP600 第 10 条 c 款规定，在受益人告知通知修改的银行其接受该修改之前，原信用证（或含有先前被接受的修改的信用证）的条款对受益人仍然有效。受益人应提供接受或拒绝修改的通知。如果受益人未能给予通知，当交单与信用证以及尚未表示接受的修改的要求一致时，即视为受益人已做出接受修改的通知，并且从此时起，该信用证被修改。

（4）UCP600 第 10 条 e 款规定，对同一修改的内容不允许部分接受，部分接受将被视为拒绝修改的通知。

（5）UCP600 第 10 条 f 款规定，修改中关于"除非受益人在某一时间内拒绝修改否则修改生效"的规定应被不予理会。

第三节　任务模块

2019 年 8 月 23 日，根据长沙鹏兴进出口有限公司与加拿大 EMS 实业有限公司签订的马克杯出口合同，对方向 A 银行申请开立了一份不可撤销跟单信用证，并由中国银行湖南省分行通知鹏兴公司。单证员李望在该项目的任务是认真对照合同审核信用证，并提出修改意见。合同及信用证内容如下：

CONTRACT

Contract No.：CB121039　　　　　　　　　　　　　　Date：JUL 5，2019

THE SELLER：PENGXING IMP&EXP COMPANY

　　　　　　　　LILING PENGXING CERAMIC FACTORY

　　　　　　　　WUSHI JIASHU LILING HUNAN，CHINA

　　　　　　　　TEL：86 – 731 – 23384199　　FAX：86 – 731 – 23384298

THE BUYER：ELBY GIFTS INC.

　　　　　　　　879 INDUSTRIEL BOIS DES FILION

　　　　　　　　QUEBEC，J6Z 4T3，CANADA

　　　　　　　　TEL：514 – 420 – 0282　　FAX：514 – 420 – 0322

This Contract is made by and between the Buyer and Seller，whereby the Buyer agrees to buy and the Seller agrees to sell the under mentioned goods on the terms and conditions stated below：

Description of Goods，Specifications，	Quantity (set)	Unit Price (U. S. D/set)	Amount (U. S. D)
Ceramic Cups and Bowls		C. I. F Prince Rupert	
V23 – 234	912	4. 05	3 693. 60
V23 – 234F	912	4. 05	3 693. 60
V23 – 235	1 520	2. 40	3 648. 00
V23 – 236	1 512	2. 10	3 175. 20
V23 – 237	1 488	1. 95	2 901. 60
V23 – 2348	1 520	2. 04	3 100. 80
36 – 062	1 528	2. 30	3 514. 40
36 – 063	1 496	2. 12	3 171. 52
As per the P/I No.：CCB23 – 36			
Total	10 888		26 898. 72

SAY TOTAL：SAY U. S DOLLARS TWENTY SIX THOUSAND EIGHT HUNDRED AND

NINETY EIGHT AND CENTS SEVENTY TWO（USD26898.72）ONLY.

PACKING：4 sets packed in a carton（V23－234/V23－234F），8 sets packed in a carton for others.

TRANSPORT DETAILS：the goods should be shipped on or before：5th Sep, 2019, from Shenzhen, China to Prince Rupert Canada, transshipment and partial shipment are all allowed.

INSURANCE：To be effected by the Seller for 110% of invoice value covering all risks and S. R. C. C as per C. I. C of PICC dated 01/01/1981.

PAYMENT：By irrevocable documentary letter of credit at sight, reaching the seller not later than Aug 5, 2019 and remain valid for negotiation in China for 15 days after shipment.

DOCUMENTS：

+ Signed commercial invoice one original and three copies.
+ Full set of clean on board ocean Bill of Lading made to order of issuing bank.
+ Packing List one original and two copies.
+ Insurance policy endorsed in blank.
+ GSP Form A certified bygovernment authority.

INSPECTION：Quality/Quantity/Weight Discrepancy and Claim：In case the quality and／or quantity/weight are found by the Buyer not to conform with the contract after arrival of the goods at the final destination, the Buyer may lodge a claim against the seller supported by a survey report issued by an inspection organization agreed upon by both parties with the exception of those claims for which the insurance company and／or the shipping company are to be held responsible. Claim for quality discrepancy should be filed by the Buyer within 60 days after arrival of the goods at the final destination while for quantity／weight discrepancy claim should be filed by the Buyer within 30 days after arrival of the goods at the final destination.

FORCE MAJEURE：The Seller shall not be held responsible for failure or delay in delivery of the entire or portion of the goods under this contract in consequence of any Force Major incidents.

ARBITRATION：All disputes in connection with this Contract or the execution thereof shall be settled through friendly negotiations. If no settlement can be reached, the case shall then be submitted to the Foreign Trade Arbitration Commission of the China Council for the Promotion of International Trade, Beijing, for settlement by arbitration in accordance with the Commission's Provisional Rules of Procedure. The award rendered by the Commission shall be final and binding on both parties. The arbitration expenses shall be borne by the losing party unless otherwise award by the arbitration organization.

Signed by：

THE SELLER：

PENGXING IMP&EXP COMPANY

LILING PENGXING CERAMIC FACTORY

李望

THE BUYER：

ELBY GIFTS INC.

Camp Wolf

以下是该业务信用证：

SEQUENCE OF TOTAL	27：	1/1
FORM OF DC	40A：	IRREVOCABLE
DC NO	20：	DC HMN214479
DATE OF ISSUE	31C：	190705
APPLICABLE RULES	40E：	UCP LATEST VERSION
EXPIRY DATE AND PLACE	31D：	190810 IN CANADA
APPLICANT	50：	ELBY GIFTS INC. 876 INDUSTRIEL BOLS DES FITION,QUEBEC,J6Z 4T3,CANADA
BENEFICIARY	59：	PENGXING IMPORT & EXPORT CO. LTD. LILING PENGXING CERAMIC FACTORY WUSHI JIASHU LILING HUNAN，CHINA
AMOUNT	32B：	USD27010,40
PCT CR AMT TOLERANCE	39A：	10/10
AVAILABLE WITH/BY	41D：	ANY BANK IN CANADA BY NEGOTIATION
DRAFTS AT	42C：	AFTER SIGHT OF 15 DAYS
DRAWEE	42A：	ISSUING BANK
PARTIAL SHIPMENTS	43P：	NOT ALLOWED
TRANSHIPMENT	43T：	ALLOWED
PORTOF LOADING	44E：	SHANGHAI, CHINA
PORT OF DISCHARGE	44F：	PRINCE RUPERT, BC
LATEST DATE OF SHIPMENT	44D：	190901
DESCRIPTION OFGOODS OR SERVICES	45A：	CERAMIC CUP AND BOWL AS PER S/C NO.：CB121089（CIF PRINCE RUPERT，BC）删 ALL PACKED IN CARTONS AND 4 SETS IN ACARTON.
DOCUMENTS REQUIRED	46A：	+ ORIGINAL SIGNED COMMERCIAL INVOICE PLUS THREE COPIES. + FULL SET OF CLEAN MULTIMODAL TRANSPORT DOCUMENT PLUS 2 N/N COPIES, MADE TO THE ORDER OF BANK OF CHINA, HUNAN

BRANCH SHOWING ON BOARD NOTATION, MARKED FREIGHT COLLECT, AND NOTIFY APPLICANT (STATING FULL NAME AND ADDRESS).

+ INSURANCE POLICY OR CERTIFICATEBLANK INDORSED, FOR THE INVOICE VALUE PLUS 20% COVERING ALL RISKS AND W. P. A. AND S. R. CC. FROM WAREHOUSE TO WAREHOUSE.

+ PACKING LIST IN ONE ORIGINAL AND TWO COPIES.

+ GSP CERTIFICATE OF ORIGIN FORM A, IN ONE ORIGINAL PLUS 2 COPIES, INDICATING COUNTRY OF ORIGIN, COUNTERCHOPPED BY GOVERNMENT OR EXPORTER'S STATMENT OF ORIGIN

+ SHIPPING NOTE INCLUDING SHIPPING MARKS, CTN NO., B/L NO., QUANTITY, VESSEL'S NAME, VOYAGE NO., SHOULD BE SENT TO THE ISSUING BANK ON THE DATE OF SHIPMENT.

ADDITIONAL CONDITIONS	47A:	+ BENEFICIARY'S DETAILS:

CTC: MILLER LEE

TEL: 86 − 731 − 2338 − 4199

FAX: 86 − 731 − 2338 − 4298

FOLLOWING CHARGES ARE FOR BENEFICIARY'S ACCOUNT:

1) REIMBURSEMENT / REMITTANCE
   CHARGES

2) DISCREPANCY FEE OF USD/CAD/EUR100 PLUS ALL RELEVANT CABLE CHARGES WILL BE DEDUCTED FROM EACH PRESENTATION OF DISCREPANT

DOCUMENTS UNDER THIS DC.

CHARGES	71B:	ALL BANKING CHARGES ARE FOR ACCOUNT OF BENEFICIARY/EXPORTER
PERIOD OF PRESENTATION	48:	WITHIN 5 DAYS AFTER THE DATE OF SHIPMENT BUT WITHIN THE VALIDITY OF THE CREDIT

CONFIRMATION INSTRUCTIONS   49：   WITHOUT

INFO TO PRESENTING BK   78：   + UPON RECEIPT OF DOCUMENTS CONFORMING TO THE TERMS OF THIS CREDIT WE UNDERTAKE TO REIMBURSE YOU IN THE CURRENCY OF THIS CREDIT IN ACCORDANCE WITH YOUR INSTRUCTIONS, LESS CABLE CHARGES,

+ FORWARD DOCUMENTS IN ONE LOT BY COURIER AT BENEFICIARY'S EXPENSES TO HSBC BANK CANADA, TRADE AND SUPPLY CHAIN, 5100 SHERBROOKE STREET EAST, SUITE 190, MONTREAL, QUEBEC, H1V 3R9 CANADA.

+ THE AMOUNT OF EACH DRAWING MUST BE ENDORSED ON THE REVERSE OF THIS DC BY THE NEGOTIATING/PRESENTING BANK.

经审核，该信用证有以下条款需要修改：

1. 31C 开证日期不符，根据合同，开证日期应为 190720 之前。

2. 31D 有效期不符，根据合同，有效期应为 190919。

3. 31D 到期地点不符，根据合同，到期地点应在中国。

4. 59 受益人名称不符，受益人名称应为 LILING PENGXING CERAMIC FACTORY。

5. 42C 汇票付款期限不符，汇票付款期限应为 AT SIGHT。

6. 41D 信用证议付行应在中国的任意银行。

7. 43P 应为允许分批装运。

8. 44E 装运港不符，装运港应为 SHENZHEN。

9. 44C 最迟装运期不符，最迟装运期应为 190905。

10. 45A 品名不符，品名应为 CERAMIC CUPS AND BOWLS。

11. 45A 合同号有误，应为 CB121039。

12. 45A 包装条款有误，应为 4 SETS PACKED IN A CARTON（V 23 – 234/V23 – 234F），8 SETS PACKED IN A CARTON FOR OTHERS。

13. 46A 提单应做成开证行抬头，运费项目错误，应注明 FREIGHT PREPAID。

14. 46A 保险单的保险金额错误，应为发票金额的 10%。

15. 46A 保险险别应为 ALL RISKS AND S. R. C. C。

16. 71B 所有费用由受益人负担不合理，应改为进口国以为的银行费用由受益人承担。

17. 48 交单期错误，应为装运日期后 15 天。

18. 50 申请人有误，应为 ELBY GIFTS INC. 879 INDUSTR, BOIS DES FILION, QUEBEC, J6Z 4T3, CANADA。

第四节　任务拓展模块

能力实训项目1：信用证审核及修改业务操作

根据上海淼睿进出口有限公司第 C－11027 号信用证的要求，2019 年 8 月 31 日，单证员彭婷根据合同开始审核信用证。

1. 合同。

SALESCONTRACT

Contract No.：SSW0803

Date：AUG 15，2019

THE SELLER：JIANGSU I－TOUCH BUSINESS SERVICE LTD，

ROOM 117，JIANGSU EDIFICE

ZHANGJIAGANG FREE TRADE ZONE，

JIANGSU，CHINA　TEL：86－512－56363783

THE BUYER：M/S．MEMORY STEEL CORPORATION

73/A，LAL MOHAN SHAHA STREET

（DHOLAIKHAL），DHAKA－1100．

BANGLADESH．

This Contract is made by and between the Buyer and Seller，whereby the Buyer agrees To buy and the Selleragrees To sell the under mentioned goods on the terms and conditions stated below：

Description of Goods，Specifications，	Quantity （set）	Unit Price （U．S．D/set）	Amount （U．S．D）
201/2B SECONDARY GRADE STAINLESS STEEL SHEET OF WIDTH 1219MM OR MORE THICKNESS 1MM TO 3MM，QTY：25，000KGSAT THE RATE OF USD1．40/KG．AS PER PROFORMA INVOIVE NO．SK20160802 －001 DATED AUG 2，2016	1．2＊1219＊2438 1．5＊1219＊2438 2．0＊1219＊2438 3．0＊1219＊2438	C．F．R 1．40 1．40 1．40 1．40	CHITTAGONG 7 806．40 4 547．20 16 282．00 6 364．40 35 000．00
Total		35 000．00	

SAY TOTAL：U．S．DOLLARS THIRTY FIVE THOUSAND ONLY．

PACKING：Standard export packing on pallets．

TRANSPORT DETAILS：the goods should shipped before：9th Oct，2016，from any Chi-

21

nese port To Chittagong Bangladesh, transshipment and partial shipment are allowed.

PAYMENT: By sight L/C and remain valid for negotiation in China for 15 days after shipment.

DOCUMENTS:

+ Signed commercial invoice in triplicate, certifying the goods are of Chinese origin and being imported against IRC No. BA – 0171646, VAT Registration No. 9141093671. .

+ Full set (3/3) of clean on board ocean Bill of Lading made out to order of shipper and blank endorsed.

+ Packing List in triplicate.

+ Certificate of origin by CCPIT.

+ Beneficiary's Declaration certifying that the country of origin has been printed on goods packing bag.

INSPECTION: Quality /Quantity/Weight Discrepancy and Claim: In case the quality and /or quantity/weight are found by the Buyer not To conform with the contract after arrival of the goods at the final destination, the Buyer may lodge a claim against the seller supported by a survey report issued by an inspection organization agreed upon by both parties with the exception of those claims for which the insurance company and /or the shipping company are To be held responsible. Claim for quality discrepancy should be filed by the Buyer within 60 days after arrival of the goods at the final destination while for quantity / weight discrepancy claim should be filed by the Buyer within 30 days after arrival of the goods at the final destination.

FORCE MAJEURE: The Seller shall not be held responsible for failure or delay in delivery of the entire or portion of the goods under this contract in consequence of any Force Major incidents.

ARBITRATION: All disputes in connection with this Contract or the execution thereof shall be settled through friendly negotiations. If no settlement can be reached, the case shall then be submitted To the Foreign Trade Arbitration Commission of the China Council for the Promotion of International Trade, Beijing, for settlement by arbitration in accordance with the Commission's Provisional Rules of Procedure. The award rendered by the Commission shall be final and binding on both parties. The arbitration expenses shall be borne by the losing party unless otherwise award by the arbitration organization.

Signed by：

THE SELLER：	**THE BUYER：**
JIANGSU I – TOUCH BUSINESS	M/S. MEMORY STEEL
CORPORATION. SERVICE LTD	
彭　婷	John Lee

2. 信用证。

SEQUENCE OF TOTAL	27：	1/1
FORM OF DC.	40A：	IRREVOCABLE
DC. NO.	20：	0684160117426
DATE OF ISSUE	31C：	190825
APPLICABLE RULES	40E：	UCP LATEST VERSION
EXPIRY DATE AND PLACE	31D：	190924, IN BANGLADESH
APPLICANT	50：	M/S. MEMORY STEEL CORPORATION 73/A, LAL MOHAN SHAHA STREET, DHAKA – 100. BANGLADESH.
BENEFICIA RY	59：	JIANGSU I – TOUCH BUSINESS SERVICE LTD, ROOM 117, JIANGSU EDIFICE ZHANG JIAGANG FREE TRADE ZONE, JIANGSU, CHINA TEL：86 – 512 – 56363783
AMOUNT	32B：	EUR 35500,00
AVAILABLE WITH/BY	41D：	ANY BANK IN CHINA BY NEGOTIATION
DRAFTS AT	42C：	AT SIGHT FOR FULL INVOICE VALUE
DRAWEE	42A：	M/S. MEMORY STEEL CORPORATION
PARTIAL SHIPMENTS	43P：	PROHIBITTED
TRANSSHIPMENT	43T：	ALLOWED
PORTOF LOADING	44A：	ANY SEA PORT, CHINA
PORT OF DISCHARGE	44B：	CHITTAGONG SEA PORT, BANGLADESH
LATEST DATE OF SHIPMENT	44C：	191109
DESCRIPTION OFGOODS	45A：	201/2B SECONDARY GRADE STAINLESS STEEL SHEET OF WIDTH 1219MM OR MORE THICKNESS 1MM TO 3MM, QTY：25,000KGS AT THE RATE OF USD1.40/KG FOR TOTAL AMOUNT OF USD35,000.00 CIF CHITTAGONG, BANGLA-DESH. AS PER BENEFICIARY'S PROFORMA IN-VOICE（形式发票）NO. SK 20160807 – 001 DATED 23. AUG, 2019, PACKED IN CARTONS.
DOCUMENTS REQUIRED	46A：	+ MANUALLY SIGNED COMMERCIAL INVOICEIN TRIPLICATE CERTIFYING MERCHANDISE TO BE

OF CHINA ORIGIN AND INDICATING THAT THE GOODS ARE BEING IMPORTED AGAINST IRC NO. BA－0171646.

＋CLEAN 'SHIPPED ON BOARD' OCEAN BILL OF LADING IN DUPLICATE, SHOWING "FREIGHT PREPAID", MADE OUT TO ORDER OF AB BANK LIMITED, NAWABPUR ROAD BRANCH, DHAKA, BANGLADESH AND NOTIFY OPENERS.

＋INSURANCE POLICY IN TRIPLICATE FOR THE 110% OF INVOICE VALUE COVERING ALL RISKS AS PER P. I. C. C.

＋PACKING LIST IN TRIPLICATE SHOWING GROSS WEIGHT, NET WEIGHT.

＋A CERTIFICATE OF 'COUNTRY OF ORIGIN' MUST BE ISSUED BY THE GOVERNMENT AP-PROVED AUTHORITY/ORGANIZATION OF THE EXPORTER'S COUNTRY.

＋BENEFICIARY SHOULD SEND A FAX OR BY COUR IER TO L/C OPENING BANK WITHIN FIVE DAYS FROM THE DATE OF SHIPMENT, ADVISING THE DATE OF SHIPMENT, VESSEL'S NAME, A-MOUNT OF BILL AND L/C NO. A COPY OF THIS FAX SHOULD SIGNED（会签）BY THE NOMINAT-ED PERSON OF THE APPLICANT AND ACCOMPA-NY（随附）THE SHIPPING DOCUMENTS.

ADDITIONAL CONDITIONS	47A：	＋FULL NAME, ADDRESS OF THE APPLICANT, L/C NO. AND DATE TO BE SHOWN IN INVOICE, PACKING LIST AND BILL OF LADING. ＋SHORT FORM, STALE, CLAUSED BILL OF LADING IS NOT ACCEPTABLE.
CHARGES	71B：	ALL FOREIGN BANK CHARGES ARE FOR THE ACCOUNT OF THE BENEFICIARY.
PERIOD OF PRESENTATION	48：	5 DAYS FROM SHIPMENT DATE BUT WITHIN VA-LIDITY OF THE CREDIT

请根据合同对信用证认真进行审核，并结合受益人实际情况对该证提出合理的修改意见。

能力实训项目 2：信用证审核修改业务操作

根据深圳普瑞玛建材有限公司第 DC 13720 号合同的要求，2019 年 8 月 5 日，单证员黄柯根据合同审核信用证。

1. 合同。

CONTRACT

Contract No. : BFF0606　　　　　　　　　　　　　Date：JUL 1, 2019

THE SELLER：PRIMA CONSTRUCTION MATERIOLS CO. , LTD

　　　　　　　　1401 ROOM, 38 BUILDING, CHUANGYE GARDEN

　　　　　　　　BAOAN DISTRICT, SHENZHEN , CHINA（这三行对齐）

THE BUYER：CONSTRUCTION MOUDULAR SPECIALIST

　　　　　　　POSTAL：13 HARVEY RD. ,

　　　　　　　SHENTON PK, WA 6008 AUSTRALIA

This Contract is made by and between the Buyer and Seller, whereby the Buyer agrees to buy and the Seller agrees to sell the under mentioned goods on the terms and conditions stated below：

Description of Goods, Specifications,	Quantity (SQM)	Unit Price (U. S. D/SQM)	Amount (U. S. D)
		CIF	FREMENTLE
BAMBOO FLOORING		20. 00	
ITEM 1	100		2 000. 00
ITEM 2	100	39. 50	3 950. 00
AS PER PI NO. : BFF0610			
Total	200		5 950. 00

SAY TOTAL：U. S DOLLARS FIFTY NINE HUNDRED AND FIFTY（USD5950）ONLY.

PACKING：All packing in seaworthy cartons.

TRANSPORT DETAILS：the goods should shipped on or before：20th Sep, 2019, from Shenzhen, China to Fremantle Australia, transshipment and partial shipment are all allowed.

INSURANCE：To be effected by the Seller for 110% of invoice value covering ICC（A）risk and ICC（War Risk）.

PAYMENT：By irrevocable documentary letter of credit at 30 days after sight, reaching the seller not later than Jul 30, 2019 and remain valid for negotiation in China for 15 days after shipment.

DOCUMENTS：

+ Signed commercial invoice three originals and three copies.

+ Full set of clean on board ocean Bill of Lading made to order.

+ Packing List three originals and two copies.

+ Insurance policy endorsed in blank and in triplicate.

+ Certificate of Origin in China issued by official authority.

2. 信用证。

SEQUENCE OF TOTAL	27:	1/1
FORM OF DC	40A:	IRREVOCABLE
DC NO.	20:	DC 160720
DATE OF ISSUE	31C:	190731
APPLICABLE RULES	40E:	UCP 600
EXPIRY DATE AND PLACE	31D:	190910 IN CHINA
APPLICANT	50:	CONSTRUCTION MOUDULAR SPECIALIST POST-AL: 13 HARVEY RD., SHENTON PK, WA 6008
BENEFICIARY	59:	PRIMA CONSTRUCTION MATERIALS CO., LTD 1041 ROOM, 38 BUILDING, HUANGYE GARDEN BAOAN DISTRICT, SHENZHEN, CHINA
AMOUNT	32B:	USD6840,00
AVAILABLE WITH/BY	41D:	ANY BANK BY NEGOTIATION
DRAFTS AT	42C:	AT SIGHT
DRAWEE	42A:	DRAWN ON US
PARTIAL SHIPMENTS	43P:	PERMITTED
TRANSHIPMENT	43T:	FORBIDDEN
LOADING PORT	44E:	CHINA MAIN PORT
DISCHARGE PORT	44F:	FREMANTLE, AUSTRALIA
LATEST DATE OF SHIPMENT	44C:	190920
DESCRIPTION OFGOODS	45A:	BAMBOO FLOORING ITEM 1 100 SQM U. S. D39. 50/SQM ITEM 2 100 SQM U. S. D20. 00/SQM ALL PACKING IN SEA WORTHY CARTONS CFR FREMANTLE AS PER PI NO.: BFF6100
DOCUMENTS REQUIRED	46A:	+ MANUALLY SIGNED COMMECIAL INVOICE 2 ORIGINALS PLUS TWO COPIES.

+FULL SET (3/3) OF MARINE BILLS OF LADING, MADE OUT TO ORDER, MARKED FREIGHT COLLECT, AND NOTIFY APPLICANT (STATING FULL NAME AND ADDRESS).

+INSURANCE POLICY OR CERTIFICATE IN TRIPLICATE, BLANK INDORSED, FOR THE INVOICE VALUE PLUS 12% COVERING ICC (A) RISK AND ICC (STRIKE). FROM WAREHOUSE TO WAREHOUSE AND I. O. P, PAYABLE AT FREMENTLE IN U. S. D.

+PACKING LIST 3 ORIGINALS AND 2 COPIES.

+ CERTIFICATE OF ORIGIN IN CHINA ISSUED BY OFFICIAL AUTHRORITY.

+ BENEFICIARY'S CERTIFICATE SHOWING THAT A SET OF ORIGINAL SHIPPING DOCUMENTS HAS BEEN MAIL TO THE APPLICANT BY EXPRESS AFTER 2 DAYS OF SHIOMENT AND COUNTER-SIGNED BY THE IMPORTER'S AGENT.

CHARGES　　　　　　　　　　71B：ALL BANKING CHARGES ARE FOR BENEFICIA-RY/'S ACCOUNT.

PERIOD OF PRESENTATION　　48：WITHIN 5 DAYS AFTER THE DATE OF SHIPMENT BUT WITHIN THE VALIDITY OF THE L/C

CONFIRMATION INSTRUCTIONS　49：WITHOUT

　　请根据合同对信用证认真进行审核，并结合受益人实际情况对该证提出合理的修改意见。

第五节　学习导航

一、参考资料

[1] 章安平. 外贸单证操作 [M]. 北京：高等教育出版社，2008.

[2] 刘启萍，周树玲. 外贸单证 [M]. 北京：对外经贸大学出版社，2008.

[3] 方士华，国际结算 [M]. 沈阳：东北财经大学出版社，2016.

[4] 吴轶群，国际商务单证操作 [M]. 青岛：中国海洋大学出版社，2018.

二、自主学习平台

[1] 全国外贸单证员考试中心。

[2] 外贸经理人微信公众号。

[3] 外贸单证课程国家教学资源库。

项目三
商业发票和装箱单的制作

第一节 项目描述与目标

一、项目描述

◆开篇业务引入

根据第 L-16017 号信用证的要求，长沙鹏兴进出口有限公司需要向进口方 ELBY GIFTS INC. 开具商业发票和装箱单，该项目任务具体由单证员李望负责。2019 年 8 月 16 日，单证员李望根据 L/C 规定："+ ORIGINAL SIGNED INVOICE PLUS THREE COPIES.""+ ORIGINAL PACKING LIST PLUS 2 COPIES"，要求完成商业发票和装箱单的缮制。

◆项目预期目标

商业发票是出口交易中最常见、最重要的单据之一，是全套出口单据的核心。装箱单是包装单据的一种，对商业发票进行补充，同时也是货运单据中的一种重要单据。通过对信用证下有关商业发票和装箱单条款的解读，理清该笔业务对商业发票和装箱单缮制的具体要求，通过介绍发票和装箱单的定义、种类和作用，引导学生熟悉商业发票和装箱单的格式及内容，重点训练学生掌握商业发票和装箱单的制作要点，并最终能独立完成符合信用证要求的商业发票和装箱单缮制。

在项目实施过程中，有效训练学生对信用证单据条款的阅读理解，培养学生认真细心制单的基本职业能力，并熟悉 UCP600 的相关条款。

表 3-1 项目预期目标

类型	商业发票和装箱单的制作
知识目标	了解发票和装箱单的含义、作用和类型
	熟悉商业发票和装箱单的格式及内容
	掌握商业发票和装箱单的缮制要点
能力目标	能根据信用证等相关信息正确制作商业发票
	能根据信用证等相关信息正确制作装箱单
职业素质目标	独立业务操作能力
	认真、细致、严谨的工作态度

二、项目实施条件

1. 教师演示工作项目和归纳技能要点。
2. 学生能够在实训室对该项目进行分组讨论并实施。

第二节　知识模块

一、商业发票的含义

商业发票（Commercial Invoice）是卖方向买方开具的载有交易货物名称、数量、价格等内容的总清单，是买卖双方交接货物、结算记账的依据，也是进出口申报关税必不可少的单证之一。在国际贸易中，也常常将商业发票简称为发票。我国各外贸公司的商业发票没有统一格式，但主要项目基本相同，主要包括发票的编号、收货人、填制日期、数量、单价、总值和支付方式等项内容。

二、商业发票的作用

1. 商业发票是交易的合法证明文件，是货运单据的中心，也是装运货物的总说明。
2. 商业发票是买卖双方收付货物和记账核算的依据。
3. 商业发票是买卖双方办理报关、纳税的计算依据。
4. 在不使用汇票结算的情况下，发票代替汇票作为付款依据。
5. 商业发票是出口方缮制其他出口单证的依据。

三、发票的类型

发票的种类很多，除了常见的商业发票外，还有形式发票（Proforma Invoice）、海关发票（Customs Invoice）、领事发票（Consular Invoice）、厂商发票（Manufacturer's Invoice）等。其中，形式发票不是一种正式发票，一般是不可接受的，仅作参考和预估，待正式成交后需重新制作商业发票。

ISSUER	COMMERCIAL INVOICE				
TO					
	NO.			DATE	
TRANSPORT DETAILS	S/C NO.			L/C NO.	
	TERMS OF PAYMENT				
Marks and Numbers	Number and kind of package Description of goods		Quantity	Unit Price	Amount
		Total:			
SAY TOTAL:					

ISSUER	形式发票 PROFORMA INVOICE				
TO					
	NO.			DATE	
TRANSPORT DETAILS	S/C NO.			L/C NO.	
	TERMS OF PAYMENT				
Marks and Numbers	Number and kind of package Description of goods		Quantity	Unit Price	Amount
		Total:			
SAY TOTAL:					

PORT TO LOADING:
PORT OF DESTINATION:
TIME OF DELIVERY:
INSURANCE:
VALIDITY:
BENEFICIARY
ADVISING BANK:
NEGOTIATING BANK:

CANADA CUSTOMS INVOICE
FACTURE DES DOUANES CANADIENNES

Customs and Excise / Douanes et Accise

1. Vendor (Name and Address) / Vendeur (Nom et adresse)	2. Date of Direct Shipment to Canada Date d'expédition directe vers le Canada	INVOICE NUMBER

AMERIWOOD
INDUSTRIES

2 SPAULDING STREET • DOWAGIAC,　　USA
Phone: +1-616-　　　　Fax: +1-616-

3. Other References (Include Purchaser's Order No.) Autres références (Include le no de commande de l'acheteur)	

4. Consignee (Name and Address) / Destinataire (Nom et adresse)	5. Purchaser's Name and Address (If other than Consignee) Nom et adresse de l'acheteur (s'il diffère de destinataire)

6. Country of Transhipment / Pays de transbordement

7. Country of Origin of Goods
Pays d'orine des marchandises

IF SHIPMENT INCLUDES GOODS OF DIFFERENT ORIGINS ENTER ORIGINS AGAINST ITEMS IN 12.
SI L'EXPÉDITION COMPREND DES MARCHANDISES D'ORIGINES DIFFÉRENTES, PRÉCISER LEUR PROVENANCE EN 12.

8. Transportation: Give Mode and Place of Direct Shipment to Canada
Transport: Préciser mode et point d'expédition directe vers le Canada

9. Conditions of Sales and Terms of Purchase
(i.e. Sale, Consignment Shipment, Leased Goods, etc.)
conditions de vente et modalités de paiement
(p. ex. vente, expédition en consignation, locate de marchandises, etc.

10. Currency of Settlement / Devises du paiement

11. No of Pkgs Nbre de colis	12. Specification of Commodities (Kind of Packages, Marks and Numbers, General Description and Characteristics i.e. Grade, Quality) Désignation des articles (nature des colis, marques et numéros, description générale et caractéristiques, p. ex. classe, qualité)	13. Quantity (State unit) Quantité (Préciser l'unité)	Selling Price / Prix de vente	
			14. Unit Price Prix unitaire	15. Total

18. If any fields 1 to 17 are included on an additional commercial invoice, check this box.
Si tout renseignement relativement aux zone 1 & 17 figure sur une ou des factures commerciales ci-attachées, cocher cette case.

Commercial Invoice No. / No de la facture commerciale

SEE ATTACHED ☐

16. Total Weight / Poids total		17. Invoice Total Total de la facture
Net	Gross / Brut	

19. Exporter's Name and Address (If other than Vendor) Nom et adresse de l'exportateur (s'il diffère du vendeur)	20. Originator (Name And Address) / Expéditeur d'originate (nom et adresse)

21. Departmental Ruling (If applicable) / Décision du Ministère(s'il y a lieu)	22. If fields 23 & 25 are not applicable, check this box. Si les zones 23 & 25 sont sans objet, cocher cette case. ☐

23. If included in field 17, indicate amount: Si compris dans le total à la zine 17, préciser:	24. If not included in field 17, indicate amount: Si non-compris dans le total à la zine 17, préciser:	25. Check (if applicable) Cocher (s'il a lieu)
(i) Transporation charges, expenses and insurance from the place of direct shipment to Canada. Les frais de transport, dépenses et assurances à partir du point d'expédition directe vers le Canada.	(i) Transporation charges, expenses and insurance to the place of direct shipment to Canada. Les frais de transport, dépenses et assurances à partir du point d'expédition directe vers le Canada.	☐ (i) Royalty payment or subsequent proceeds are paid or payable by the purchaser. Des redevance ou produits ont été or seront versés par l'acheteur.
(ii) Costs for construction, erection and assembly incurred after importation into canada. Les coûts de construction, d'érection et d'assemblage après importation au Canada.	(ii)Amounts for commissions other than buying commissions. Les commissions autres que celles versées pour l'achat.	☐ (ii) The purchaser has supplied goods or services for use in the production or these goods. L'acheteur a fourni des marchandises ou des services pour la production des marchandises.
(iii) Export Packing Le cout de l'emballage d' exportation	(iii) Export Packing Le cout de l'emballage d' exportation	

四、商业发票的缮制

（一）具体操作

1. 出口方公司名称和地址（Name and Address of Seller）。

（1）填写内容：

根据 UCP600 的规定，若信用证无另外规定，商业发票的出票人为受益人（即出口方）。发票的顶端往往要有醒目的出票人名称和详细地址，且应与信用证或合同一致。许多出口企业在印刷空白发票时已印制这些内容，或将这些内容编入电脑程序一并打印。

（2）实例：

LILING PENGXING CERAMIC FACTORY

WUSHI JIASHU LILING HUNAN, CHINA

TEL：86 – 731 – 23384199　　　FAX：86 – 731 – 23384298

2. 商业发票名称（Name of Invoice）。

（1）填写内容：

根据来证要求填写，若无另外规定，一般标为"商业发票"或"发票"的单据均可接受。

（2）实例：

COMMERCIAL INVOICE 或 INVOICE

3. 收货人或抬头名称和地址（To）。

（1）填写内容：

根据 UCP600 的规定，若信用证无另外规定，商业发票的收货人或抬头为开证申请人（即进口方）。名称和地址应与信用证或合同一致。

（2）实例：

To

ELBY GIFTS INC.

879 INDUSTRIEL BOIS DES FILION,

QUEBEC, J6Z 4T3, CANADA

4. 商业发票号码（Invoice No. ）。

（1）填写内容：

由出口商统一编制，一般采用顺序号，便于查对。商业发票作为中心票据，其他票据的号码一般与此号码保持一致。如：汇票号码、出口报关单号码及附属单据号码等一般都与发票号码一致。

（2）实例：

Invoice No. ：PX12IVN1039

5. 商业发票日期（Invoice Date）。

（1）填写内容：

通常是指商业发票签发的日期，发票日期应早于提单日期和汇票日期，但不能迟于信用证的议付日期或有效期。根据 UCP600 的规定，如果信用证没有特殊规定，银行可以接受签发日期早于开证日的发票。

（2）实例：

Invoice Date：2019/8/16

6. 合同号码或信用证号码（S/C No. Or L/C No.）。

（1）填写内容：

参照合同和信用证填制。

（2）实例：

S/C No.：CB121039

L/C No.：DC HMN214479

7. 运输路线及工具（From…To…By…）。

（1）填写内容：

该栏目为非必须栏目，可以省略。如不省略，起运地和目的地均应明确具体，不能笼统。且按实际情况填制，起讫地应与提单一致。如果货物系转运，转运地点也应明确表示。

（2）实例：

From Shanghai to London, U. K. W/T at Rotterdam by sea

8. 唛头及件号（Marks & Numbers）。

（1）填写内容：

凡是来证有指定唛头的，必须完全按照规定制唛。若无指定，出口商可自行设计唛头，唛头一般以简明、易于识别为原则。唛头通常由收货人名称缩写、参考号码（合同号/发票号码/订单号码等）、目的港、件号四部分组成。如系散装或裸装货物时，无唛头，则可打上 N/M（No Mark）。

（2）实例：

Marks & Numbers

MOMO

HNT（04）021

KOBE

NO. 1～240

9. 货物描述（Description of Goods）。

（1）填写内容：

商业发票的货物描述必须与信用证保持一致，但并不要求如同镜子反射那样一致。货物细节可以在发票中的若干地方表示，当合并在一起与信用证规定一致即可。同时，商业发票中的货物描述必须反映实际装运的货物。

（2）实例：

Description of Goods

12,000 KGS Pu-er Tea PACKED IN 240 CARTONS AS PER CONTRACT NO. HNT

（04）021

10. 商品的数量（Quantity）。

（1）填写内容：

商品的重量或数量应与其他单据相一致，且数量单位应与单价中的数量单位一致。凡出现"约"（About/ABT/more or less）"大概""大约"或类似词语，用于信用证数量时，应理解为有关数量不超过 10% 的增减幅度。

（2）实例：

Quantity

100PCS

11. 单价与总值（Unit Price & Amount）。

（1）填写内容：

完整的商品单价应由计价货币、单位价格金额、计量单位、价格术语四部分组成。其中特别注意不要漏填或错填价格术语，且必须与信用证指明的价格术语保持一致，因为它涉及买卖双方责任的承担、费用的负担和风险的划分等问题。另外，它也是海关核定关税的依据。

商业发票中使用的币种应与信用证中使用的币种严格一致。同时，商业发票总金额应该是计算后得出的商品的总价值，且总金额不能超过信用证规定的最大金额。特别注意的是，当来证要求商业发票必须显示折扣或佣金时，应如实照办。当出现既含折扣又含佣金时，应先减扣折扣，再减扣佣金。例如，来证要求"5% DISCOUNT AND 5% COMMISSION TO BE DEDUCTED FROM INVOICE VALUE"，那么商业发票应显示如下：

Quantity	Unit price	Amount
4000PCS	USD3.10/PC CIFC5 NEWYORK	USD 12,400.00
	LESS 5% DISCOUNT	USD 620.00
		USD 11,780.00
	LESS 5% COMMISSION	USD 589.00
	NET:	USD 11,191.00

如果来证要求显示 FOB 价格或者分离 CIF/CFR 价格，应分别注明运费、保险费和 CIF 价格，严格按信用证要求来制作商业发票。如：

Quantity	Unit price CIF Montreal	Amount
500 sets	USD50.00/set	USD 25,000.00
	Freight	USD 1,000.00
	Insurance	USD 1,500.00
	TOTAL FOB value	USD 22,500.00

单价和总值是商业发票的重要项目，必须准确计算、正确缮打，并认真复核。特别要注意小数点的位置是否正确，金额和数量的横乘、竖加是否有矛盾。凡出现"约"（About/ABT/more or less）"大概""大约"或类似词语，用于信用证金额、单价时，应理解为有关金额或单价有不超过10%的增减幅度。

（2）实例：

Quantity	Unit price	Amount
200 PCS	EUR80.00/PC CFR BANGKOK	EUR16,000.00

12. 来证要求加注特殊内容（Other special requirements）。

（1）填写内容：

有时信用证要求在商业发票上加注各种费用金额、特定号码、某些权威机构认证等证明文句，在可以接受和做到的情况下，一般将这些内容打在商业发票商品栏以下的空白处。常见的有：加注运费或保费等，注明许可证号码等，注明货物原产自中国，加注"发展中国家声明"等等。因此，在审证时，则应将这些特殊条款标出，以免遗漏。如若难以办到，则应及时要求对方修改条款。

（2）实例：

WE HEREBY CERTIFY THAT THE ABOVE GOODS ARE TRUE AND CORRECT.

或 WE HEREBY CERTIFY THAT THE ABOVE GOODS ARE OF CHINESE ORIGIN.

13. 出票人签章（Signature）。

（1）填写内容：

除非信用证另有规定，商业发票只能由信用证中规定的受益人出具，且一般由出票人在发票正面右下角签章。如果以影印、自动或电脑处理货复写方法制作的商业发票作为正本者，应在商业发票上注明"正本"（ORIGINAL）字样，并由出单人签字。

UCP600 规定商业发票可不必签字，但有时来证规定商业发票需要签字的，则必须照办，如来证要求"SIGNED COMMERCIAL INVOICE…"。在没有手签要求的情况下，可以使用印鉴；但若来证明确要求手签（MANULLY SIGNED 或 HAND SIGNED），则必须手签。

（2）实例：

HUNAN TEA IMPORT & EXPORT COPORATION

WUYI ROAD，CHANGSHA，HUNAN，CHINA

李萍

（二）《UCP600》对商业发票的规定和注意事项

1. 《UCP600》第 18 条规定：

a. 商业发票：

i. 必须看似由受益人出具。

ii. 必须出具成以申请人为抬头。

iii. 必须与信用证的货币相同。

iv. 无须签名。

b. 按指定行事的指定银行、保兑行（如有的话）或开证行可以接受金额大于信用证允许金额的商业发票，其决定对有关各方均有约束力，只要该银行对超过信用证允许金额的部分未作承付或者议付。

c. 商业发票上的货物、服务或履约行为的描述应该与信用证中的描述一致。

2. 制作商业发票的注意事项。

（1）应根据来证要求，提交数量准确的正本与副本商业发票。

（2）注意商业发票的格式整齐。若出现多种货号的商品，每一货号的商品内容和总数排列要有序，做到：横排是每一货号的商品内容，竖排是个货号商品内容的总和。

五、装箱单的含义及作用

装箱单（Packing List）又称为花色码单或包装单，是列明出口商品的包装形式、规格、数量、毛净重、体积等的一种包装单据。它是商业发票的补充，同时也是货运单据中的一项重要单据。通常可以将其有关内容加列在商业发票上，但是在信用证有明确要求时，就必须严格按信用证约定制作。

装箱单主要用于补充商业发票内容的不足，通过列明包装件数、规格、体积、重量、运输标志等，详尽描述了商品的包装情况，便于进口方掌握和核查交易商品的包装及数量等细节情况，同时也便于进口国海关查验核对货物。

装箱单的内容应与商品实际包装情况相符，并与其他单据所列内容保持一致。一般包括：合同号码、发票号码、唛头、货物描述、体积、重量、收货人名称及地址、运输路线等等。有的来证规定"SEAWORTHY PACKING"（适用于海运包装）、"PACKING SUITABLE FOR LONG VOYAGE"（适合于长途海运包装）或"STRONG WOODEN CASE PACKING"（坚固木箱装运）等等，信用证中的这些表达都应在商业发票和装箱单中照抄。

ISSUER						
TO		**PACKING LIST**				
		INVOICE NO.		DATE		
Marks and Numbers	Number and kind of package / Description of goods	Quantity	PACKAGE	G.W	N.W	Meas.
	Total:					
SAY TOTAL:						

装箱单式样图

六、装箱单的缮制

（一）具体操作

1. 单据名称（Name of document）。

（1）填写内容：

按信用证要求的类型和名称提供，如要求"Detailed Packing List"，可通过在单据中详细显示单件货物的毛、净重和体积加以实现；如要求"Neutral Packing List"（中性装箱单），所提供的单据只要不打印受益人名称、不签章就可满足要求；如要求提供重量单，则名称应写为"Weight List"；如要求提供尺码单，则名称应写为"Measurement List"。ISBP 规定，只要单据中包括了装箱细节，即使没有单据名称也视为符合信用证规定。

（2）实例：

PACKING LIST

2. 抬头（To）。

（1）填写内容：

内容与商业发票相同，一般填写开证申请人即买方的公司名称及地址。也有不列抬头而注明"As per Inv."或"To whom it may concern"。除非信用证特别要求，否则银行可以接受装箱单表面无抬头的表示。

（2）实例：

TO：ELBY GIFTS INC.

879 INDUSTRIEL BOIS DES FILION　QUEBEC，J6Z 4T3，CANADA

3. 出单日期（Date）。

（1）填写内容：

实务中，因为装箱单通常是商业发票内容的补充，所以装箱单的出单日期可以按商业发票的日期填写，也可晚于发票日，但不能晚于提单的签发日。如信用证未做规定，也可不注明出单日。

（2）实例：

Date：APR. 15，2019

4. 合同号码或销售确认书号码或商业发票号码（Contract No. /Sales Confirmation No. /Invoice No. ）。

（1）填写内容：

根据合同、销售确认书、商业发票如实填写即可。

（2）实例：

S/C NO.：DD145

L/C NO.：DE4578FF

INVOICE NO.：RT084

5. 唛头（Marks & No. s）。

（1）填写内容：

唛头须与商业发票、信用证及实物印刷完全一致，也可以只注明"As Per Invoice

No. xxx"。

（2）实例：

Marks & No. s

TOTO

BHI7821

DUBAI

NO. 1 – 565

6. 货物描述及数量（Description of Goods & Quantity）。

（1）填写内容：

装箱单中所列明的货物应与商业发票中所描述的货物一致，但可用与其他单据无矛盾的统称表示。

（2）实例：

Description of Goods	Quantity
LADIES JACKET NO. 112 NO. 113	1 520PCS 1 230PCS

7. 包装件数（Number & kind of package/Package/PKGS）。

（1）填写内容：

该栏填写货物的运输包装单位及小写数量，而不是计价单位的数量。注意，包装件数大写应缮制在正文下方，大小写件数应保持一致。

（2）实例：

Package

560CTNS

Say FIVE HUNDRED AND SIXTY CARTONS ONLY.

8. 毛重（Gross Weight/G. W. ）、净重（Net Weight/N. W. ）和体积（Measurement/Meas. ）。

（1）填写内容：

毛重应注明每个包装件的毛重和此包装件内不同规格、品种、花色货物各自的总毛重，最后在合计栏处标注所有货物的总毛重。净重应注明每个包装件的净重和此包装件内不同规格、品种、花色货物各自的总净重，最后在合计栏处标注所有货物的总净重。注意重量都是以千克（KG）为单位，保留整数。

体积则要求注明每个包装件的尺寸和总体积。注意体积单位是立方米（m3 或 CBM），且保留三位小数。

注意：如商品有多种规格，则包装件数、毛重、净重、体积均应按不同规格描述再合计。

（2）实例：

Package	G. W.	N. W.	Measurement
560CTNS	3500KGS	3250KGS	35.876CBM

9. 签署（Signature）。

（1）填写内容：

通常由受益人完成，如信用证没有要求，可以不签字盖章。

（2）实例：

SHANGHAI GARMENT CORPORATION

王晓丽

（二）注意事项

1. 装箱单的内容必须完全符合信用证的要求，既包括包装的货物内容，也包括包装的种类和件数、每件毛净重和总毛净重、总体积。

2. 装箱单可以不显示货物的价格、运输路线和收货人，除非特别规定。

3. 若信用证对装箱单有特殊规定，必须在单据中充分体现出来。如：要求加注信用证号或者详细描述货物的包装细节。

第三节　任务模块

上接项目二，根据信用证审核并修改后的条款并结合合同的要求，鹏兴公司完成了该笔业务货物的准备，接下来单证员李望应完成的工作任务包括：

任务1：根据资料和信用证相关条款要求，完成商业发票的缮制。

任务2：根据资料和信用证相关条款要求，完成装箱单的缮制。

1. 信用证。

SEQUENCE OF TOTAL	27：	1/1
FORM OF DC	40A：	IRREVOCABLE
DC NO	20：	DC HMN214479
DATE OF ISSUE	31C：	190720
APPLICABLE RULES	40E：	UCP LATEST VERSION
EXPIRY DATE AND PLACE	31D：	190919 IN COUNTRY OF BENEFICIARY
APPLICANT	50：	ELBY GIFTS INC. 879 INDUSTRIEL BOIS DES FILION, QUEBEC, J6Z 4T3, CANADA
BENEFICIARY	59：	LILING PENGXING CERAMIC FACTORY WUSHI JIASHU LILING HUNAN, CHINA
AMOUNT	32B：	USD27010,40
PCT CR AMT TOLERANCE	39A：	10/10
AVAILABLE WITH/BY	41D：	ANY BANK BY NEGOTIATION

DRAFTS AT	42C：	AT SIGHT FOR FULL INVOICE VALUE
DRAWEE	42A：	ISSUING BANK
PARTIAL SHIPMENTS	43P：	ALLOWED
TRANSHIPMENT	43T：	ALLOWED
PORTOF LOADING	44E：	SHENZHEN, CHINA
PORT OF DISCHARGE	44F：	PRINCE RUPERT, BC
LATEST DATE OF SHIPMENT	44D：	160905
DESCRIPTION OFGOODS OR SERVICES	45A：	CERAMIC CUPS AND BOWLS AS PER S/C NO.：CB121039 CIF PRINCE RUPERT, BC ALL PACKED IN CARTONS.

DOCUMENTS REQUIRED　　　46A： +ORIGINAL SIGNED INVOICE PLUS THREE COPIES.

+FULL SET OF CLEAN MULTIMODAL TRANSPORT DOCUMENT PLUS 2 N/N COPIES, MADE TO THE ORDER OF HSBC BANK CANADA, SHOWING ON BOARD NOTATION, MARKED FREIGHT PREPAID, AND NOTIFY APPLICANT (STATING FULL NAME AND ADDRESS).

+ INSURANCE POLICY OR CERTIFICATE-BLANK INDORSED, FOR THE INVOICE VALUE PLUS 10% COVERING ALL RISKS AND S. R. CC. FROM WAREHOUSE TO WAREHOUSE.

+ORIGINAL PACKING LIST PLUS 2 COPIES

+GSP CERTIFICATE OF ORIGIN FORM A, IN ONE ORIGINAL PLUS 2 COPIES, INDICATING COUNTRY OF ORIGIN, COUNTERCHOPPED BY GOVERNMENT AUTHORITIES OR EXPORTER'S STATMENT OF ORIGIN

+ SHIPPING NOTE INCLUDING SHIPPING MARKS, CTN NO., B/L NO., QUANTITY, VESSEL'S NAME, VOYAGE NO., SHOULD BE SENT TO THE ISSUING BANK ON THE DATE OF SHIPMENT.

ADDITIONAL CONDITIONS　　47A： +BENEFICIARY'S DETAILS：

CTC：MILLER LEE

TEL：86－731－2338－4199

FAX：86 - 731 - 2338 - 4298

FOLLOWING CHARGES ARE FOR BENEFICIARY'S ACCOUNT：

1）REIMBURSEMENT / REMITTANCE CHARGES

2）DISCREPANCY FEE OF USD/CAD/EUR100 PLUS ALL RELEVANT CABLE CHARGES WILL BE DEDUCTED FROM EACH PRESENTATION OF DISCREPANT

DOCUMENTS UNDER THIS DC.

CHARGES   71B： ALL BANKING CHARGES OUTSIDE COUNTRY OF ISSUE FOR ACCOUNT OF BENEFICIARY/EXPORTER

PERIOD OF PRESENTATION   48： WITHIN 15 DAYS AFTER THE DATE OF SHIPMENT BUT WITHIN THE VALIDITY OF THE CREDIT

CONFIRMATION INSTRUCTIONS   49： WITHOUT

INFO TO PRESENTING BK   78： + UPON RECEIPT OF DOCUMENTS CONFORMING TO THE TERMS OF THIS CREDIT WE UNDERTAKE TO REIMBURSE YOU IN THE CURRENCY OF THIS CREDIT IN ACCORDANCE WITH YOUR INSTRUCTIONS, LESS CABLE CHARGES,

+ FORWARD DOCUMENTS IN ONE LOT BY COURIER AT BENEFICIARY'S EXPENSES TO HSBC BANK CANADA, TRADE AND SUPPLY CHAIN, 5100 SHERBROOKE STREET EAST, SUITE 190, MONTREAL, QUEBEC, H1V 3R9 CANADA.

+ THE AMOUNT OF EACH DRAWING MUST BE ENDORSED ON THE REVERSE OF THIS DC BY THE NEGOTIATING/PRESENTING BANK.

2. 合同。

SALES CONTRACT

ContractNo.：SSW0803

Date：AUG 15，2019

THE SELLER：PENGXING IMP&EXP COMPANY

LILING PENGXING CERAMIC FACTOR

WUSHI JIASHU LILING HUNAN，CHINA

TEL：86 – 731 – 23384199   FAX：86 – 731 – 23384298

THE BUYER：ELBY GIFTS INC.

879 INDUSTRIEL BOIS DES FILION

QUEBEC，J6Z 4T3，CANADA

TEL：514 – 420 – 0282   FAX：514 – 420 – 0322

This Contract is made by and between the Buyer and Seller，whereby the Buyer agrees to buy and the Selleragrees to sell the under mentioned goods on the terms and conditions stated below：

Description of Goods，Specifications，	Quantity (set)	Unit Price (U. S. D/set)	Amount (U. S. D)
Ceramic Cups and Bowls		C. I. F Prince Rupert	
V23 – 234	912	4. 05	3 693. 60
V23 – 234F	912	4. 05	3 693. 60
V23 – 235	1 520	2. 40	3 648. 00
V23 – 236	1 512	2. 10	3 175. 20
V23 – 237	1 488	1. 95	2 901. 60
V23 – 2348	1 520	2. 04	3 100. 80
36 – 062	1 528	2. 30	3 514. 40
36 – 063	1 496	2. 12	3 171. 52
As per the P/I No.：CCB23 – 36			
Total	10 888		26 898. 72

Say Total：U. S DOLLARS TWENTY SIX THOUSAND EIGHT HUNDRED AND NINETY EIGHT AND CENTS

SEVENTY TWO（USD26898. 72）ONLY.

PACKING：4 sets packed in a carton（V 23 – 234/V23 – 234F），8 sets packed in a carton for others.

TRANSPORT DETAILS：the goods should shipped on or before：5th Sep，2019，from Shenzhen，China to Prince Rupert

Canada，transshipment and partial shipment are all allowed.

INSURANCE：To be effected by the Seller for 110% of invoice value covering all risks and S. R. C. C as per C. I. C of PICC dated 01/01/1981.

PAYMENT：By irrevocable documentary letter of credit at sight, reaching the seller not later than Aug 5, 2019 and remain valid for negotiation in China for 15 days after shipment.

DOCUMENTS：

+ Signed commercial invoice one original and three copies.

+ Full set of clean on board ocean Bill of Lading made to order of issuing bank.

+ Packing List one original and two copies.

+ Insurance policy endorsed in blank.

+ GSP Form A certified bygovernment authority.

INSPECTION：Quality/Quantity/Weight Discrepancy and Claim：In case the quality and /or quantity/weight are found by the Buyer not to conform with the contract after arrival of the goods at the final destination, the Buyer may lodge a claim against the seller supported by a survey report issued by an inspection organization agreed upon by both parties with the exception of those claims for which the insurance company and /or the shipping company are to be held responsible. Claim for quality discrepancy should be filed by the Buyer within 60 days after arrival of the goods at the final destination while for quantity/weight discrepancy claim should be filed by the Buyer within 30 days after arrival of the goods at the final destination.

FORCE MAJEURE：The Seller shall not be held responsible for failure or delay in delivery of the entire or portion of the goods under this contract in consequence of any Force Major incidents.

ARBITRATION：All disputes in connection with this Contract or the execution thereof shall be settled through friendly negotiations. If no settlement can be reached, the case shall then be submitted to the Foreign Trade Arbitration Commission of the China Council for the Promotion of International Trade, Beijing, for settlement by arbitration in accordance with the Commission's Provisional Rules of Procedure. The award rendered by the Commission shall be final and binding on both parties. The arbitration expenses shall be borne by the losing party unless otherwise award by the arbitration organization.

Signed by：

THE SELLER：	**THE BUYER**：
PENGXING IMP&EXP COMPANY	ELBY GIFTS INC.
LILING PENGXING CERAMIC FACTORY	
李　望	Camp Wolf

据此，单证员李望完成了该笔业务下商业发票和装箱单的制作。

PENGXING IMP&EXP COMPANY

LILING PENGXING CERAMIC FACTORY

WUSHI JIASHU LILING HUNAN CHINA

TEL：86 – 731 – 23384199   FAX：86 – 731 – 23384298

COMMERCIAL INVOICE

To:	ELBY GIFTS INC. 879 INDUSTRIEL BOIS DES FILION QUEBEC, J6Z 4T3, CANADA	InvoiceNo.:	PX12IVN1039
		InvoiceDate:	AUG 16,2019
		S/C No.:	CB121039
		S/C Date:	JUL 5,2019
From:	SHENZHEN,CHINA	To:	PRINCE RUPERT,BC,CANADA
Letter of Credit No.:	DC HMN214479	Issued By:	HSBC BANK, MONTREAL CANADA

Marks and Numbers	Number and kind of package		Quantity	Unit Price	Amount
	Description of goods			**U.S.D/set**	
	CERAMIC CUPS AND BOWLS			CIF PRINCE RUPERT ,BC	
ELBY		CTN	Set	U.S.D	U.S.D
S/C NO.:CB121039	V23-234	228	912	4.05	3693.60
NO: 1-1589	V23-234F	228	912	4.05	3693.60
	V23-235	190	1520	2.40	3648.00
	V23-236	189	1512	2.10	3175.20
	V23-237	186	1488	1.95	2901.60
	V23-238	190	1520	2.04	3100.80
	36-062	191	1528	2.30	3514.40
	36-063	187	1496	2.12	3171.52
	Total:	1,589	10,888		26,898.72

Say Total：U. S DOLLARSTWENTY SIX THOUSAND EIGHT HUNDRED AND NINETY EIGHT AND CENTS SEVENTY TWO（USD26898. 72）ONLY

PENGXING IMP&EXP COMPANY

李望

PENGXING IMP&EXP COMPANY

LILING PENGXING CERAMIC FACTORY

WUSHI JIASHU LILING HUNAN CHINA

TEL：86 - 731 - 23384199　　FAX：86 - 731 - 23384298

PACKING LIST

To：　ELBY GIFTS INC.　　　　　　　　Date　　AUG 16, 2019

879 INDUSTRIEL BOIS DES FILION　　Invoice No.：PX12IVN1039

QUEBEC, J6Z 4T3, CANADA

From：　SHENZHEN, CHINA　　　　　To：PRINCE RPERT, BC, CANADA

Item No.	Description of goods	Quantity	Sets/CTN		CTN		G. W/ N. W (KGS)		Dimension (CM)			Meas. (CBM)
V23 - 234	CERAMIC CUPS AND BOWLS	912	SETS	228	CTNS	4	11.8	9.6	38.9 *	29.0 *	26.6	6.84
V23 - 234F	CERAMIC CUPS AND BOWLS	912	SETS	228	CTNS	4	11.8	9.6	38.9 *	29.0 *	26.6	6.84
V23 - 235	CERAMIC CUPS AND BOWLS	1520	SETS	190	CTNS	8	15.0	12.8	48.6 *	31.6 *	43.6	12.72
V23 - 236	CERAMIC CUPS AND BOWLS	1512	SETS	189	CTNS	8	10.6	8.4	50.4 *	27.0 *	.34.8	8.95
V23 - 237	CERAMIC CUPS AND BOWLS	1488	SETS	186	CTNS	8	8.4	6.4	31.0 *	28.2 *	39.2	6.37
V23 - 238	CERAMIC CUPS AND BOWLS	1520	SETS	190	CTNS	8	10.5	8.0	48.6	28.2 *	39.2	10.21
36 - 062	CERAMIC CUPS AND BOWLS	1528	SETS	191	CTNS	8	12.0	9.6	49.0 *	28.9 *	38.2	10.33
36 - 063	CERAMIC CUPS AND BOWLS	1496	SETS	187	CTNS	8	8.4	6.4	34.4 *	33.0 *	27.6	5.86

ALL PACKED IN CARTONS

SAY TOTAL：ONE THOUSAND FIVE HUNDRED AND EIGHTY NINE （1589CTNS）
CARTONS ONLY

第四节　任务拓展模块

能力实训项目1：商业发票和装箱单业务操作

根据出口商 Jiangsu 1 – Touch Business Service Ltd. 第 0684160117426 号信用证及合同的要求，2019 年 9 月 13 日，单证员彭婷制作了商业发票和装箱单。

1. 信用证。

SEQUENCE OF TOTAL	27：	1/1
FORM OF DC.	40A：	IRREVOCABLE
DC. NO.	20：	0684160117426
DATE OF ISSUE	31C：	190825
APPLICABLE RULES	40E：	UCP LATEST VERSION
EXPIRY DATE AND PLACE	31D：	191024，CHINA
APPLICANT	50：	M/S. MEMORY STEEL CORPORATION 73/A，LAL MOHAN SHAHA STREET （DHOLAIKHAL），　DHAKA – 1100. BANGLADESH.
BENEFICIARY	59：	JIANGSU I – TOUCH BUSINESS SERVICE LTD, ROOM 117，JIANGSU EDIFICE ZHANGJIAGANG FREE TRADE ZONE, JIANGSU，CHINA　TEL：86 – 512 – 56363783
AMOUNT	32B：	USD35000,00
AVAILABLE WITH/BY	41D：	ANY BANK IN CHINA BY NEGOTIATION
DRAFTS AT	42C：	AT SIGHT FOR FULL INVOICE VALUE
DRAWEE	42A：	DRAWN ON US
PARTIAL SHIPMENTS	43P：	ALLOWED
TRANSSHIPMENT	43T：	ALLOWED
PORTOF LOADING	44A：	ANY SEA PORT，CHINA
PORT OF DISCHARGE	44B：	CHITTAGONG SEA PORT，BANGLADESH
LATEST DATE OF SHIPMENT	44C：	191009
DESCRIPTION OFGOODS	45A：	201/2B SECONDARY GRADE STAINLESS STEEL SHEET OF WIDTH 1219MM THICKNESS 1MM TO 3MM，QTY：25,000 KGS AT THE RATE OF USD1. 40/KG FOR TOTAL AMOUNT OF USD35000,00 CFR CHIT-TAGONG，BANGLADESH. AS PER BENEFICIARY'S

PROFORMA INVOICE NO. SK20160802 – 001 DATED AUG 2，2019

DOCUMENTS REQUIRED	46A：	+ MANUALLY SIGNED COMMERCIAL INVOICE IN TRIPLICATE CERTIFYING MERCHANDISE TO BE OF CHINA ORIGIN AND INDICATING THAT THE GOODS ARE BEING IMPORTED AGAINST IRC NO. BA – 0171646，TI NO. 157 – 107 – 0121，VAT REGISTRATION NO. 9141093671.

+ FULL SET OF CLEAN 'SHIPPED ON BOARD' O-CEAN BILL OF LADING SHOWING ' FREIGHT PREPAID' MADE OUT TO ORDER AND BLANK IN-DORSED, NOTIFY APPLICANT.

+ PACKING LIST IN TRIPLICATE SHOWING GROSS WEIGHT, NET WEIGHT.

+ CERTIFICATE OF ORIGIN ISSUED AND LE-GALED BY CCPIT

+ BENEFICIARY'S DECLARATION SHOULD CERTIFY THAT THE COUNTRY OF ORIGIN HAS BEEN PRINTED ON GOODS PACKING BAG.

+ BENEFICIARY SHOULD SEND A FAX OR BY COUR IER TO L/C OPENING BANK WITHIN FIVE DAYS FROM THE OF SHIPMENT, ADVISING THE DATE OF SHIPMENT, VESSEL'S NAME, AMOUNT OF BILL AND L/C NO. AND A COPY OF THIS FAX SHOULD ACCOMPANY THE SHIPPING DOCU-MENTS.

+ SHIPMENT BY ISRAELI LINER IS PROHIBITED AND A CERTIFICATE TO THIS EFFECT ISSUED BY THE SHIPPING COMPANY MUST ACCOMPANY THE ORIGINAL DOCUMENTS.

CHARGES	71B：	ALL FOREIGN BANK CHARGES ARE FOR THE ACCOUNT OF THE BENEFICIARY.
PERIOD OF PRESENTATION	48：	15 DAYS FROM SHIPMENT DATE BUT WITHIN VALIDITY OF THE CREDIT

2. 合同。

SALES CONTRACT

ContractNo.：SSW0803

Date：AUG 15，2019

THE SELLER：JIANGSU I – TOUCH BUSINESS SERVICE LTD，

ROOM 117，JIANGSU EDIFICE

ZHANGJIAGANG FREE TRADE ZONE，

JIANGSU，CHINA TEL：86 – 512 – 56363783

THE BUYER：M/S. MEMORY STEEL CORPORATION

73/A，LAL MOHAN SHAHA STREET

（DHOLAIKHAL），DHAKA – 1100.

BANGLADESH.

This Contract is made by and between the Buyer and Seller，whereby the Buyer agrees to buy and the Selleragrees to sell the under mentioned goods on the terms and conditions stated below：

Description of Goods，Specifications	Quantity (set)	Unit Price (U. S. D/set)	Amount (U. S. D)
201/2B SECONDARY GRADE STAINLESS STEEL SHEET OF WIDTH 1219MM OR MORETHICKNESS 1MM TO 3MM, QTY：25，000KGS AT THE RATE OF USD1. 40/KG. AS PER BENEFICIARY'S PROFORMA INVOIVE NO. SK20160802 – 001 DATED AUG 2，2019			
	C. F. R	CHITTAGONG	
1. 2 * 1219 * 2438	5 576	1. 40	7 806. 40
1. 5 * 1219 * 2438	3 248	1. 40	4 547. 20
2. 0 * 1219 * 2438	11 630	1. 40	16 282. 00
3. 0 * 1219 * 2438	4 546	1. 40	6 364. 40
Total	25 000		35 000. 00

Say Total：U. S DOLLARS THIRTY FIVE THOUSAND ONLY.

PACKING：Standard export packing on pallets.

TRANSPORT DETAILS：the goods should shipped before：9th Oct，2019，from any Chinese port to Chittagong Bangladesh，

transshipment and partial shipment are allowed.

PAYMENT：By sight L/C and remain valid for negotiation in China for 15 days after shipment.

DOCUMENTS：

+ Signed commercial invoice in triplicate，certifying the goods are of Chinese origin and being imported against IRC No. BA – 0171646，VAT Registration No. 9141093671. .

+ Full set （3/3） of clean on board ocean Bill of Lading made out to order of shipper and blank endorsed.

+ Packing List in triplicate.

+ Certificate of origin by CCPIT.

+ Beneficiary's Declaration certifying that the country of origin has been printed on goods packing bag.

INSPECTION：Quality /Quantity/Weight Discrepancy and Claim：In case the quality and /or quantity/weight are found by the Buyer not to conform with the contract after arrival of the goods at the final destination, the Buyer may lodge a claim against the seller supported by a survey report issued by an inspection organization agreed upon by both parties with the exception of those claims for which the insurance company and /or the shipping company are to be held responsible. Claim for quality discrepancy should be filed by the Buyer within 60 days after arrival of the goods at the final destination while for quantity / weight discrepancy claim should be filed by the Buyer within 30 days after arrival of the goods at the final destination.

FORCE MAJOR：The Seller shall not be held responsible for failure or delay in delivery of the entire or portion of the goods under this contract in consequence of any Force Major incidents.

ARBITRATION：All disputes in connection with this Contract or the execution thereof shall be settled through friendly negotiations. If no settlement can be reached, the case shall then be submitted to the Foreign Trade Arbitration Commission of the China Council for the Promotion of International Trade, Beijing, for settlement by arbitration in accordance with the Commission's Provisional Rules of Procedure. The award rendered by the Commission shall be final and binding on both parties. The arbitration expenses shall be borne by the losing party unless otherwise award by the arbitration organization.

Signed by：

<table>
<tr><td>**THE SELLER**：</td><td>**THE BUYER**：</td></tr>
<tr><td>JIANGSU I – TOUCH BUSINESS SERVICE LTD</td><td>M/S. MEMORY STEEL CORPORATION.</td></tr>
<tr><td>彭　婷</td><td>**John Lee**</td></tr>
</table>

3. 货物资料：

毛重：180KGS/160KGS/195KGS/200KGS

净重：178KGS/157KGS/190KGS/198KGS

体积：35M3/42M3/40M3/38MS

发票日期：2019 年 9 月 20 日

唛头：请自制国际标准唛头

据此，请完成商业发票与装箱单制作：

ISSUER		COMMERCIAL INVOICE	
TO			
		NO.	DATE
TRANSPORT DETAILS		S/C NO.	L/C NO.
		TERMS OF PAYMENT	

Marks and Numbers	Number and kind of package Description of goods	Quantity	Unit Price	Amount
	Total:			

SAY

TOTAL:

×××× Import & Export Co. , Ltd
Add: No. 1 , ××× Road , ××× District , ××× City , ××× Prov. , P R China
Tel: Fax:

PACKING LIST

Contract No.		Date: .			
C/I No.		Date:			
From:		To:			

Marks	Description	Quantity	G. W.	N. W.	Meas.

Total:

能力实训项目2：商业发票和装箱单业务操作

　　根据出口商 PRIMA CONSTRUCTION MATERIALS CO.，LTD 第 DC 13724 号信用证的要求，2019 年 8 月 22 日，单证员黄柯制作了商业发票和装箱单。

　　1. 信用证。

SEQUENCE OF TOTAL	27：	1/1
FORM OF DC	40A：	IRREVOCABLE
DC NO.	20：	DC 190720
DATE OF ISSUE	31C：	190720
APPLICABLE RULES	40E：	UCP 600
EXPIRY DATE AND PLACE	31D：	160920 IN CHINA
APPLICANT	50：	CONSTRUCTION MOUDULAR SPECIALIST POSTAL：13 HARVEY RD.， SHENTON PK，WA 6008 AUSTRALIA
BENEFICIARY	59：	PRIMA CONSTRUCTION MATERIOLS CO.，LTD 1401 ROOM，38 BUILDING，CHUANGYE GARDEN BAOAN DISTRICT，SHENZHEN，CHINA
AMOUNT	32B：	USD6840,00
AVAILABLE WITH/BY	41D：	ANY BANK BY NEGOTIATION
DRAFTS AT	42C：	AT 30DAYS AFTER SIGHT
DRAWEE	42A：	DRAWN ON US
PARTIAL SHIPMENTS	43P：	ALLOWED
TRANSHIPMENT	43T：	ALLOWED
LOADING PORT	44E：	CHINA MAIN PORT
DISCHARGE PORT	44F：	FREMANTLE，AUSTRALIA
LATEST DATE OF SHIPMENT	44C：	190905
DESCRIPTION OFGOODS	45A：	BAMBOO FLOORING ITEM 1 100 SQM　U. S. D20.00/SQM ITEM 2 100 SQM　U. S. D39.50/SQM ALL PACKING IN SEA WORTHY CARTONS CIF FREMANTLE AS PER PI NO.：BFF0610
DOCUMENTS REQUIRED	46A：	+MANUALLY SIGNED COMMECIAL INVOICE 3 ORIGINALS PLUS THREE COPIES. +FULL SET（3/3）OF MARINE BILLS OF LADING，MADE OUT TO ORDER，MARKED FREIGHT PREPAID，AND NOTIFY APPLICANT（STATING FULL NAME AND ADDRESS）. +INSURANCE POLICY OR CERTIFICATE IN TRIPLICATE，BLANK INDORSED，FOR THE INVOICE VALUE PLUS 10% COVERING ICC（A）

RISK AND ICC（STRIKE）. FROM WAREHOUSE TO WAREHOUSE AND I. O. P, PAYABLE AT FREMENTLE IN U. S. D.

+ PACKING LIST 3 ORIGINALS AND 2 COPIES.

+ CERTIFICATE OF ORIGIN IN CHINA ISSUED BY OFFICIAL AUTRORITY.

+ BENEFICIARY'S CERTIFICATE SHOWING THAT A SET OF ORIGINAL SHIPPING DOCUMENTS HAS BEEN MAIL TO THE APPLICANT BY EXPRESS AFTER 2 DAYS OF SHIOMENT.

CHARGES   71B：ALL BANKING CHARGES OUTSIDE COUNTRY OF ISSUE ARE FOR BENEFICIARY/'S ACCOUNT.

PERIOD OF PRESENTATION   48：WITHIN 15 DAYS AFTER THE DATE OF SHIPMENT BUT WITHIN THE VALIDITY OF THE L/C

CONFIRMATION INSTRUCTIONS 49：WITHOUT

2. 合同。

CONTRACT

Contract No. ：BFF0606   Date：JUL 1，2019

THE SELLER：PRIMA CONSTRUCTION MATERIOLS CO. ，LTD

1401 ROOM，38 BUILDING，CHUANGYE GARDEN

BAOAN DISTRICT，SHENZHEN，CHINA

THE BUYER：CONSTRUCTION MOUDULAR SPECIALIST

POSTAL：13 HARVEY RD. ，

SHENTON PK，WA 6008 AUSTRALIA

This Contract is made by and between the Buyer and Seller，whereby the Buyer agrees to buy and the Seller agrees to sell the under mentioned goods on the terms and conditions stated below：

Description of Goods，Specifications，	Quantity（SQM）	Unit Price（U. S. D/SQM）	Amount（U. S. D）
BAMBOO FLOORING CIF FREMENTLE		CIF	FREMANTLE
ITEM 1	100	20. 00	2 000. 00
ITEM 2	100	39. 50	3 950. 00
AS PER PI NO. ：BFF0610			
Total	200		5 950. 00

Say total：U. S DOLLARS FIFTY NINE HUNDRED AND FIFTY （USD5950）ONLY.

PACKING：ALL PACKING IN SEA WORTHY CARTONS.

TRANSPORT DETAILS：the goods should shipped on or before：5th Sep，2019，from

Shenzhen，China to Fremantle Australia，transshipment and partial shipment are all allowed.

INSURANCE：To be effected by the Seller for 110% of invoice value covering ICC（A）risk and ICC（War Risk）.

PAYMENT：By irrevocable documentary letter of credit at 30 days after sight，reaching the seller not later than Jul 30，2019 and remain valid for negotiation in China for 15 days after shipment.

DOCUMENTS：

　+ Signed commercial invoice three originals and three copies.

　+ Full set of clean on board ocean Bill of Lading made to order.

　+ Packing List three originals and two copies.

　+ Insurance policy endorsed in blank and in triplicate.

　+ Certificate of Origin in China issued by official authority.

3. 货物资料。

C/I No：13BBF016 C/I Date：SEP. 11，2013

G/W：102KG /SQM ；110KG/SQM

N/W：97KG /SQM ；108KG/SQM

据此，请完成商业发票及装箱单制作：

ISSUER	COMMERCIAL INVOICE		
TO			
	NO.		DATE
TRANSPORT DETAILS	S/C NO.		L/C NO.
	TERMS OF PAYMENT		
Marks and Numbers	Number and kind of package Description of goods	Quantity	Unit Price	Aount
	Total:			
SAY				
TOTAL:				

XXXX Import & Export Co. , Ltd Add：No. 1 , xxx Road, xxx District, xxx City, xxx Prov. , P R China Tel： Fax：					
PACKING LIST					
Contract No.		Date： .			
C/I No.		Date：			
From：		To：			
Marks	Description	Quantity	G. W.	N. W.	Meas.

Total：

第五节　学习导航

一、参考资料

［1］章安平. 外贸单证操作［M］. 北京：高等教育出版社，2008.

［2］刘启萍，周树玲. 外贸单证［M］. 北京：对外经贸大学出版社，2008.

［3］方士华，国际结算［M］. 沈阳：东北财经大学出版社，2016.

［4］吴轶群，国际商务单证操作［M］. 青岛：中国海洋大学出版社，2018.

二、自主学习平台

［1］全国外贸单证员考试中心。

［2］外贸经理人微信公众号。

［3］外贸单证课程国家教学资源库。

项目四
保险单据制作业务

第一节 项目描述与目标

一、项目描述

◆开篇业务引入

完成托运手续确认船期后，长沙鹏兴进出口有限公司向中国人民保险公司办理投保手续。该项目任务具体由单证员李望负责。2019 年 8 月 15 日，单证员李望根据 L/C 规定："+ INSURANCE POLICY OR CERTIFICATE BLANK INDORSED，FOR THE INVOICE VALUE PLUS 10% COVERING ALL RISKS AND S. R. CC. FROM WAREHOUSE TO WAREHOUSE"，以及缮制好的商业发票、装箱单正本，制作投保单，向保险公司办理投保手续。

◆项目预期目标

通过对信用证项下保险条款的认真解读，结合该项目提供的商业发票等相关单据，介绍保险的相关知识，使同学们了解保险单据的种类，熟悉保险险别和保险条款，掌握保险单的缮制。

在项目实施过程中，通过对填制保险单和办理投保手续的任务训练，培养学生的审核、制单、业务核算等国际商务单证基本职业能力，亦培养学生独立操作业务和沟通能力。

表 4 -1 项目预期目标

目标类型	制作投保单和办理保险操作
知识目标	了解国际货物运输保险的有关知识、投保程序以及保单的种类
	掌握国际货物运输保险单的基本格式及内容
	掌握其签订和履行的基本过程
能力目标	能够缮制国际货物运输保险单
	掌握填写保险单据的技巧
职业素质目标	独立的业务操作能力
	沟通衔接能力

二、项目实施条件

1. 组织学生参观中国人民保险公司。
2. 学生能够在实训室对该项目进行分组讨论并实施。
3. 指导教师掌握扎实的国际贸易政策，具备扎实的外贸业务基础。

第二节　知识模块

一、保险单的含义

保险单据一般被理解为保险单，简称保单，是保险人对被保险人的承保证明，又是双方之间权利义务的契约。在被保险货物遭受损失时，它是被保险人索赔和保险人理赔的主要依据。

由于国际贸易大多数是通过海上运输来实现的，在海上运输途中，船只和货物都有可能由于自然灾害和意外事故而造成各种损失，因而进行保险是十分必要的。因此，海上运输保险单也就成为国际贸易中不可或缺的货运单据之一。

二、保险单据的内容

国际贸易中保单的格式不尽相同，但内容基本一致，一份完整的保险单据其基本内容应该包括如下几点：

（1）发票号码和保单号码。
（2）投保人即被保险人名称。
（3）货物描述、唛头、件数、包装情况。
（4）船名、起讫地、预计起运日期。
（5）保险金额和货币单位。
（6）承保险别、投保加成。
（7）保费给付地点及理赔地点。
（8）出单日期。
（9）保险公司签章。

三、保险单据的种类

（一）保险单（Insurance Policy）

俗称大保单，这是一种正规的保险合同，是完整独立的保险文件。除载明被保险人（投保人）的名称、被保险货物（标的物）的名称、数量或重量、唛头、运输工具、保险的起讫地点、承保险别、保险金额、出单日期等项目外，还在保险单的背面列有保险人的责任范围，以及保险人与被保险人各自的权利、义务等方面的详细条款。可由被保险人背书，随物权的转移而转让。

（二）保险凭证（Insurance certificate）

俗称小保单，中国人民保险公司发出的保险凭证是表示保险公司已经接受保险的一种证明文件，这是一种比较简化的保险单据。它包括了保险单的基本内容，但不附有保险条款全文。这种保险凭证与保险单有同等的法律效力。

（三）联合凭证（Combined Certificate），又称承保证明（Risk Note）

是我国保险公司特别使用的，比保险凭证更简化的保险单据。保险公司仅将承保险别、保险金额及保险编号加注在我国进出口公司开具的出口货物发票上，并正式签章即作为已经保险的证据。这种单据不能转让，是最简单的保险单据。

（四）预约保险单（Open Policy）

预约保险单又称开口保险单，它一般适用于经常有相同类型货物需要陆续装运的保险条款。预约保险单上载明保险货物的范围、险别、保险费率、每批运输货物的最高保险金额以及保险费的结付、赔款处理等项目，凡属于此保险单范围内的进出口货物，一经起运，即自动按保险单所列条件承保。但被保险人在获悉每批保险货物起运时，应立即将货物装船详细情况包括货物名称、数量、保险金额、运输工具种类和名称、航程起讫地点、开船日期等情况通知保险公司和进口商。

（五）保险批单

保险单出立后，如需变更其内容，可由保险公司另出的凭证注明更改或补充的内容，称为批单。其须粘在保险单上并加盖骑缝章，作为保险单不可分割的一部分。

四、保险条款和险别

我国为适应对外经济贸易业务发展的需要，由中国人民保险公司（PICC）根据我国的实际情况，分别制定了海洋、陆地、航空等多种运输方式的货物保险条款，总称为《中国保险条款》（China insurance clause，CIC）。

在国际保险市场上，最有影响力的保险条款当属英国伦敦保险协会制定的《协会货物条款》（Institute cargo clauses，ICC）。

我国现行的货物保险条款是1981年1月1日的修订本，根据不同的运输方式分别有不同的保险条款，以《海洋运输货物保险条款》使用最普遍，其主要内容有：保险人承保责任范围、除外责任、责任起讫、被保险人的义务和索赔期限。

保险人的承保责任范围：海运货物保险险别分为基本险和附加险两类。基本险又称主险，是可以独立投保的险别，包括平安险、水渍险和一切险；附加险是对基本险的补充和扩展，它不能单独投保，只能在投保了基本险的基础上加保，包括一般附加险和特殊附加险。

1. 基本险。

（1）平安险（F. P. A）

平安险是我国保险业的习惯叫法，英文原意是"单独海损不赔"。平安险承诺以下八项责任：

①被保险货物在运输途中由于恶劣气候、雷电、海啸、地震、洪水自然灾害造成整批

货物的全部损失或推定全损。当被保险人要求赔付推定全损时，须将受损货物及其权利委付给保险公司。

②由于运输工具遭搁浅、触礁、沉没、互撞，与其他物体碰撞以及失火、爆炸等意外事故造成被保险货物的全部或部分损失。

③只要运输工具曾经发生搁浅、触礁、沉没、焚毁等意外事故，不论这个意外事故发生之前或者以后曾在海上遭恶劣气候、雷电、海啸等自然灾害所造成的被保险货物的部分损失。

④在装卸转船过程中，被保险货物一件或数件落海所造成的全部损失或部分损失。

⑤被保险人对遭受承保责任内危险的货物采取抢救，防止或减少货损的措施而支付的合理费用，但以不超过这批被救货物的保险金额为限。

⑥运输工具遭自然或灾害或意外事故，需要在中途的港口或者在避难港口停靠，因而引起的卸货、装货、存仓以及运送货物所产生的特别费用。

⑦发生共同海损所引起的牺牲、公摊费和救助费用。

⑧运输契约订有"船舶互撞责任"条款，根据该条款规定应由货方偿还船方的损失。

（2）水渍险（W. P. A）

水渍险亦是我国保险业的习惯叫法，英文原意是"负责单独海损"。水渍险承保的责任范围是：

①平安保险承担的全部责任。

②被保险货物由于恶劣气候、雷电、海啸、地震、洪水自然灾害所造成的部分损失。

（3）一切险（All risks）

一切险的承保范围是：

①水渍险承保的全部责任一切险均给予承保。

②一切险负责被保险货物在运输途中，由于一般外来风险所致的全部或部分损失。

2. 附加险。

（1）一般附加险（General additional risks）

一般附加险承保一般外来风险所造成的损失，共有11种。

①偷窃、提货不着险（Theft, Pilferage and non-delivery risks, T. P. N. D）；②淡水雨淋险（Fresh water and damage risks, F. W. R. D）；③渗漏险（Leakage risks）；④短量险（Shortage risks）；⑤混杂、玷污险（Intermixture and contamination risks）；⑥碰撞、破碎险（Clash and breakage risks）；⑦钩损险（Hook damage risks）；⑧锈损险（Rust risks）；⑨串味险（risk of odour）；⑩包装破裂险（Breakage of packing risks）；⑪受潮受热险（sweating and heating risks）。

（2）特殊附加险（Special additional risks）

①交货不到险（Failure to deliver risks）；②进口关税险（Import duty risks）；③舱面险（On deck risks）；④黄曲霉素险（Aflatoxin risk）；⑤拒收险（Rejection risk）；⑥出口货物到香港（包括九龙在内）或澳门存仓火险责任扩展条款（Fine risk extension clause for storage of cargo at destination Hong Kong, including Kowloon, or Macao，简称 F. R. E. C）；⑦战争险（War risks）；⑧罢工险（Strikes risks）。

（3）英国伦敦保险协会海运货物保险条款

现行英国伦敦《协会货物条款》是 1982 年 1 月 1 日的修订本，与我国现行保险条款相比，其形式和内容都有所不同。该条款共有六种险别。它们是：

①协会货物条款（A）［ICC（A）］；②协会货物条款（B）［ICC（B）］；③协会货物条款（C）［ICC（C）］；④协会战争险条款；⑤协会罢工险条款；⑥恶意损害险条款。

前三种是主险，后三种是附加险，其中战争险条款和罢工险条款在征得保险人同意时，可以作为独立的险别进行投保。

（4）保险责任起讫

保险的责任起讫，是指保险人对被保险货物承担保险责任的有效时间。被保险货物如果在保险有效期内发生保险责任范围内的风险损失，被保险人有权进行索赔，否则就无权进行索赔。

根据国际保险市场的习惯做法，我们应注意以下两个保险条款：

①仓至仓条款（Warehouse to Warehouse clause，简称 W/W）。

它是指保险人的承保责任从被保险货物运离保险单所载明的起运地发货人仓库开始，直至该项货物被运抵保险单所载明的收货人仓库或被保险人用作分配、分派或非正常运输的其他储存处所为止。

如未抵达上述仓库或储存处所，则以被保险货物在最后卸货港全部卸离海轮后满 60 天为止。

如在上述 60 天内被保险货物需转运至非保险单所载明的目的地时，则该项货物开始转运时终止。

②水上条款。

战争险的责任起讫与基本险所采用的"仓之仓条款"不同，而是以"水上危险"为限，是指保险人的承保责任自货物装上保险单所载明的启运港的海轮或驳船开始，到卸离保险单所载明的目的港的海轮或驳船为止。

如果货物不卸离海轮或驳船，则从海轮到达目的港当日午夜起算满 15 日为上，等再装上续运海轮时，保险责任才继续有效。

五、保险金额和保险费

（一）保险金额

保险金额的定义：保险公司承担赔偿或者给付保险金责任的最高限额，也是保险公司计算保险费的基础。

保险金额一般是根据保险价值确定的。

保险金额的计算公式：

$$保险金额 = CIF（CIP）价 \times （1 + 投保加成率）$$

保险费的计算：

$$保险费 = 保险金额 \times 保险费率$$

PICC	中国人民保险公司
	The People's Insurance Company of China
	总公司设于北京　　　　　　一九四九年创立
	Head Office Beijing　　　　Established in 1949

货物运输保险单
CARGO TRANSPORTATION INSURANCE POLICY

发票号（INVOICE NO.）		保单号次
合同号（CONTRACT NO.）		POLICY NO.
信用证号（L/C NO.）		
被保险人：INSURED：		

　　中国人民保险公司（以下简称本公司）根据被保险人的要求，由被保险人向本公司缴付约定的保险费，按照本保险单承保险别和背面所载条款与下列特款承保下述货物运输保险，特立本保险单。

　　THIS POLICY OF INSURANCE WITNESSES THAT THE PEOPLE'S INSURANCE COMPANY OF CHINA (HEREINAFTER CALLED "THE COMPANY") AT THE REQUEST OF THE INSURED AND IN CONSIDERATION OF THE AGREED PREMIUM PAID TO THE COMPANY BY THE INSURED, UNDERTAKES TO INSURE THE UNDERMENTIONED GOODS IN TRANSPORTATION SUBJECT TO THE CONDITIONS OF THIS OF THIS POLICY AS PER THE CLAUSES PRINTED OVERLEAF AND OTHER SPECIAL CLAUSES ATTACHED HEREON.

标记 MARKS&NOS	包装及数量 QUANTITY	保险货物项目 DESCRIPTION OF GOODS	保险金额 AMOUNT INSURED

总保险金额 TOTAL AMOUNT INSURED：			
保费： PERMIUM：	AS ARRANGED	启运日期 DATE OF COMMENCEMENT：	装载运输工具： PER CONVEYANCE：
自 FROM：		经 VIA	至 TO

承保险别：
CONDITIONS：

　　所保货物，如发生保险单项下可能引起索赔的损失或损坏，应立即通知本公司下述代理人查勘。如有索赔，应向本公司提交保单正本（本保险单共有份正本）及有关文件。如一份正本已用于索赔，其余正本自动失效。

　　IN THE EVENT OF LOSS OR DAMAGE WITCH MAY RESULT IN A CLAIM UNDER THIS POLICY, IMMEDIATE NOTICE MUST BE GIVEN TO THE COMPANY'S AGENT AS MENTIONED HEREUNDER. CLAIMS, IF ANY, ONE OF THE ORIGINAL POLICY WHICH HAS BEEN ISSUED IN ORIGINAL (S) TOGETHER WITH THE RELEVANT DOCUMENTS SHALL BE SURRENDERED TO THE COMPANY. IF ONE OF THE ORIGINAL POLICY HAS BEEN ACCOMPLISHED. THE OTHERS TO BE VOID.

	中国人民保险公司 The People's Insurance Company of China
赔款偿付地点 CLAIM PAYABLE AT	
出单日期 ISSUING DATE	Authorized Signature

图 4-1　中国人民保险公司保险单样本

六、具体单据业务操作

1. 被保险人（Insured）。

（1）填写内容：

填在"at the request of"后面，被保险人有以下几种填法：

①如 L/C 和合同无特别定，或要求"Endorsed in blank"此栏一般填信用证的受益人，即出口公司名称。可不填详细地址，但出口公司应在保险单背面背书。

②若来证指定以 XX 公司为被保险人，则应在此栏填 XX CO.。出口公司不要背书。

③若来证规定以某银行为抬头，如："TO ORDER OF XXX BANK"，则在此栏先填上受益人名称，再填上"HELD TO THE ORDER OF XXX BANK"。受益人均须在背面作空白背书。

如：TO ORDER，则应填 THE APPLICANT + 出口企业名称，FOR THE ACCOUNT OF WHOM IT MAY CONCERN。

（2）实例：

①at the request of：JIANGXI JINYUAN IMPORT & EXPORT CO.，LTD.

②at the request of：JIANGXI JINYUAN IMPORT & EXPORT CO.，LTD. HELD TO THE ORDER OF XXX BANK

2. 发票号码、合同号和信用证号（Invoice no.，contract no. and L/C no.）。

（1）填写内容：

该栏目要根据商业发票以及合同、信用证信息进行填写。

（2）实例：

发票号（INVOICE NO.）LJ08071

合同号（CONTRACT NO.）ZJJY0739

信用证号（L/C NO.）YZF07599

3. 标记 & 唛头（Marks & Nos.）。

（1）填写内容：

按信用证规定，保险单上标记应与发票、提单上一致。可单独填写，若来证无特殊规定，一般可简单填成"AS PER INV. NO. XXX"。

（2）实例：

Marks & Nos：

　SIK

ZJJY0739

L357/L358

DUBAI，U. A. E.

C/NO：1 - 66

4. 包装及数量（Quantity）。

（1）填写内容：

此栏填制大包装件数，并应与提单上同一栏目内容相同。有包装但以重量计价的，应把包装重量与计价重量都注上；裸装货物要注明本身件数；煤炭、石油等散装货应注明"IN BULK"再填净重；如以单位包装件数计价者，可只填总件数。

（2）实例：

    Quantity：166　BALES

5. 保险物资项目（Description of goods）。

（1）填写内容：

根据投保单填写，要与提单此栏目的填写一致。一般允许使用统称，但不同类别的多种货物应注明不同类别的各自总称。

（2）实例：

    Description of Goods：LADIES JACKET

6. 保险金额（Amount Insured）和总保险金额（Total Amount Insured）。

（1）填写内容：

保险金额可小写，例如：USD70,638.00。

总保险金额大写。

注意：

①保险货币与信用证一致，大小写要一致。

②保险金额应严格按照信用证和合同上的要求填制，保险金额应为发票金额加上投保加成后的金额，如信用证和合同无明确规定，一般都以发票金额加一成（即110%的发票金额）填写。

③保险金额不要小数，出现小数时无论多少一律向上进位。

（2）实例：

Amount Insured：USD70,638.00

Total Amount Insured：SAY U.S. DOLLARS SEVENTY THOUSAND SIX HUNDRED THIRTY EIGHT ONLY

7. 保险费及保险费率（Premium and Rate）。

此栏一般由保险公司填制或已印好 AS ARRANGED，除非信用证另有规定，如"IN-OURANCE POLICY ENDORSED IN BLANK FULL INVOICE VALUE PLUS10% MARKED PREMIUM PAID"时，此栏就填入"PAID"或把已印好的"AS ARRANGED"删去加盖校对章后打上"PAID"字样。

8. 装载运输工具（Per Conveyance S. S）。

（1）填写内容：

要与运输单据一致，并应按照实际情况填写。

海运方式下填写船名和航次；如整个运输由两段或两段以上运程完成时，应分别填写一程船名及二程船名，中间用"/"隔开。例如：提单中一程船名为"DOGXING"，二程船为"HUAIHAI"，则填"DONGXING/HUAIHAI"。

铁路运输加填运输方式为 BY RAILWAY 或 BY TRAI，最好再加车号，如：BY TRAIN：WAGON NO. ××；航空运输为"BY AIR"；邮包运输为"BY PARCEL POST"。

（2）实例：

Per conveyance：MSC SARAH VOY. NO. 60A

9. 启运日期（date of commencement）。

（1）填写内容

此栏填制应按 B/L 中的签发日期或签发日期前 5 天内的任何一天填，或可简单填上 AS PER B/L。

（2）实例：

date of commencement：MAR. 20，2016

10. 起讫地点（FROM...TO...）。

（1）填写内容：

与提单一致。填装运港，目的港及转运港。当信用证中未明确列明具体的起运港口和目的的港口时，如：ANY CHINESE PORT 或 ANY JAPANESE PORT，填制时应根据货物实际装运选定一个具体的港口，如 SHANGHAI 或 OSAKA 等。

（2）实例：

FROM SHANGHAI TO NEW YORK

11. 承保险别（Conditions）。

（1）填写内容：

本栏系保险单的核心内容，填写时应注意保险险别及文句与信用证严格一致，应根据信用证或合同中的保险条款要求填写，即使信用证中有重复语句，为了避免混乱和误解，最好按信用证规定的顺序填写。

注意：

①应严格按照信用证的险别投保。最好注明险别的依据及生效时间。

②如信用证没有规定具体险别，或只规定"MARINE RISK" "USUAL RISK" 或 "TRANSPORT RISK" 等，则可投保一切险（ALL RISKS）、水渍险（WA 或 WPA）、平安险（FPA）三种基本险中的任何一种。另外，还可以加保一种或几种附加险。

③如来证要求的险别超出了合同规定，或成交价格为 FOB 或 CFR，但来证却由卖方保险，这种情况下，如果买方同意支付额外保险费，可按信用证办理。

④保险单据可以援引任何除外责任条款（An insurance document may contain reference to any exclusion clause）

⑤保险单据可以注明受免赔率或免赔额（减除额）约束。如果信用证要求的保险不计免索赔（Irrespective of percentage，I. O. P.），那么该保单不能含有免赔率和超过部分减扣（an excess deductible）的约束条款。

（2）实例：

CONDITIONS：COVERING ALL RISKS AND WAR RISK OF PICC（1/1/1981）INCL. WAREHOUSE TO WAREHOUSE AND I. O. P

12. 赔款偿付地点（Claim payable at）。

（1）填写内容：

①此栏应严格按照信用证或合同规定填制地点和币种两项内容，地点按信用证或投保单，币种应与保险金额一致。

②如来证未具体规定，一般将目的地作为赔付地点。

③如信用证规定不止一个目的港或赔付地，则应全部照填。

（2）实例：

CLAIM PAYABLE AT：DUBAI，U. A. E.

13. 投保日期（Date）。

（1）填写内容：

此栏填制保险单的日期。以保险手续要求货物离开出口仓库前办理，保险单的签发日期应为货物离开仓库的日期或至少填写早于提单签发的日期、发运日或接受监管日。

（2）实例：

Apr. 10，2019

14. 保险公司签章（Authorized signature）。

（1）填写内容：

此栏盖与第一栏相同的保险公司印章及其负责人的签字。实际操作中其签章一般已经印刷在保险单上。保险单需经保险公司签章后方才生效。

（2）实例：

PICC Property and Casualty Limited Qingdao Branch

李阳

15. 保险单的正本份数（Originals of the policy）。

正本保险单上必须有"ORIGINAL"字样。UCP600 规定：如保险单据表明所出具正本单据系一份以上，则必须提交全部正本保险单据；如保险单据表明有要求或信用证条款要求，所有正本必须表面看来已被会签。

第三节　任务模块

在该项目中单证员李望应完成的工作任务包括：

任务1：认真审核信用证中的保险条款并准备好商业发票和装箱单。

任务2：根据上述资料及具体业务要求缮制保险单。

任务3：办理投保手续。

1. 信用证中的保险条款：" + INSURANCE POLICY OR CERTIFICATE BLANK INDORSED, FOR THE INVOICE VALUE PLUS 10% COVERING ALL RISKS AND S. R. CC. FROM WAREHOUSE TO WAREHOUSE"。

2. 商业发票。

单据略。

3. 装箱单。

单据略。

据此，单证员李望缮制了保险单。

Policy of insurance

PICC	中国人民保险公司
	The People's Insurance Company of China
	总公司设于北京　　　一九四九年创立
	Head Office Beijing　　Established in 1949

货物运输保险单
CARGO TRANSPORTATION INSURANCE POLICY

发票号（INVOICE NO.）	PX16IVN1039	保单号次	SH01/173071
合同号（CONTRACT NO.）	CB161039	POLICY NO.	
信用证号（L/C NO.）	DC HMN214479		
被保险人：INSURED：	LILING FENGXING CERAMIC FACTORY WUSHI JIASHU LILING HUNAN, CHINA		

　　中国人民保险公司（以下简称本公司）根据被保险人的要求，由被保险人向本公司缴付约定的保险费，按照本保险单承保险别和背面所载条款与下列特款承保下述货物运输保险，特立本保险单。

THIS POLICY OF INSURANCE WITNESSES THAT THE PEOPLE'S INSURANCE COMPANY OF CHINA (HEREINAFTER CALLED "THE COMPANY") AT THE REQUEST OF THE INSURED AND IN CONSIDERATION OF THE AGREED PREMIUM PAID TO THE COMPANY BY THE INSURED, UNDERTAKES TO INSURE THE UNDERMENTIONED GOODS IN TRANSPORTATION SUBJECT TO THE CONDITIONS OF THIS OF THIS POLICY AS PER THE CLAUSES PRINTED OVERLEAF AND OTHER SPECIAL CLAUSES ATTACHED HEREON.

标记 MARKS&NOS	包装及数量 QUANTITY	保险货物项目 DESCRIPTION OF GOODS	保险金额 AMOUNT INSURED
AS PRE INVOICE NO. PX16IVN1039	1589 CTNS	CERAMIC CUPS AND BOWLS	USD 29,589.00

总保险金额 TOTAL AMOUNT INSURED：	SAY U. S. DOLLARS TWENTY NINE THOUSAND FIVE HUNDRED AND EIGHTY NINE ONLY

保费： PERMIUM：	AS ARRANGED	启运日期 DATE OF COMMENCEMENT：	AS PER B/L	装载运输工具： PER CONVEYANCE：	COSCO　SEATTLE VOY. NO. C078E
自 FROM：	SHENZHEN	经 VIA		至 TO	PRINCE RUPERT

承保险别：
CONDITIONS：

COVERING ALL RISKS AND S. R. C. C. OF C. I. C. OF PICC (1/1/1981) INCL. WAREHOUSE TO WAREHOUSE

　　所保货物，如发生保险单项下可能引起索赔的损失或损坏，应立即通知本公司下述代理人查勘。如有索赔，应向本公司提交保单正本（本保险单共有 份正本）及有关文件。如一份正本已用于索赔，其余正本自动失效。

IN THE EVENT OF LOSS OR DAMAGE WITCH MAY RESULT IN A CLAIM UNDER THIS POLICY, IMMEDIATE NOTICE MUST BE GIVEN TO THE COMPANY'S AGENT AS MENTIONED HEREUNDER. CLAIMS, IF ANY, ONE OF THE ORIGINAL POLICY WHICH HAS BEEN ISSUED IN ORIGINAL (S) TOGETHER WITH THE RELEVANT DOCUMENTS SHALL BE SURRENDERED TO THE COMPANY. IF ONE OF THE ORIGINAL POLICY HAS BEEN ACCOMPLISHED. THE OTHERS TO BE VOID.

		中国人民保险公司 The People's Insurance Company of China
赔款偿付地点 CLAIM PAYABLE AT	PRINCE RUPERT IN USD	SHENZHEN
出单日期 ISSUING DATE	Aug. 15, 2019	＊＊＊＊＊＊

第四节 任务拓展模块

能力实训项目1：保险单业务操作

根据以下资料填制保险单

1. 信用证。

+ INSURANCE POLICY/CERTIFICATE IN DUPLICATEENDORSED IN BLANK FOR 110% INVOICE VALUE, COVERING ALL RISKS OF CIC OF PICC（1/1/1981）INCL. WAREHOUSE TO WAREHOUSE AND I. O. P AND SHOWING THE CLAIMING CURRENCY IS THE SAME AS THE CURRENCY OF CREDIT

2. 商业发票。

ZHEJIANG INTERNATIONAL IMP. & EXP. CORP.
8TH FLOOR FOREIGN TRADER BUILDING
200 ZHANQIAN ROAD, JIANGWANG BUILDING

COMMERCIAL INVOICE

TO:	MCHIME CORPORATION 2-2 NAKANOSHINA 3-CHOME, KITA-KU KOBE, 632-8620, JAPAN	INVOICE NO.:	05AO-P001
		INVOICE DATE:	MAR. 10, 2019
		S/C NO.:	J515
		S/C DATE:	FEB.2,2019
		L/C NO.:	DCMTN55163
		L/C DATE:	FEB. 16, 2019

FROM :	SHANGHAI		TO:	KOBE

Marks and Numbers	Number and kind of package Description of goods	Quantity	Unit Price CIF KOBE	Amount CIF KOBE
J-515 KOBE PKG. NO. 1-166	100PCT COTTON GREIGE PRINT CLOTH ART. NO. 3042 FIRST QUALITY SIZE:30×30 68×68 50"EXPORT PACKING IN 166 SEAWORTHY BALES OF 1600 EACH THISIS TO CERTIFY THAT THE GOODS IS CHINESE ORIGIN	199,200YDS	CIF KOBE USD 0.32/YD	USD63,744.00
	Total:	199,200YDS		USD63,744.00
SAY TOTAL:	U.S. DOLLARS SIXTY THREE THOUSAND SEVEN HUNDRED AND FORTY FOUR ONLY			
	ZHEJIANG INTERNATIONAL IMP. & EXP. CORP. XXX			

3. 海运提单。

1. Shipper Insert Name, Address and Phone	许可证号
ZHEJIANG INTERNATIONAL IMP. & EXP. CORP. 8TH FLOOR FOREIGN TRADER BUILDING 200 ZHANQIAN ROAD, JIANGWANG BUILDING	B/L No. MSCU42014737

中远集装箱运输有限公司
COSCO CONTAINER LINES

2. ConsigneeInsert Name, Address and Phone	
TO ORDER	TLX: 33057 COSCO CN
	FAX: +86(021) 6545 8984 ORIGINAL

3. Notify Party Insert Name, Address and Phone (It is agreed that no responsibility shall attach to the Carrier or his agents for failure to notify)
MCHIME CORPORATION 2-2 NAKANOSHINA 3-CHOME, KITA-KU KOBE, 632-8620, JAPAN

Port-to-Port or Combined Transport

BILL OF LADING

4. Combined Transport *	5. Combined Transport*
Pre -carriage by	Place of Receipt

6. Ocean Vessel Vo. No.	7. Port of Loading
MC SARAH VOY.6A	SHANGHAI, CHINA

8. Port of Discharge	9. Combined Transport *
	Place of Delivery
KOBE, JAPAN	

RECEIVED in external apparent good order and condition except as otherwise noted. The total number of packages or unites stuffed in the container, the description of the goods and the weights shown in this Bill of Lading are furnished by the Merchants, and which the carrier has no reasonable means of checking and is not a part of this Bill of Lading contract. The carrier has issued the number of Bills of Lading stated below, all of this tenor and date, one of the original Bills of Lading must be surrendered and endorsed or signed against the delivery of the shipment and whereupon any other original Bills of Lading shall be void. The Merchants agree to be bound by the terms and conditions of this Bill of Lading as if each had personally signed this Bill of Lading

SEE clause 4 on the back of this Bill of Lading (Terms continued on the back hereof, please read carefully)

*Applicable Only When Document Used as a Combined Transport Bill of Lading

Marks & Nos. Container / Seal No.	No. of Containers or Packages	Description of Goods (If Dangerous Goods, See Clause 20)	Gross Weight Kgs	Measurement
J-515 KOBE PKG. NO. 1-166	166 BALES	100PCT COTTON GREIGE PRINT CLOTH	23406KGS	53.618M^3
		Description of Contents for Shipper's Use Only (Not part of This B/L Contract)		

10. Total Number of containers and/or packages (in words) SAY ONE HUNDRED SIXTY SIX BALES ONLY
Subject to Clause 7 Limitation

11. Freight & Charges	Revenue Tons	Rate	Per	Prepaid	Collect
	AS ARRANGED				

Ex. Rate:	Prepaid at	Payable at	Place and date of issue
			SHANGHAI MAR. 20,2019
	Total Prepaid	No. of Original B(s)/L	Signed for the Carrier, COSCO CONTAINER LINES
		THREE	COSCO AS CARRIER XXXX

LADEN ON BOARD THE VESSEL			AS AGENT FOR THE CARRIER NAMED ABOVE
DATE	MAR. 20, 2019	BY	CHINA NATIONAL FOREIGN TRADE TRANSPORT CORPRATION AS AGENT
(COSCO STANDARD FORM 9803)			XXXX

能力实训项目 2：保险单业务操作

上接项目六，根据深圳比高进出口有限公司第 NK2－166 号信用证的要求，2016 年 10 月 18 日，单证员黄柯备齐信用证、商业发票和装箱单等资料向中国人民保险公司办理保险手续。

1. 信用证。

SEQUENCE OF TOTAL	27：	1/1
FORM OF DC	40A：	IRREVOCABLE
DC NO	20：	DC 19810
DATE OF ISSUE	31C：	190810
APPLICABLE RULES	40E：	UCP 600
EXPIRY DATE AND PLACE	31D：	190920 IN CHINA
APPLICANT	50：	CONSTRUCTION MOUDULAR SPECIALIST POSTAL：16 HARVEY RD., SHENTON PK, WA 6008
BENEFICIARY	59：	PRIMA CONSTRUCTION MATERIALS CO., LTD 1401 ROOM, 38 BUILDING, CHUANGYE GARDEN BAOAN DISTRICT, SHENZHEN, CHINA
AMOUNT	32B：	USD6,840.00
AVAILABLE WITH/BY	41D：	ANY BANK BY NEGOTIATION
DRAFTS AT	42C：	AT 30DAYS AFTER SIGHT
DRAWEE	42A：	DRAWN ON US
PARTIAL SHIPMENTS	43P：	ALLOWED
TRANSHIPMENT	43T：	ALLOWED
LOADING PORT	44E：	CHINA MAIN PORT
DISCHARGE PORT	44F：	FREMANTLE, AUSTRALIA
LATEST DATE OF SHIPMENT	44C：	190905
DESCRIPTION OF GOODS	45A：	BAMBOO FLOORING ITEM 1 100 SQM U.S.D20.00/SQM ITEM 1 100 SQM U.S.D39.50/SQM ALL PACKING IN SEA WORTHY CARTONS CIF FREMANTLE AS PER PI NO.：BFF0610
DOCUMENTS REQUIRED	46A：	+ MANUALLY SIGNED COMMECIAL INVOICE 3 ORIGINALS PLUS THREE COPIES. + FULL SET (3/3) OF MARINE BILLS OF LADING, MADE OUT TO ORDER, MARKED FREIGHT PREPAID, AND NOTIFY APPLICANT (STATING FULL NAME AND ADDRESS). + INSURANCE POLICY OR CERTIFICATE IN TRIPLICATE, BLANK INDORSED, FOR THE IN-

VOICE VALUE PLUS 10% COVERING ICC（A）RISK AND ICC（STRIKE）. FROM WAREHOUSE TO WAREHOUSE AND I. O. P, PAYABLE AT FREMENTLE IN U. S. D.

+ PACKING LIST 3 ORIGINALS AND 2 COPIES.

+ CERTIFICATE OF ORIGIN IN CHINA ISSUED BY OFFICIAL AUTRORITY.

+ BENEFICIARY'S CERTIFICATE SHOWING THAT A SET OF ORIGINAL SHIPPING DOCUMENTS HAS BEEN MAIL TO THE APPLICANT BY EXPRESS AFTER 2 DAYS OF SHIOMENT.

CHARGES　　　　　　　　　　71B：ALL BANKING CHARGES OUTSIDE COUNTRY OF ISSUE ARE FOR BENEFICIARY/'S ACCOUNT.

PERIOD OF PRESENTATION　　48：WITHIN 15 DAYS AFTER THE DATE OF SHIPMENT

BUT WITHIN THE VALIDITY OF THE L/C

CONFIRMATION INSTRUCTIONS　49：WITHOUT

2. 商业发票。

Prima Construction Materials Co. , Ltd
Add：1401Room，38building，Chuangye Gardern，Baoan District，Shenzhen China
Tel：0086－755－32076630　　　　Fax：0086－755－32076630

COMMERCIAL INVOICE

Contract No. : CBF160724	No. : PR－20190820
L/C No. : DC 16724	Date：AUG 22，2019
From：SHENZHEN	To：FREMENTLE

Marks&Nos. No	Description of Goods	Quantity	Unit Price	Amount
CMS FREMENTLE CBF160724 NO. : 1－109	BAMBOO FLOORING			CIF FREMENTLE
	CARBONISED BAMBOO FLOORING	100SQM	$ 20. 00	$ 2,000. 00
		100SQM	$ 39. 50	$ 3,950. 00
	STRAND WOVEN BAMBOO FLOOR－ING DECKING			
		TOTAL EXW PRICE		$ 5,950. 00
		LCL CHARGE		$ 450. 00
		INSURANCE COST		$ 60. 00
		FREIGHT		$ 380. 00
		CIF VALUE		$ 6,480. 00

3. 其他信息。

VESSEL/VOYAGE：MOL INTEGRITY /102W

第五节　学习导航

一、参考资料

[1] 章安平. 外贸单证操作［M］. 北京：高等教育出版社，2008.

[2] 刘启萍，周树玲. 外贸单证［M］. 北京：对外经贸大学出版社，2008.

[3] 方士华，国际结算［M］. 沈阳：东北财经大学出版社，2016.

[4] 吴轶群，国际商务单证操作［M］. 青岛：中国海洋大学出版社，2018.

二、自主学习平台

[1] 全国外贸单证员考试中心。

[2] 外贸经理人微信公众号。

[3] 外贸单证课程国家教学资源库。

项目五
原产地证的申领和制作

第一节　项目描述与目标

一、项目描述

◆开篇业务引入

根据第 DC HMN214479 号信用证的要求，长沙鹏兴进出口有限公司可以向长沙海关申领普惠制原产地证。该项目任务具体由单证员李望负责。2019 年 4 月 10 日，单证员李望根据 L/C 规定："+ CETIFICATE OF GSP FORM A CETIFIED BY OFFICIAL AUTHOR-IZED"，以及缮制好的商业发票、装箱单正本，申领和制作普惠制原产地证。

◆项目预期目标

通过对信用证项下原产地证条款的认真解读，结合该项目提供的商业发票等相关单据，并介绍几种原产地证的背景知识，使同学们了解原产地证的申领流程，熟悉普惠制原产地证的产生背景，掌握原产地证的缮制。

在项目实施过程中，通过对产地证申领和制作任务的分解，在分工与合作中逐渐培养审核、制单、归类等国际商务单证基本职业能力，亦培养独立操作业务和与其他业务或政府部门有效沟通的能力。

表 5-1　项目预期目标

目标类型	原产地证的申领与制作
知识目标	熟悉原产地制度及贸易政策
	理解原产地证的申领程序
	掌握几种重要的产地证制作
能力目标	能办理原产地证的申领业务
	能根据实际业务需要缮制不同的原产地证
职业素质目标	独立业务操作能力
	与政府部门的沟通衔接能力

二、项目实施条件

1. 组织学生参观贸促会或出入境检验检疫局。
2. 学生能够在实训室对该项目进行分组讨论并实施。
3. 学生能够登陆产地证网上申报系统界面。
4. 指导教师掌握扎实的国际贸易政策，具备扎实的外贸业务基础。

第二节　知识模块

一、原产地证的含义及使用场合

原产地证明书，简称产地证。它是由出口国政府相关机构签发的一种证明货物的原产地或制造地的法律文件。它主要用于进口国海关实行差别关税、进口限制、不同进口配额和税率的依据，同时也是进出口通关和贸易统计的重要依据。原产地证明书是出口商按进口商的要求提供的，有着多种形式，其中应用最多的是一般原产地证书和普惠制产地证，通常多用于不需要提供海关发票或领事发票的国家或地区。

二、原产地证的主要种类

1. 普惠制原产地证（Generalized System of Preference Certificate of Origin，简称 GSP 产地证）。

普遍优惠制是发达国家对发展中国家向其出口的制成品或半成品货物，普遍给予的一种关税优惠待遇的制度。它使发展中国家与发达国家在贸易上能开展有效的竞争。至今，世界上目前给予我国普惠制待遇的国家共 37 个：欧盟 28 国（比利时、丹麦、英国、德国、法国、爱尔兰、意大利、卢森堡、荷兰、希腊、葡萄牙、西班牙、奥地利、芬兰、瑞典、波兰、捷克、斯洛伐克、拉脱维亚、爱沙尼亚、立陶宛、匈牙利、马耳他、塞浦路斯、斯洛文尼亚、保加利亚、罗马尼亚、克罗地亚）、挪威、瑞士、土耳其、俄罗斯、白俄罗斯、乌克兰、哈萨克斯坦、加拿大、澳大利亚和新西兰。

受惠国凡是要求享受普惠制待遇的出口商品，都必须持有能证明其原产资格和符合直运规则的证明文件。证明原产资格的文件就是《普遍优惠制原产地证明书（申报与证明联合）格式 A》，简称 GSP FORM A 格式（见图 1）。它是受惠国的产品出口到给惠国时，产品享受普惠制关税减免待遇时必备的凭证。

签发机构通常不接受货物出运后才递交的原产地证申请。

此外，还有如中国 – 澳大利亚自贸协定原产地证书、中国 – 新西兰自贸协定原产地证书、中国 – 新加坡自贸协定原产地证书、中国 – 韩国自贸协定原产地证书等 15 种原产地证书均可在单一窗口自助打印。

ORIGINAL

1. Goods consigned form (Exporter's business name, address, country)	Reference No. GENERALIZED SYSTEM OF PREFERENCES CERTIFICAT OF ORIGIN (Combined declaration and certificate) FORM A issued in the people's republic of china (country) See Notes Overleaf			
2. Goods consigned to (consignee's name, address, country)				
3. Means of transport and route (as far as known)	4. For official use			
5. item number	6. Marks & No. XYZSLACKS TOK	7. Number and kind of packages; description of goods 100PCT COTTO	8. Origin criterion (see Notes overleaf) " "	9. Gross weight or other quantity 180KGS	10. Number and date of invoices DATE:

11. Certification It is hereby certified, on the basis of control carried out, that the declaration by the exporter is correct. 中国海关 -------------------------------- Place and date, signature and stamp of certifying authority	16. Declaration by the exporter The undersigned hereby declares that above details and statements are correct; that all goods were produced in ------------------------ CHINA ------------------------ (country) and that they comply with the original requirements specified for those goods in the generalized system of preferences for goods exported to -------------------------------- -------------------------------- Place and date, signature and stamp of certifying authority

图 5-1　普惠制原产地证样本

2. 一般原产地证（Certificate of Origin）。

简称 C/O，它是证明中国出口货物符合《中华人民共和国出口货物原产地规则》，货物确系中华人民共和国原产的证明文件，也是进口国海关采取不同国别政策和关税待遇的依据。我国使用的一般原产地证书主要由中国贸促会（CCPIT）签发。

ORIGINAL

1. Exporter	Certificate No.
	CERTIFICATE OF ORIGIN
2. Consignee	**OF**
	THE PEOPLE'S REPUBLIC OF CHINA
3. Means of transport and route	5. For certifying authority use only
4. Country / region of destination	

6. Marks and numbers	7. Number and kind of packages; description of goods	8. H. S. Code	9. Quantity	10. Number and date of invoices

11. Declaration by the exporter	16. Certification
The undersigned hereby declares that the above details and statements are correct, that all the goods were produced in China and that they comply with the Rules of Origin of the People's Republic of China.	It is hereby certified that the declaration by the exporter is correct.
-------------------------------	-------------------------------
Place and date, signature and stamp of authorized signatory	Place and date, signature and stamp of certifying authority

图 5 - 2   一般原产地证样本

3. 区域性经济集团互惠原产地证。

区域性经济集团互惠原产地证主要有《〈中国－东盟自由贸易区〉优惠原产地证明书》（FORM E）、《亚太贸易协定》原产地证明书（FORM B）、《〈中国与巴基斯坦优惠贸易安排〉优惠原产地证明书》（FORM P）、《〈中国—智利自贸区〉原产地证书》（FORM F）等。区域优惠原产地证书是具有法律效力的在协定成员国之间就特定产品享受互惠减免关税待遇的官方凭证。

4. 专用原产地证。

专用原产地证书是国际组织和国家根据政策和贸易措施的特殊需要，针对某一特殊行业的特定产品规定的原产地证书。主要有对美国出口的原产地声明书（Declaration of Country Origin），简称 DCO 产地证；输往欧盟纺织品产地证（Certificate of Origin of Textile Products），该证书的效用等同于配额，因此在我国由商务部签发；此外，还有输往欧盟蘑菇罐头原产地证明书、烟草真实性证书等。

三、具体单据业务操作

（一）一般原产地证的缮制

1. 产地证编号（Certificate No.）。

（1）填写内容：

该栏填写由签证机关编订的证书号。

（2）实例：

    Certificate No. ：CCPIT040377950

2. 出口方（Exporter）。

（1）填写内容：

该栏填写出口公司的名称、详细地址以及国家（地区）名。如有中间商，则先在出口商信息后填写 VIA，再写中间商名称地址及国家（地区）名。

（2）实例：

    Exporter

        HUNAN TEXTILE IMP & EXP CORP.

        4E WUYI RD. ，CHANGSHA，CHINA

3. 收货方（Consignee）。

（1）填写内容：

该栏填写最终收货人的名称、详细地址以及国家（地区）名，一般为合同中的买方或信用证提单条款中的被通知人。如有中间商，则先在收货人信息后填写 VIA，再写中间商名称地址及国家（地区）名。

有时在转口贸易中信用证要求所有单据的收货人一栏留空，而原产地证该栏不得留空，此时，我们应在该栏注明"TO WHOM IT MAY CONCERN"或"TO ORDER"。

（2）实例：

    Consignee

K. ASLAM AND CO：16 – A DUBAI MAKET,

SHORAB KATRAK MARKET,

SADDAR KARACHI

4. 运输方式及路线（Means of Transport and Route）。

（1）填写内容：

该栏填写货物的装运港、目的港以及运输方式，如有转运港也必须注明。

（2）实例：

Means of Transport and Route

FORM CHANGSHA TO KARACHI BY TRAIN AND BY VESSEL VIA SHANGHAI

5. 最终目的国（地区）（Country/Region of Destination）。

（1）填写内容：

不论货物是否发生转运，该栏应填实际的最终收货人所在国家或地区名称。

（2）实例：

Country/Region of Destination

PAKISTAN

6. 签证机关用栏（For Certifying Authority Use Only）。

该栏一般留空，仅供签证机关在签发后发、补发证书或加注其他声明时使用。

7. 运输标志（Marks and Numbers）。

（1）填写内容：

该栏参照信用证的要求或者按商业发票填写商品的详细唛头，不能填写诸如（As per invoice No.）之类统称，无唛头时填写（N/M）。

（2）实例：

Marks and Numbers

KAAC

KARACHI

JWBS01611

NO. 1 – 500 CTNS

8. 商品描述、包装数量及种类（Number and Kind of Packages，Description of Goods）。

（1）填写内容：

该栏填写商品描述及包装数量。品名应避免使用食品（Food）之类的泛称，包装数量应用中英文描述，通常格式为在阿拉伯数字后加英文描述。最后可在该栏加注表示结束的分隔符。

（2）实例：

Number and Kind of Packages，Description of Goods

TRANSISTOR

500 CTNS（FIVE HUNDRED CARTONS）

9. 商品编码（H. S. Code）。

（1）填写内容：

该栏填写统一的海关商品编码。多种商品应分别填写商品编码。

（2）实例：

    H. S. Code

    2106. 1000

10. 数量（Quantity）。

（1）填写内容

该栏填写货物的毛重或净重或其他计量单位。

（2）实例：

  Quantity

    25 ,200. 00KGS（G. W）

11. 发票号码及日期（Number and Date of Invoice）。

（1）填写内容：

该栏应按照国际标准格式填写商业发票的号码及日期。

（2）实例：

  Number and Date of Invoice

    SEP 1ST, 2019

12. 出口方声明（Declaration by the Exporter）

（1）填写内容：

该栏填写申报单位地点、申报日期及经手人签名。

（2）实例：

  Declaration by the Exporter

    CHANGSHA，SEP 7TH, 2019

      雷淼

13. 签证机关证明（Certification）。

（1）填写内容：

该栏填写签证地点及日期，并由签证机关官员在审查合格后在此栏签名盖章。

（2）实例：

  Certification

    CHANGSHA，SEP 7TH, 2019

      章小东

（二）普惠制原产地证（格式 A）的缮制

1. 证书编号（Reference No. ）。

（1）填写内容：

该栏填写由检验检疫机构编订的证书号。

（2）实例：

ReferenceNo.：XSW893489027

2. 货物产自（Goods Consigned From）。

（1）填写内容：

该栏必须填写出口公司的名称、详细地址包括街道名、门牌号以及国家（地区）名。

（2）实例：

Goods Consigned From

HUNAN TEXTILE IMP & EXP CORP.

4E WUYI RD.，CHANGSHA，CHINA

3. 货物运至（Goods Consigned to）。

（1）填写内容：

该栏应参照信用证的要求填写给惠国最终收货人的名称、详细地址以及国家（地区）名，但不得填写中间商。欧盟成员国一般对该栏不作要求。

（2）实例：

Goods Consigned to

ABC HAND TOOL INC.

P. O. BOX 235，QUEEN AVENUE，

LIVERPOOR，U. K

4. 运输方式及路线（Means of Transport and Route）。

（1）填写内容：

该栏填写货物的装运港、目的港以及运输方式，如有转运港也必须注明。

（2）实例：

Means of Transport and Route

FORM CHANGSHA TO KARACHI BY TRAIN AND BY VESSEL VIA SHANGHAI

5. 供官方使用（For Official Use）。

申报单位一般将该栏留空，由签证机关在特殊情况下使用。签发后发、补发证书或加注其他声明时使用。

6. 商品类别序号（Item No. …）。

（1）填写内容：

单一种类商品出口，该填"1"，出现多种商品填对应的阿拉伯数字。注意，这里的类别是指的不同编码的商品，而不是同种商品下的不同规格，因此该栏切忌填写货号或规格号。

（2）实例：

Item No.

1

7. 唛头及包装号（Marks & Nos no. ...）。

（1）填写内容：

该栏请参照商业发票填写国际标准唛头，如无唛头则填写"N/M"（No marks）。

8. 包装数量及种类和货描（No. and kind of Pkgs, Description）。

（1）填写内容：

该栏填写商品的品名品牌、外包装小写数量、大写数量及包装种类，所述内容填写完毕后请在下面一行打上"＊＊＊"等截止符，表示受惠商品所列截止。填写的方式一般分为两种，具体如实例所示。

（2）实例

① PRINTED SHIRTS

　　2000 CARTONS

　　SAY：TWO THOUSAND CARTONS PACKING IN CARTONS

＊＊＊＊＊＊＊＊＊＊＊＊＊＊＊＊＊＊＊＊＊＊＊＊＊＊＊＊＊＊＊＊＊＊

② ONE THOUSAND FIVE HUNDRED（1500）CARTONS OF MEN`S 100% COTTON WOVEN SHIRTS

＊＊＊＊＊＊＊＊＊＊＊＊＊＊＊＊＊＊＊＊＊＊＊＊＊＊＊＊＊＊＊＊＊＊

9. 原产地标准（Origin Criterion...）。

（1）填写内容：

原产程度不同或给惠国家不同的受惠商品按照国际标准统一填写原产地标准，一般用字母或字母加注关键信息表示。具体如下：

货物完全自产，不含任何进口成分，则不管销往哪个国家或地区，该栏都填"P"。

输往欧盟含有给惠国进口成分，该栏仍填"P"，即仍视为完全自产。

输往欧盟、瑞士的产品，含有进口国成分但符合原产地标准，该栏填"W"，并在后面填上税目号（H. S Code）。例如："W" 6205. 2000。

输往加拿大，含有进口成分，但不超过出厂价的40%，则该栏填"F"。

输往澳大利亚、新西兰，符合原产地标准的，该栏" "（留空），或无需出具 Form A，只需在商业发票中注明"发展中国家声明条款"，即：出口商品最后一道工序在中国完成，在中国创造的商品和劳务价值不低于一定的百分比（X%）。

输往东欧国家的，如俄罗斯、波兰、捷克、斯洛伐克，含有进口成分但不超过产品 FOB 价的50%，该栏填"Y"，并在其后加注进口成分在商品（FOB 价）中的百分比，例如：Y40%。

10. 毛重或其他数量（G. W or other quantity）。

（1）填写内容：

该栏一般填写毛重，如货物无毛重，也可以填写净重，但其后需标注"N. W"字样，或者填写商品的内包装件数。

11. 发票号码及日期（No. & date of invoice）。

（1）填写内容：

该栏参照商业发票填写其号码及出票日期，填写时号码在前，日期在后。

（2）实例：

No. & date of invoice

2016A - 001

SEP. 24，2019

12. 证明（Certification）。

（1）填写内容

该栏由系统自动生成签证及印章或者现场申领签证盖章。一般为提单签发日期之前的 5 - 7 天为宜。

（2）实例：

Certification

CHANGSHA，SEP 7TH，2016

章小东

13. 出口商声明（Declaration by the Exporter）。

（1）填写内容：

该栏由出口企业经办人员填写申报地点及日期，填写时注意地点在前日期在后。此外，该栏最好与第 16 栏的时间保持一致，填同一天或稍早，填制完毕后由申报人员手签，并加盖中英文对照的出口企业印章，最后填写给惠国国名，受惠国国名已经印制的则无需填写。

（2）实例：

Declaration by the Exporter

CHANGSHA，SEP 7TH 2019

雷淼

CHINA（已印制）

CANADA

SHANGHAI. SEP. 27，2019

第三节   任务模块

上接项目二、项目三，根据信用证审核的结果及商业发票的制作情况，在该项目中单证员李望应完成的工作任务包括：

任务 1：认真审核信用证中的原产地证书条款并准备好商业发票和装箱单。

任务 2：根据上述资料及具体业务要求缮制原产地证。

任务 3：办理一般原产地证或普惠制原产地证。

1. 信用证。

SEQUENCE OF TOTAL   27： 1/1

FORM OF DC   40A： IRREVOCABLE

DC NO   20： DC HMN214479

DATE OF ISSUE   31C： 190720

APPLICABLE RULES	40E：	UCP LATEST VERSION
EXPIRY DATE AND PLACE	31D：	190919 IN COUNTRY OF BENEFICIARY
APPLICANT	50：	ELBY GIFTS INC. 879 INDUSTRIEL
		BOIS DES FILION, QUEBEC, J6Z 4T3, CANADA
BENEFICIARY	59：	LILING PENGXING CERAMIC FACTORY
		WUSHI JIASHU LILING HUNAN, CHINA
AMOUNT	32B：	USD27,010.40
AVAILABLE WITH/BY	41D：	ANY BANK BY NEGOTIATION
DRAFTS AT	42C：	AT SIGHT FOR FULL INVOICE VALUE
DRAWEE	42A：	ISSUING BANK
PARTIAL SHIPMENTS	43P：	ALLOWED
TRANSHIPMENT	43T：	ALLOWED
PORTOF LOADING	44E：	SHENZHEN, CHINA
PORT OF DISCHARGE	44F：	PRINCE RUPERT, BC
LATEST DATE OF SHIPMENT	44D：	190905
DESCRIPTION OFGOODS OR SERVICES	45A：	CERAMIC CUPS AND BOWLS AS PER S/C NO.： CB161039 CIF PRINCE RUPERT. BC ALL PACKED IN CARTONS.

DOCUMENTS REQUIRED　46A：　+ ORIGINAL SIGNED INVOICE PLUS THREE COPIES.

+ FULL SET OF CLEAN MULTIMODAL TRANSPORT DOCUMENT PLUS 2 N/N COPIES, MADE TO THE ORDER OF HSBC BANK CANADA, SHOWING ON BOARD NOTATION, MARKED FREIGHT PREPAID, AND NOTIFY APPLICANT (STATING FULL NAME AND ADDRESS).

+ INSURANCE POLICY OR CERTIFICATEBLANK INDORSED, FOR THE INVOICE VALUE PLUS 10% COVERING ALL RISKS AND S. R. CC. FROM WAREHOUSE TO WAREHOUSE.

+ ORIGINAL PACKING LIST PLUS 2 COPIES

+ GSP CERTIFICATE OF ORIGIN FORM A, IN ONE ORIGINAL PLUS 2 COPIES, INDICATING COUNTRY OF ORIGIN, COUNTERCHOPPED BY GOVERNMENT AUTHORITIES

+ SHIPPING NOTE INCLUDING SHIPPING MARKS,

CTN NO., B/L NO., QUANTITY, VESSEL'S NAME, VOYAGE NO., SHOULD BE SENT TO THE ISSUING BANK ON THE DATE OF SHIPMENT.

ADDITIONAL CONDITIONS 47A: + BENEFICIARY'S DETAILS:
CTC: MILLER LEE
TEL: 86 – 731 – 2338 – 4199
FAX: 86 – 731 – 2338 – 4298
FOLLOWING CHARGES ARE FOR BENEFICIARY'S ACCOUNT:
1) REIMBURSEMENT / REMITTANCE CHARGES
2) DISCREPANCY FEE OF USD/CAD/EUR100 PLUS ALL RELEVANT CABLE CHARGES WILL BE DEDUCTED FROM EACH PRESENTATION OF DIS-CREPANT
DOCUMENTS UNDER THIS DC.

CHARGES 71B: ALL BANKING CHARGES OUTSIDE COUNTRY OF ISSUE FOR ACCOUNT OF BENEFICIARY/EX-PORTER

PERIOD OF PRESENTATION 48: WITHIN 15 DAYS AFTER THE DATE OF SHIP-MENT
BUT WITHIN THE VALIDITY OF THE CREDIT

CONFIRMATION INSTRUCTIONS 49: WITHOUT

INFO TO PRESENTING BK 78: + UPON RECEIPT OF DOCUMENTS CONFORMING TO THE TERMS OF THIS CREDIT WE UNDER-TAKE TO REIMBURSE YOU IN THE CURRENCY OF THIS CREDIT IN ACCORDANCE WITH YOUR INSTRUCTIONS, LESS CABLE CHARGES,
+ FORWARD DOCUMENTS IN ONE LOT BY COURIER AT BENEFICIARY'S EXPENSES TO HS-BC BANK CANADA, TRADE AND SUPPLY CHAIN, 5100 SHERBROOKE STREET EAST, SUITE 190, MONTREAL, QUEBEC, H1V 3R9 CANADA.
+ THE AMOUNT OF EACH DRAWING MUST BE ENDORSED ON THE REVERSE OF THIS DC BY THE NEGOTIATING/PRESENTING BANK.

2. 商业发票。

PENGXING IMP&EXP COMPANY

LILING PENGXING CERAMIC FACTORY

WUSHI JIASHU LILING HUNAN CHINA

TEL：86－731－23384199　　FAX：86－731－23384298

COMMERCIAL INVOICE

To:	ELBY GIFTS INC. 879 INDUSTRIEL BOIS DES FILION QUEBEC, J6Z 4T3, CANADA		Invoice No.:	PX12IVN1039
			Invoice Date:	AUG 16,2019
			S/C No.:	S/C NO.:CB161039
			S/C Date:	JUL 5,2019
From:	SHENZHEN,CHINA	To:	PRINCE RUPERT,BC,CANADA	
Letter of Credit No.:	DC HMN214479	Issued By:	HSBC BANK, MONTREAL CANADA	

Marks and Numbers	Number and kind of package	Quantity	Unit Price	Amount
	Description of goods		U.S.D/set	
ELBY	CERAMIC CUPS AND BOWLS		CIF PRINCE RUPERT, BC	
		CTN	U.S.D	U.S.D
S/C NO.:CB121039	V23-234	228	4.05	3693.60
NO: 1-1589	V23-234F	228	4.05	3693.60
	V23-235	190	2.40	3648.00
	V23-236	189	2.10	3175.20
	V23-237	186	1.95	2901.60
	V23-238	190	2.04	3100.80
	36-062	191	2.30	3514.40
	36-063	187	2.12	3171.52
	Total:	1589 CTNS		U.S.D 26,398.72

Say Total：U. S DOLLARS TWENTY SIX THOUSAND EIGHT HUNDRED AND NINETY EIGHT AND CENTS SEVENTY TWO（USD26898. 72）ONLY

PENGXING IMP&EXP COMPANY
李望

据此，单证员李望缮制了一份普惠制原产地证。

ORIGINAL

1. Goods consigned from (Exporter's business name, address, country) PENGXIANG IMP&EXP CORP. WUSHI JIASHU LILING HUNAN, CHINA	Reference No. Z16470ZC40401688 **GENERALIZED SYSTEM OF PREFERENCES** **CERTIFICATE OF ORIGIN** (Combined declaration and certificate) **FORM A**
2. Goods consigned to (Consignee's name, address, country) ELBY GIFTS INC. 879 INDUSTRIEL BOIS DES FILION, QUEBEC, J6Z 4T3, CANADA	Issued in ——issued in the people's republic of china—— (country) See Notes Overleaf
3. Means of transport and route (as far as known) FROM SHENZHEN CHINA TO BOIS DES FILION, CANADA BY VESSEL	4. For official use

5. item number	6. Marks and numbers of packages	7. Number and kind of packages; description of goods	8. Origincriterion (see Notes overleaf)	9. Gross weight or other quantity	10. Numberand date ofinvoices DATE：
1	N/M	CERAMIC CUPS AND BOWLS TOTAL：ONE THOUSAND FIVE HUNDRED EIGHTY NINE (1589) CARTONS COUNTRY OF ORIGIN：CHINA *	"P" 10888SETS PX16IVN1039 AUG 16，2019		

11. Certification It is hereby certified, on the basis of control carried out, that the declaration by the exporter is correct. 长沙海关（签章） SHENZHEN, AUG 16, 2019 ———————————————————— Place and date, signature and stamp of certifying authority	16. Declaration by the exporter The undersigned hereby declares that the above details and statements are correct, that all the goods were produced in ————————CHINA———————— (country) and that they comply with the origin requirements specified for those goods in the Generalized System of Preferences for goods exported to ————————CANADA———————— SHENZHEN, AUG 16, 2019 ———————————————————— Place and date, signature and stamp of certifying authority

第四节　任务拓展模块

能力实训项目1： 一般原产地证业务操作

根据上海淼睿进出口有限公司第 C –11027 号信用证的要求，2019 年 5 月 20 日，单证员彭婷备齐信用证、商业发票等资料向上海市贸促会申领一般原产地证。

1. 信用证。

SEQUENCE OF TOTAL	27：	1/1
FORM OF DC.	40A：	IRREVOCABLE
DC. NO.	20：	0684160117426
DATE OF ISSUE	31C：	190825
APPLICABLE RULES	40E：	UCP LATEST VERSION
EXPIRY DATE AND PLACE	31D：	191024，CHINA
APPLICANT	50：	M/S. MEMORY STEEL CORPORATION
		73/A，LAL MOHAN SHAHA STREET
		（DHOLAIKHAL），DHAKA –1100.
		BANGLADESH.
BENEFICIARY	59：	JIANGSU I –TOUCH BUSINESS SERVICE LTD，
		ROOM 117，JIANGSU EDIFICE
		ZHANGJIAGANG FREE TRADE ZONE，
		JIANGSU，CHINA　　TEL：86 –516 –56363783
AMOUNT	32B：	USD35,000. 00
AVAILABLE WITH/BY	41D：	ANY BANK IN CHINA BY NEGOTIATION
DRAFTS AT	42C：	AT SIGHT FOR FULL INVOICE VALUE
DRAWEE	42A：	DRAWN ON US
PARTIAL SHIPMENTS	43P：	ALLOWED
TRANSSHIPMENT	43T：	ALLOWED
PORTOF LOADING	44A：	ANY SEA PORT, CHINA
PORT OF DISCHARGE	44B：	CHITTAGONG SEA PORT，BANGLADESH
LATEST DATE OF SHIPMENT	44C：	191009
DESCRIPTION OFGOODS	45A：	201/2B SECONDARY GRADE STAINLESS STEEL SHEET OF WIDTH 1619MM THICKNESS 1MM TO 3MM，QTY：25,000KGS AT THE RATE OF USD1. 40/KG FOR TOTAL AMOUNT OF USD35, 000. 00 CFR CHITTAGONG，BANGLADESH. AS PER BENEFICIARY'S PROFORMA INVOICE

		NO. SK20160802 – 001 DATED AUG 2，2019

DOCUMENTS REQUIRED   46A：   + MANUALLY SIGNED COMMERCIAL INVOICE IN TRIPLICATE CERTIFYING MERCHANDISE TO BE OF CHINA ORIGIN AND INDICATING THAT THE GOODS ARE BEING IMPORTED AGAINST IRC NO. BA – 0171646，TI NO. 157 – 107 – 0161，VAT REGISTRATION NO. 9141093671.

+ FULL SET OF CLEAN 'SHIPPED ON BOARD' OCEAN BILL OF LADING SHOWING' FREIGHT PREPAID' MADE OUT TO ORDER AND BLANK INDORSED，NOTIFY APPLICANT.

+ PACKING LIST IN TRIPLICATE SHOWING GROSS WEIGHT，NET WEIGHT.

+ CERTIFICATE OF ORIGIN ONE ORIGINAL AND TWO COPIES ISSUED AND LEGALED BY CCPIT

+ BENEFICIARY'S DECLARATION SHOULD CERTIFY THAT THE COUNTRY OF ORIGIN HAS BEEN PRINTED ON GOODS PACKING BAG.

+ BENEFICIARY SHOULD SEND A FAX OR BY COURIER TO L/C OPENING BANK WITHIN FIVE-DAYS FROM THE OF SHIPMENT，ADVISING THE DATE OF SHIPMENT，VESSEL'S NAME，AMOUNT OF BILL AND L/C NO. AND A COPY OF THIS FAX SHOULD ACCOMPANY THE SHIPPING DOCUMENTS.

+ SHIPMENT BY ISRAELI LINER IS PROHIBITED AND ACERTIFICATE TO THIS EFFECT ISSUED BY THE SHIPPING COMPANY MUST ACCOMPANY THE ORIGINAL DOCUMENTS.

CHARGES   71B：   ALL FOREIGN BANK CHARGES ARE FOR THE ACCOUNT OF THE BENEFICIARY.

PERIOD OF PRESENTATION   48：   15 DAYS FROM SHIPMENT DATE BUT WITHIN VALIDITY OF THE CREDIT

2. 合同。

SALES CONTRACT

Contract   No. ：SSW0803

Date：AUG 15，2019

THE SELLER：JIANGSU I – TOUCH BUSINESS SERVICE LTD,

ROOM 117，JIANGSU EDIFICE

ZHANGJIAGANG FREE TRADE ZONE，

JIANGSU，CHINA TEL：86 – 512 – 56363783

THE BUYER：M/S. MEMORY STEEL CORPORATION

73/A，LAL MOHAN SHAHA STREET

（DHOLAIKHAL），DHAKA – 1100.

BANGLADESH.

This Contract is made by and between the Buyer and Seller，whereby the Buyer agrees to buy and the Seller agrees to sell the under mentioned goods on the terms and conditions stated below：

Description of Goods，Specifications	Quantity（set）	Unit Price（U. S. D/set）	Amount（U. S. D）
201/2B SECONDARY GRADE STAINLESS STEEL SHEET OF WIDTH 1219MM OR MORETHICKNESS 1MM TO 3MM，QTY：25，000KGS AT THE RATE OF USD1. 40/KG. AS PER BENEFICIARY'S PROFORMA INVOIVE NO. SK20160802 – 001 DATED AUG 2，2019			
	C. F. R	CHITTAGONG	
1. 2 * 1219 * 2438	5 576	1. 40	7 806. 40
1. 5 * 1219 * 2438	3 248	1. 40	4 547. 20
2. 0 * 1219 * 2438	11 630	1. 40	16 282. 00
3. 0 * 1219 * 2438	4 546	1. 40	6 364. 40
Total	25 000		35 000. 00

Say total：U. S DOLLARS THIRTY FIVE THOUSAND ONLY.

PACKING：Standard export packing on pallets.

TRANSPORT DETAILS：the goods should shipped before：Oct 9th，2019，from any Chinese port to Chittagong Bangladesh，transshipment and partial shipment are allowed.

PAYMENT：By sight L/C and remain valid for negotiation in China for 15 days after shipment.

DOCUMENTS：

+ Signed commercial invoice in triplicate，certifying the goods are of Chinese origin and being imported against IRC No. BA – 0171646，VAT Registration No. 9141093671.

+ Full set （3/3） of clean on board ocean Bill of Lading made out to order of shipper and blank endorsed.

+ Packing List in triplicate.

+ Certificate of origin by CCPIT.

+ Beneficiary's Declaration certifying that the country of origin has been printed on goods packing bag.

3. 其他信息。

商品编码：6200. 2100

产地证编号：CCPIT11051039

发票号码及日期：INV190022，Sep 20th，2019

起运港：张家港市

据此，请完成一般原产地证的填制：

ORIGINAL

1. Exporter	Certificate No.
	CERTIFICATE OF ORIGIN OF
2. Consignee	
	THE PEOPLE'S REPUBLIC OF CHINA
3. Means of transport and route	5. For certifying authority use only
4. Country / region of destination	

6. Marks and numbers	7. Number and kind of packages；description of goods	8. H. S. Code	9. Quantity	10. Number and date of invoices

11. Declaration by the exporter	16. Certification
The undersigned hereby declares that the above details and statements are correct，that all the goods were produced in China and that they comply with the Rules of Origin of the People's Republic of China.	It is hereby certified that the declaration by the exporter is correct.
----------------------------------	----------------------------------
Place and date，signature and stamp of authorized signatory	Place and date，signature and stamp of certifying authority

能力实训项目 2：普惠制原产地证业务操作

根据深圳普瑞玛建材有限公司笃 DC 16810 号信用证的要求，2019 年 8 月 29 日，单证员黄柯备齐信用证、商业发票等资料向深圳海关申领普惠制原产地证

1. 信用证。

SEQUENCE OF TOTAL	27：	1/1
FORM OF DC	40A：	IRREVOCABLE
DC NO	20：	DC 16810
DATE OF ISSUE	31C：	190810
APPLICABLE RULES	40E：	UCP 600
EXPIRY DATE AND PLACE	31D：	190920 IN CHINA
APPLICANT	50：	CONSTRUCTION MOUDULAR SPECIALIST
		POSTAL：16 HARVEY RD. ,
		SHENTON PK，WA 6008
BENEFICIARY	59：	PRIMA CONSTRUCTION MATERIALS CO. ，LTD
		1401 ROOM，38 BUILDING，CHUANGYE GARDEN
		BAOAN DISTRICT，SHENZHEN，CHINA
AMOUNT	32B：	USD6840 ,00
AVAILABLE WITH/BY	41D：	ANY BANK BY NEGOTIATION
DRAFTS AT	42C：	AT 30DAYS AFTER SIGHT
DRAWEE	42A：	DRAWN ON US
PARTIAL SHIPMENTS	43P：	ALLOWED
TRANSHIPMENT	43T：	ALLOWED
LOADING PORT	44E：	CHINA MAIN PORT
DISCHARGE PORT	44F：	FREMANTLE，AUSTRALIA
LATEST DATE OF SHIPMENT	44C：	190905
DESCRIPTION OFGOODS	45A：	BAMBOO FLOORING
		ITEM 1 100 SQM　U. S. D20. 00/SQM
		ITEM 1 100 SQM　U. S. D39. 50/SQM
		ALL PACKING IN SEA WORTHY CARTONS
		CIF FREMENTLE AS PER PI NO. ：BFF0610
DOCUMENTS REQUIRED	46A：	+MANUALLY SIGNED COMMECIAL INVOICE 3 ORIGINALS PLUS THREE COPIES.
		+FULL SET（3/3）OF MARINE BILLS OF LADING, MADE OUT TO ORDER，MARKED FREIGHT PREPAID，AND NOTIFY APPLICANT（STATING FULL NAME AND ADDRESS）.
		+ INSURANCE POLICY OR CERTIFICATE IN TRIPLICATE，BLANK INDORSED，FOR THE INVOICE VALUE PLUS 10% COVERING ICC（A）

RISK AND ICC（STRIKE）. FROM WAREHOUSE TO WAREHOUSE AND I. O. P, PAYABLE AT FREMENTLE IN U. S. D.

+ PACKING LIST 3 ORIGINALS AND 2 COPIES.

+ CERTIFICATE OF ORIGIN IN CHINA ISSUED BY OFFICIAL AUTRORITY.

+ BENEFICIARY'S CERTIFICATE SHOWING THAT A SET OF ORIGINAL SHIPPING DOCUMENTS HAS BEEN MAIL TO THE APPLICANT BY EXPRESS AFTER 2 DAYS OF SHIOMENT.

CHARGES   71B： ALL BANKING CHARGES OUTSIDE COUNTRY OF ISSUE ARE FOR BENEFICIARY/'S ACCOUNT.

PERIOD OF PRESENTATION   48： WITHIN 15 DAYS AFTER THE DATE OF SHIP-MENT

BUT WITHIN THE VALIDITY OF THE L/C

CONFIRMATION INSTRUCTIONS 49： WITHOUT

2. 商业发票。

Prima Construction Materials Co. ，Ltd
Add：1401Room，38building，Chuangye Gardern，Baoan District，Shenzhen China
Tel：0086－755－32076630   Fax：0086－755－32076630

COMMERCIAL INVOICE

Contract No. ：CBF160724	No. ：PR－20160820
L/C No. ：DC 16724	Date：AUG 22，2019
From：SHENZHEN	To：FREMANTLE

Marks&Nos. No	Description of Goods	Quantity		Unit Price	Amount
	BAMBOO FLOORING			CIF FREMENTLE	
CMS FREMENTLE CBF160724 NO. ：1－109	CARBONISED BAMBOO FLOORING	100SQM		$ 20. 00	$ 2,000. 00
	STRAND WOVEN BAMBOO FLOOR－ING DECKING	100SQM		$ 39. 50	$ 3,950. 00
			TOTAL EXW PRICE		$ 5,950. 00
			LCL CHARGE		$ 450. 00
			INSURANCE COST		$ 60. 00
			FREIGHT		$ 380. 00
			CIF VALUE		$ 6,480. 00

Prima Construction Materials Co. ，Ltd

黄柯

3. 其他信息。

该商品全部生产环节均在中国完成。

普惠制产地证编号：BF2016810

毛重：1500.00KGS

据此，请完成普惠制原产地证的真制：

ORIGINAL

1. Goods consigned form (Exporter's business name, address, country)	Reference No. GENERALIZED SYSTEM OF PREFERENCES CERTIFICAT OF ORIGIN (Combined declaration and certificate) FORM A issued in the people's republic of china (country) See Notes Overleaf		
2. Goods consigned to (consignee's name, address, country)			
3. Means of transport and route (as far as known)	4. For official use		
5. item number	6. Marks & No.	7. Number and kind of packages; description of goods	8. Origin criterion (see Notes overleaf)	9. Gross weight or other quantity	10. Number and date of invoices
11. Certification It is hereby certified, on the basis of control carried out, that the declaration by the exporter is correct. ------------------------------------ Place and date, signature and stamp of certifying authority	16. Declaration by the exporter The undersigned hereby declares that above details and statements are correct; that all goods were produced in ------------------------------ CHINA ------------------------------ (country) and that they comply with the original requirements specified for those goods in the generalized system of preferences for goods exported to ------------------------------------ ------------------------------------ Place and date, signature and stamp of certifying authority		

第五节　学习导航

一、参考资料

[1] 章安平. 外贸单证操作 [M]. 北京：高等教育出版社，2008.

[2] 吴轶群. 国际商务单证操作 [M]. 北京：对外经贸大学出版社，2014.

[3] 林文斌，涂奇. 外贸单证 [M]. 南京：南京大学出版社，2011.

3. 采用"集中申报"通关方式办理报关手续的，报关单填报归并的集中申报清单的进出口起止日期〔按年（4 位）月（2 位）日（2 位）年（4 位）月（2 位）日（2 位）〕。

4. 无实际进出境的货物，免予填报。

编码规则：自由文本，与运输部门向海关申报的舱单（载货清单）所列相应内容一致。

12 栏　消费使用单位/生产销售单位

项目类型：该申报项目为必填项。该项目为字符型。

录入要求：进口填报消费使用单位，出口填报生产销售单位。编码可以选择填报 18 位法人和其他组织统一社会信用代码、10 位海关代码或 10 位检验检疫编码之一。无 18 位法人和其他组织统一社会信用代码的，在统一社会信用代码栏目填报"NO"；未取得 10 位检验检疫编码的，空置 10 位检验检疫编码栏目，不填写内容。人工录入企业代码后，系统可返填企业中文名称。

注意事项：

1. 消费使用单位填报已知的进口货物在境内的最终消费、使用单位的名称，包括：

（1）自行进口货物的单位。

（2）委托进出口企业进口货物的单位。

2. 生产销售单位填报出口货物在境内的生产或销售单位的名称，包括：

（1）自行出口货物的单位。

（2）委托进出口企业出口货物的单位。

（3）免税品经营单位经营出口退税国产商品的，填报该免税品经营单位统一管理的免税店。

3. 减免税货物报关单的消费使用单位/生产销售单位应与《中华人民共和国海关进出口货物征免税证明》（以下简称《征免税证明》）的"减免税申请人"一致；保税监管场所与境外之间的进出境货物，消费使用单位/生产销售单位填报保税监管场所的名称（保税物流中心（B 型）填报中心内企业名称）。

4. 海关特殊监管区域的消费使用单位/生产销售单位填报区域内经营企业（"加工单位"或"仓库"）。

编码规则：

1. 填报 18 位法人和其他组织统一社会信用代码。

2. 无 18 位统一社会信用代码的，填报"NO"。

3. 进口货物在境内的最终消费或使用以及出口货物在境内的生产或销售的对象为自然人的，填报身份证号、护照号、台胞证号等有效证件号码及姓名。

13 栏　监管方式

项目类型：该申报项目为必填项。该项目为字符型。

录入要求：监管方式是以国际贸易中进出口货物的交易方式为基础，结合海关对进出口货物的征税、统计及监管条件综合设定的海关对进出口货物的管理方式。其代码由 4 位数字构成，前两位是按照海关监管要求和计算机管理需要划分的分类代码，后两位是参照国际标准编制的贸易方式代码。

二、自主学习平台

[1] 全国外贸单证员考试中心。

[2] 外贸经理人微信公众号。

[3] 外贸单证课程国家教学资源库。

项目六
报关单据制作业务

第一节　项目描述与目标

一、项目描述

◆开篇业务引入

根据第 L-16017 号信用证的要求，长沙鹏兴出口有限公司业务员李望在办理好订舱手续后，根据以下相关信息马上办理、制作和备齐出口货物报关单、报关委托书等单证，同时备齐报检委托书、出境货物换证凭单等单证，寄给深圳货运代理，委托其向大鹏海关申请办理出口报关手续。该项目任务具体由报关员李艳负责。

◆项目预期目标

熟悉报关单各栏目规范填制要求，能熟练运用海关使用手册寻找海关代码、出口货物监管条件、出口货物应征税率；能准确填制出口货物报关单及其他通关所需的随附单据。

在项目实施过程中，通过对报关单填制、申报、配合查验、计算和缴纳税费、装运货等任务的分解，在分工与合作中逐渐培养学生通关基本能力，培养学生团队合作能力以及与海关等政府部门有效沟通的能力。

表 6-1　预期项目目标

目标类型	报关单的填制
知识目标	熟悉中国人民共和国海关法及其他法律法规
	掌握出口货物报关程序
	掌握不同性质货物的通过程序
能力目标	能按照我国《海关法》规范填制报关单
	能办理货物的通关手续
职业素质目标	学生团队合作能力
	与政府部门沟通衔接能力

二、项目实施条件

1. 组织学生参观长沙海关以及长沙霞凝新港口岸、长沙保税物流中心。

2. 学生能够在实训室对该项目进行分组讨论并实施。

3. 学生能够登陆出口货物申报系统界面。

4. 指导教师掌握扎实的国家对外贸易管制法、海关法及其他相关法律法规，具备扎实的外贸业务基础。

第二节　知识模块

进出口货物的收发人或其代理人向海关办理报关手续时，应当按照海关《进出口货物申报项目录入指南》及《报关单填制规范》，填制《中华人民共和国海关进（出）口货物报关单》，备齐相关的商业货运单证、相关的许可证件，向海关报告实际进出口货物的情况，并接受海关监管。能否正确规范填制报关单将直接影响通关率、企业的经济利益和国际营商环境。因此，正确规范填制报关单是海关对报关企业和报关员的基本要求，也是报关员必须履行的义务。

一、进出口货物报关单的含义

进出口货物报关单是指进出口货物的收发货人或其代理人，按照海关规定的格式对进出口货物的实际情况作出书面申明，以此要求海关对其货物按照适用的海关制度办理通关手续的法律文书。

二、进出口货物报关单的填制

1 栏　预录入编号

预录入编号指预录入报关单的编号，一份报关单对应一个预录入编号，由系统自动生成。

报关单预录入编号为 18 位，其中第 1－4 位为接受申报海关的代码（海关规定的《关区代码表》中相应海关代码），第 5－8 位为录入时的公历年份，第 9 位为进出口标志（"1"为进口，"0"为出口；集中申报清单"I"为进口，"E"为出口），后 9 位为顺序编号。

2 栏　海关编号

海关编号指海关接受申报时给予报关单的编号，一份报关单对应一个海关编号，由系统自动生成。

报关单海关编号为 18 位，其中第 1－4 位为接受申报海关的代码（海关规定的《关区代码表》中相应海关代码），第 5－8 位为海关接受申报的公历年份，第 9 位为进出口标志（"1"为进口，"0"为出口；集中申报清单"I"为进口，"E"为出口），后 9 位为顺序编号。

3 栏　境内发货人

项目类型：该申报项目为必填项。该项目为字符型。

录入要求：填报在海关备案的对外签订并执行进出口贸易合同的中国境内法人、其他组织名称及编码。编码填报 18 位法人和其他组织统一社会信用代码，没有统一社会信用代码的，填报其在海关的备案编码。

注意事项：

1. 进出口货物合同的签订者和执行者非同一企业的，填报执行合同的企业。

2. 外商投资企业委托进出口企业进口投资设备、物品的，填报外商投资企业，并在标记唛码及备注栏注明"委托某进出口企业进口"，同时注明被委托企业的18位法人和其他组织统一社会信用代码。

3. 有代理报关资格的报关企业代理其他进出口企业办理进出口报关手续时，填报委托的进出口企业。

4. 海关特殊监管区域收发货人真报该货物的实际经营单位或海关特殊监管区域内经营企业。

5. 免税品经营单位经营出口退税国产商品的，填报免税品经营单位名称。

4 栏　境外收货人

项目类型：该申报项目为必填项。该项目为字符型。

录入要求：境外收货人通常指签订并执行出口贸易合同中的买方或合同指定的收货人，境外发货人通常指签订并执行进口贸易合同中的卖方。填报境外收发货人的名称及编码。名称一般填报英文名称，检验检疫要求填报其他外文名称的，在英文名称后填报，以半角括号分隔；特殊情况下无境外收发货人的，名称及编码填报"NO"。

注意事项：对于 AEO 互认国家（地区）企业的，编码填报 AEO 编码，填报样式按照海关总署发布的相关公告要求填报（如新加坡 AEO 企业填报样式为 SG123456789012，韩国 AEO 企业填报样式为 KR1234567，具体见相关公告要求）；非互认国家（地区）AEO 企业等其他情形，编码免于填报。

编码规则：编码引用《国别地区代码表》。

5 栏　进出境关别

项目类型：该项目为必填项。该项目为字符型。

录入要求：根据货物实际进出境的口岸海关，填报海关规定的《关区代码表》中相应口岸海关的名称及代码。例如：货物实际进出境的口岸海关为"广州机场时，录入"5141"。

注意事项：进口转关运输货物，填报货物进境地海关名称及代码，出口转关运输货物填报货物出境地海关名称及代码。按转关运输方式监管的跨关区深加工结转货物，出口报关单填报转出地海关名称及代码，进口报关单填报转入地海关名称及代码。在不同海关特殊监管区域或保税监管场所之间调拨、转让的货物，填报对方海关特殊监管区域或保税监管场所所在的海关名称及代码。其他无实际进出境的货物，填报接受申报的海关名称及代码。

编码规则：进出境关别代码：由四位数字组成，前两位采用直属海关关别代码，后两位为隶属海关或海关监管场所的代码。参数引用《关区代码表》。

6 栏　进出口日期

项目类型：该申报项目为必填项。该项目为字符型。

录入要求：进口日期填报运载进口货物的运输工具申报进境的日期。出口日期指运载出口货物的运输工具办结出境手续的日期，在申报时免予填报。无实际进出境的货物，填报海关接受申报的日期。进口日期为人工录入，入库后系统自动返填；出口日期在申报时免于填报，入库后系统自动返填。

编码规则：本栏目为 8 位数字，顺序为年（4 位）月（2 位）日（2 位），格式为YYYYMMDD。

7 栏　申报日期

项目类型：该申报项目为系统返填项。该项目为字符型。

录入要求：申报日期指海关接受进出口货物收发货人、受委托的报关企业申报数据的日期以电子数据报关单方式申报的，申报日期为海关计算机系统接受申报数据时记录的日期。以纸质报关单方式申报的，申报日期为海关接受纸质报关单并对报关单进行登记处理的日期。申报后系统自动返填。

编码规则：申报日期为 8 位数字，顺序为年（4 位）月（2 位）日（2 位）

8 栏　备案号

项目类型：该申报项目为选填项。该项目为字符型。

录入要求：填报进出口货物收发货人、消费使用单位、生产销售单位在海关办理加工贸易合同备案或征、减、免税审核确认等手续时，海关核发的《加工贸易手册》、海关特殊监管区域和保税监管场所保税账册、《征免税证明》或其他备案审批文件的编号。

注意事项：一份报关单只允许填报一个备案号。具体填报要求如下

1. 加工贸易项下货物，除少量低值辅料按规定不使用《加工贸易手册》及以后续补税监管方式办理内销征税的外，填报《加工贸易手册》编号。使用异地直接报关分册和异地深加工结转出口分册在异地口岸报关的，填报分册号；本地直接报关分册和本地深加工结转分册限制在本地报关，填报总册号。加工贸易成品凭《征免税证明》转为减免税进口货物的，进口报关单填报《征免税证明》编号，出口报关单填报《加工贸易手册》编号。对加工贸易设备、使用账册管理的海关特殊监管区域内减免税设备之间的结转转入和转出企业分别填制进、出口报关单，在报关单"备案号"栏目填报《加工贸易手册》编号。

2. 涉及征、减、免税审核确认的报关单，填报《征免税证明》编号。

3. 减免税货物退运出口，填报《中华人民共和国海关进口减免税货物准予退运证明》的编号；减免税货物补税进口，填报《减免税货物补税通知书》的编号；减免税货物进口或结转进口（转入），填报《征免税证明》的编号；相应的结转出口（转出），填报《中华人民共和国海关进口减免税货物结转联系函》的编号。

4. 免税品经营单位经营出口退税国产商品的，免予填报。

编码规则：备案号为 12 位字符，结构如下：

（1）第 1 位为备案或审批文件的标记。

A 外商投资企业为生产内销产品进口料件

B 来料加工进出口货物

C 进料加工进出口货物

D 加工贸易不作价进口设备

E 加工贸易电子帐册

G 加工贸易深加工结转异地报关手册

F 加工贸易异地报关手册

H 出口加工区电子账册

J 保税仓库记账式电子账册

K 保税仓库备案式电子账册

Y 原产地证书

Z《征免税证明》

Q 汽车零部件电子账册

（2）第 2 - 5 位为核发《加工贸易手册》、《征免税证明》等海关关区代码。

（3）第 6 位为年份最后一位，出口加工区设备电子账册第 6 位为"D

（4）第 7 位区分不同类型分别定义

① 保税仓库电子账册（K、J）第 7 位为保税仓库类型代码。

②《加工贸易手册》第 7 位为企业经济类别代码。

③ 深加工结转分册第 7 位为"H"，用于出口加工区深加工结转分册。

④《征免税证明》第 7 位为归档标志。

（5）第 8 - 12 位数为顺序码。

9 栏　运输方式

项目类型：该申报项目为必填项。该项目为字符型。

录入要求：运输方式包括实际运输方式和海关规定的特殊运输方式，前者指货物实际进出境的运输方式，按进出境所使用的运输工具分类；后者指货物无实际进出境的运输方式，按货物在境内的流向分类。根据货物实际进出境的运输方式或货物在境内流向的类别，按照海关规定的《运输方式代码表》选择填报相应的运输方式。

注意事项：

1. 特殊情况填报要求如下：

（1）非邮件方式进出境的快递货物，按实际运输方式填报。

（2）进口转关运输货物，按载运货物抵达进境地的运输工具填报；出口转关运输货物，按载运货物驶离出境地的运输工具填报。

（3）不复运出（入）境而留在境内（外）销售的进出境展览品、留赠转卖物品等，填报"其他运输"（代码 9）。

（4）进出境旅客随身携带的货物，填报"旅客携带"（代码 L）。

（5）以固定设施（包括输油、输水管道和输电网等）运输货物的，填报"固定设施运输"（代码 G）。

2. 无实际进出境货物在境内流转时填报要求如下：

（1）境内非保税区运入保税区货物和保税区退区货物，填报"非保税区"（代码 0）。

（2）保税区运往境内非保税区货物，填报"保税区"（代码 7）。

（3）境内存入出口监管仓库和出口监管仓库退仓货物，填报"监管仓库"（代码 1）。

（4）保税仓库转内销货物或转加工贸易货物，填报"保税仓库"（代码 8）。

（5）从境内保税物流中心外运入中心或从中心运往境内中心外的货物，填报"物流中心"（代码 W）。

（6）从境内保税物流园区外运入园区或从园区内运往境内园区外的货物，填报"物流园区"（代码 X）。

（7）保税港区、综合保税区与境内（区外）（非海关特殊监管区域、保税监管场所）之间进出的货物，填报"保税港区/综合保税区"（代码 Y）。

（8）出口加工区、珠澳跨境工业区（珠海园区）、中哈霍尔果斯边境合作中心（中方配套区）与境内（区外）（非海关特殊监管区域、保税监管场所）之间进出的货物，填报"出口加工区"（代码 Z）。

（9）境内运入深港西部通道港方口岸区的货物以及境内进出中哈霍尔果斯边境合作中心中方区域的货物，填报"边境特殊海关作业区"（代码 H）。

（10）经横琴新区和平潭综合实验区（以下简称综合试验区）二线指定申报通道运往境内区外或从境内经二线指定申报通道进入综合试验区的货物，以及综合试验区内按选择性征收关税申报的货物，填报"综合试验区"（代码 T）。

（11）海关特殊监管区域内的流转、调拨货物，海关特殊监管区域、保税监管场所之间的流转货物，海关特殊监管区域与境内区外之间进出的货物，海关特殊监管区域外的加工贸易余料结转、深加工结转、内销货物，以及其他境内流转货物，填报"其他运输"（代码 9）。

10 栏　运输工具名称及航次号

项目类型：该申报项目为有条件必填项。载运货物进出境运输工具有具体名称好编号时，为必填项。该项目为字符型。

录入要求：填报载运货物进出境的运输工具名称或编号及航次号。填报内容应与运输部门向海关申报的舱单（载货清单）所列相应内容一致。

注意事项：

运输工具名称具体填报要求如下：

1. 直接在进出境地或采用全国通关一体化通关模式办理报关手续的报关单填报要求如下：

（1）水路运输：填报船舶编号（来往港澳小型船舶为监管簿编号）或者船舶英文名称。

（2）公路运输：启用公路舱单前，填报该跨境运输车辆的国内行驶车牌号，深圳提前报关模式的报关单填报国内行驶车牌号 + "／" + "提前报关"。启用公路舱单后，免予填报。

（3）铁路运输：填报车厢编号或交接单号。

（4）航空运输：填报航班号。

（5）邮件运输：填报邮政包裹单号。

（6）其他运输：填报具体运输方式名称，例如：管道、驮畜等。

2. 转关运输货物的报关单填报要求如下：

（1）进口。

A. 水路运输：直转、提前报关填报"@" + 16 位转关申报单预录入号（或 13 位载货清单号）；中转填报进境英文船名。

B. 铁路运输：直转、提前报关填报"@"＋16 位转关申报单预录入号；中转填报车厢编号。

C. 航空运输：直转、提前报关填报"@"＋16 位转关申报单预录入号（或 13 位载货清单号）；中转填报"@"。

D. 公路及其他运输：填报"@"＋16 位转关申报单预录入号（或 13 位载货清单号）。

E. 以上各种运输方式使用广东地区载货清单转关的提前报关货物填报"@"＋13 位载货清单号。

（2）出口。

A. 水路运输：非中转填报"@"＋16 位转关申报单预录入号（或 13 位载货清单号）。如多张报关单需要通过一张转关单转关的，运输工具名称字段填报"@"。

中转货物，境内水路运输填报驳船船名；境内铁路运输填报车名（主管海关 4 位关区代码＋"TRAIN"）；境内公路运输填报车名（主管海关 4 位关区代码＋"TRUCK"）。

B. 铁路运输：填报"@"＋16 位转关申报单预录入号（或 13 位载货清单号），如多张报关单需要通过一张转关单转关的，填报"@"。

C. 航空运输：填报"@"＋16 位转关申报单预录入号（或 13 位载货清单号），如多张报关单需要通过一张转关单转关的，填报"@"。

D. 其他运输方式：填报"@"＋16 位转关申报单预录入号（或 13 位载货清单号）。

3. 采用"集中申报"通关方式办理报关手续的，报关单填报"集中申报"。

4. 免税品经营单位经营出口退税国产商品的，免予填报。

5. 无实际进出境的货物，免予填报。

编码规则：自由文本，与运输部门向海关申报的舱单（载货清单）所列相应内容一致。

航次号具体填报要求如下：

1. 直接在进出境地或采用全国通关一体化通关模式办理报关手续的报关单

（1）水路运输：填报船舶的航次号。

（2）公路运输：启用公路舱单前，填报运输车辆的 8 位进出境日期〔顺序为年（4位）、月（2 位）、日（2 位），下同〕。启用公路舱单后，填报货物运输批次号。

（3）铁路运输：填报列车的进出境日期。

（4）航空运输：免予填报。

（5）邮件运输：填报运输工具的进出境日期。

（6）其他运输方式：免予填报。

2. 转关运输货物的报关单

（1）进口。

A. 水路运输：中转转关方式填报"@"＋进境干线船舶航次。直转、提前报关免予填报。

B. 公路运输：免予填报。

C. 铁路运输："@"+8位进境日期。

D. 航空运输：免予填报。

E. 其他运输方式：免予填报。

（2）出口。

A. 水路运输：非中转货物免予填报。中转货物：境内水路运输填报驳船航次号；境内铁路、公路运输填报6位启运日期〔顺序为年（2位）、月（2位）、日（2位）〕。

B. 铁路拼车拼箱捆绑出口：免予填报。

C. 航空运输：免予填报。

D. 其他运输方式：免予填报。

3. 免税品经营单位经营出口退税国产商品的，免予填报。

4. 无实际进出境的货物，免予填报。

5. 该项目最多支持32支付。

11栏　提运单号

项目类型：该申报项目为有条件必填项。该项目为字符型。

录入要求：填报进出口货物提单或运单的编号。一份报关单只允许填报一个提单或运单号，一票货物对应多个提单或运单时，应分单填报。

注意事项：

1. 直接在进出境地或采用全国通关一体化通关模式办理报关手续的。

（1）水路运输：填报进出口提单号。如有分提单的，填报进出口提单号+"*"+分提单号。

（2）公路运输：启用公路舱单前，免予填报；启用公路舱单后，填报进出口总运单号。

（3）铁路运输：填报运单号。

（4）航空运输：填报总运单号+"_"+分运单号，无分运单的填报总运单号。

（5）邮件运输：填报邮运包裹单号。

2. 转关运输货物的报关单。

（1）进口。

① 水路运输：直转、中转填报提单号。提前报关免予填报。

② 铁路运输：直转、中转填报铁路运单号。提前报关免予填报。

③ 航空运输：直转、中转货物填报总运单号+"_"+分运单号。提前报关免予填报。

④ 其他运输方式：免予填报。

⑤ 以上运输方式进境货物，在广东省内用公路运输转关的，填报车牌号。

（2）出口。

① 水路运输：中转货物填报提单号；非中转货物免予填报；广东省内汽车运输提前报关的转关货物，填报承运车辆的车牌号。

② 其他运输方式：免予填报。广东省内汽车运输提前报关的转关货物，填报承运车辆的车牌号。

根据实际对外贸易情况按海关规定的《监管方式代码表》选择填报相应的监管方式简称及代码。一份报关单只允许填报一种监管方式。

注意事项：

1. 进口少量低值辅料（即 5000 美元以下，78 种以内的低值辅料）按规定不使用《加工贸易手册》的，填报"低值辅料"。使用《加工贸易手册》的，按《加工贸易手册》上的监管方式填报。

2. 加工贸易料件转内销货物以及按料件办理进口手续的转内销制成品、残次品、未完成品，填制进口报关单，填报"来料料件内销"或"进料料件内销"；加工贸易成品凭《征免税证明》转为减免税进口货物的，分别填制进、出口报关单，出口报关单填报"来料成品减免"或"进料成品减免"，进口报关单按照实际监管方式填报。

3. 加工贸易出口成品因故退运进口及复运出口的，填报"来料成品退换"或"进料成品退换"；加工贸易进口料件因换料退运出口及复运进口的，填报"来料料件退换"或"进料料件退换"；加工贸易过程中产生的剩余料件、边角料退运出口，以及进口料件因品质、规格等原因退运出口且不再更换同类货物进口的，分别填报"来料料件复出"、"来料边角料复出"、"进料料件复出"、"进料边角料复出"。

4. 加工贸易边角料内销和副产品内销，填制进口报关单，填报"来料边角料内销"或"进料边角料内销"。

5. 企业销毁处置加工贸易货物未获得收入，销毁处置货物为料件、残次品的，填报"料件销毁"；销毁处置货物为边角料、副产品的，填报"边角料销毁"。

企业销毁处置加工贸易货物获得收入的，填报为"进料边角料内销"或"来料边角料内销"。

6. 免税品经营单位经营出口退税国产商品的，填报"其他"。

14 栏　征免性质

项目类型：该申报项目为选填项。该项目数据类型为 3 位字符型。

录入要求：根据实际情况，按海关规定的《征免性质代码表》选择填报相应的征免性质简称及代码，持有海关核发的《征免税证明》的，按照《征免税证明》中批注的征免性质填报。

录入时可根据下拉菜单选择征免性质或按海关规定的《征免性质代码表》录入相应的征免性质代码。例如：一般征税的货物，下拉菜单时可选择"101 一般征税"或录入"101"，栏目自动生成"一般征税"。

一份报关单只允许填报一种征免性质。

注意事项：加工贸易货物报关单按照海关核发的《加工贸易手册》中批注的征免性质简称及代码填报。特殊情况填报要求如下：

1. 加工贸易转内销货物，按实际情况填报（如一般征税、科教用品、其他法定等）。

2. 料件退运出口、成品退运进口货物填报"其他法定"。

3. 加工贸易结转货物，免予填报。

4. 免税品经营单位经营出口退税国产商品的，填报"其他法定"。

15 栏　许可证号

项目类型：该申报项目为选填项。该项目数据类型字符型，最多支持录入 20 位。

录入要求：填报进（出）口许可证、两用物项和技术进（出）口许可证、两用物项和技术出口许可证（定向）、纺织品临时出口许可证、出口许可证（加工贸易）、出口许可证（边境小额贸易）的编号。

注意事项：一份报关单只允许填报一个许可证号。

16 栏　合同协议号

填报进出口货物合同（包括协议或订单）编号。未发生商业性交易的免予填报。

免税品经营单位经营出口退税国产商品的，免予填报。

17 栏　贸易国（地区）

项目类型：该申报项目为必填项。该项目为字符型。

录入要求：发生商业性交易按海关规定的《国别（地区）代码表》选择填报相应的贸易国（地区）中文名称及代码。进口填报购自国（地区），出口填报售予国（地区）。

注意事项：未发生商业性交易的填报货物所有权拥有者所属的国家（地区）。

编码规则：贸易国别（地区）代码由3位英文字母构成。例如：美国代码为"USA美国"。参数引用《国别（地区）代码表》。

18 栏　启运/运抵国（地区）

项目类型：该申报项目为必填项。该项目为字符型。

录入要求：启运国（地区）按海关规定的《国别（地区）代码表》填报进口货物启始发出直接运抵我国或者在运输中转国（地）未发生任何商业性交易的情况下运抵我国的国家（地区）例如：申报进口货物的启运国为美国时，根据下拉菜单选择填报"USA美国"，也可在本栏录入中文"美国"。运抵国（地区）按海关规定的《国别（地区）代码表》填报出口货物，离开我国关境直接运抵或者在运输中转国（地区）未发生任何商业性交易的情况下最后运抵的国家（地区）。例如：申报出口货物的运抵国为马来西亚时，根据下拉菜单选择填报代码为"MYS马来西亚"，也可在本栏录入中文"马来西亚"。

注意事项：不经过第三国（地区）转运的直接运输进出口货物，应在启运国（地区）项目中填报进口货物的装货港所在国（地区），在运抵国（地区）项目中填报出口货物的指运港所在国（地区 经过第三国（地区）转运的进出口货物，如在中转国（地区）发生商业性交易，则以中转国（地区）作为启运/运抵国（地区）填报在本栏。无实际进出境的货物，填报"中国"或"CHN"。

编码规则：启运/运抵国（地区）代码由3位英文字母构成。例如：美国代码为"USA美国"。参数引用《国别（地区）代码表》。

19 栏　经停/指运港

项目类型：该申报项目为必填项。该项目为字符型。

录入要求：经停港按海关规定的《港口代码表》选择填报进口货物在运抵我国关境前的最后一个境外装运港。指运港按海关规定的《港口代码表》选择填报出口货物运往境外的最终目的港。

注意事项：

1. 出口货物的最终目的港不可预知的，按尽可能预知的目的港作为指运港填报

2. 经停/指运港在《港口代码表》中无港口名称及代码的，可选择填报相应的国家名

称及代码。例如：若来自或去往的柬埔寨港口在《港口代码表》无港口名称和对应代码，则填报"柬埔寨"或代码"KHM000"。

3. 无实际进出境的货物，填报"中国境内"或代码"CHN000"。

4. 该项目数据类型为6位字符型。

编码规则：一般港口代码由3位英文字母和3位数字组成，例如：缅甸仰光的港口代码为"MMR018"；海关特殊监管区域或保税监管场所的代码由6位数字组成，例如：珠海保税区货场的港口代码为"994802"参数引用《港口代码表》。

20栏　入境口岸/离境口岸

项目类型：该申报项目为必填项。该项目为字符型。

录入要求：入境口岸填报进境货物从跨境运输工具卸离的第一个境内口岸的中文名称及代码；采取多式联运跨境运输的，填报多式联运货物最终卸离的境内口岸中文名称及代码；过境货物填报货物进入境内的第一个口岸的中文名称及代码；从海关特殊监管区域或保税监管场所进境的，填报海关特殊监管区域或保税监管场所的中文名称及代码。其他无实际进境的货物，填报货物所在地的城市名称及代码。

注意事项：离境口岸填报装运出境货物的跨境运输工具离境的第一个境内口岸的中文名称及代码；采取多式联运跨境运输的，填报多式联运货物最初离境的境内口岸中文名称及代码；过境货物填报货物离境的第一个口岸的中文名称及代码；从海关特殊监管区域或保税监管场所离境的，填报海关特殊监管区域或保税监管场所的中文名称及代码。其他无实际出境的货物，填报货物所在地的城市名称及代码。

编码规则：入境口岸/离境口岸类型包括港口、码头、机场、机场货运通道、边境口岸、火车站、车辆装卸点、车检场、陆路港、坐落在口岸的海关特殊监管区域等。按海关规定的《国内口岸编码表》选择填报相应的境内口岸名称及代码。

21栏　包装种类

项目类型：该申报项目为必填项，该项目为字符型。

录入要求：按照海关规定的《包装种类代码表》选择填报进出口货物的所有包装材料，包括运输包装和其他包装。其中，运输包装指提运单所列货物件数单位对应的包装，按照海关规定的《包装种类代码表》，填报运输包装对应的2位包装种类代码或中文名称。例如：使用再生木托作为运输包装的，在本栏填报中文"再生木托"或代码"92"。若还有其他包装，则在"其他包装栏目中，按照海关规定的《包装种类代码表》勾选包装材料种类。例如其他包装中含有天然木质托盘的在本栏勾选"93天然木托"。"其他包装为选填项，动植物性包装物、铺垫材料进境时必须填报。

编码规则：参数引用《包装种类代码表》。

22栏　件数

项目类型：该申报项目为必填项。该项目数据类型为数字型，最多支持录入9位。

录入要求：填报进出口货物运输包装的件数（按运输包装计），不得填报为零，裸装货物填报为"1"。运输包装指提运单所列货物件数单位对应的包装。

注意事项：

（1）舱单件数为集装箱的，填报集装箱个数。

（2）舱单件数为托盘的，填报托盘数。

23 栏　毛重（千克）

项目类型：该申报项目为必填项。该项目数据类型为数字型，最多支持录入 19 位，19 位中小数点后最多支持录入 5 位。

录入要求：填报进出口货物及其包装材料的重量之和，计量单位为千克，不足一千克的填报为"1"。

注意事项：报关单毛重栏目不得为空，毛重应大于或等于1，不得为"0"。

24 栏　净重（千克）

项目类型：该申报项目为必填项。该项目数据类型为数字型，最多支持录入 19 位，19 位中小数点后最多支持录入 5 位。

录入要求：填报进出口货物的毛重减去外包装材料后的重量，即货物本身的实际重量，计量单位为千克，不足一千克的填报为"1"。

注意事项：报关单净重栏目不得为空，净重应大于或等于1，不得为"0"。

25 栏　成交方式

项目类型：该申报项目为必填项。该项目数据类型为 1 位字符型。

录入要求：根据进出口货物实际成交价格条款，按海关规定的《成交方式代码表》选择填报相应的成交方式代码。例如：该货物的成交方式为 CIF，下拉菜单时可选择"1－CIF"或录入"1"，栏目自动生成"CIF"。

注意事项：无实际进出境的货物，进口录入 CIF，出口录入 FOB。

编码规则：根据进出口货物实际成交价格条款，按海关规定的《成交方式代码表》选择填报相应的成交方式代码。

成交方式名称	成交方式代码	成交方式名称	成交方式代码
CIF	1	市场价	5
CFR（C&F/CNF）	2	垫仓	6
FOB	3	EXW	7
C&I	4		

26 栏　运费

（一）"运费标记"栏

项目类型：该申报项目为选填项。"运费标志"、"运费/率"和"运费币制"共同填报。该项目为字符型。

录入要求：运费为进口货物运抵我国境内输入地点起卸前的运输费用，出口货物运至我国境内输出地点装载后的运输费用。运费可按运费单价、总价或运费率三种方式之一填报。

"运费标志"为"运费"项下第一栏。当按照运费率申报时，"运费标志"栏选择填报"1－率"；当按照每吨货物的运费单价申报时，"运费标志"栏选择填报"2－单价"；

按照运费总价申报时，"运费标志"栏选择填报"3 - 总价"。

编码规则："1 - 率"/"2 - 单价"/"3 - 总价"。

（二）"运费率"栏

项目类型：该申报项目为选填项。"运费标志"、"运费/率"和"运费币制"共同填报。该项目为字符型。

录入要求：运费为进口货物运抵我国境内输入地点起卸前的运输费用，出口货物运至我国境内输出地点装载后的运输费用。运费可按运费单价、总价或运费率三种方式之一填报。

"运费/率"为"运费"项下第二栏。

当"运费标记"为"1 - 率"，在本栏填报运费率；当"运费标记"为"2 - 单价"，在本栏填报运费单价；当"运费标记"为"3 - 总价"，在本栏填报运费总价。

该项目数据类型为数字型，最多支持录入19位，19位中小数点后最多支持录入5位。

编码规则：数字

（三）"运费币制"栏

项目类型：该申报项目为选填项。该项目数据类型为3位字符型。

录入要求：填报进口货物运抵我国境内输入地点起卸前的运输费用，出口货物运至我国境内输出地点装载后的运输费用。运费可按运费单价、总价或运费率三种方式之一填报。

"运费"项下第三栏为"运费币制"栏。

当"运费标记"栏为"1 - 率"是，本栏免予录入；如"运费标记"为"2 - 单价"或"3 - 总价"时，本栏按海关规定的《货币代码表》录入相应的币种代码。

编码规则：保险费市制代码由3位英文字母构成。例如：美元代码为"USD 美元"。参数引用《货币代码表》。

27栏　保费

（一）"保费标记"栏

项目类型：该申报项目为选填项。"保险费标志"、"保险费/率"和"保险费币制"共同填报；该项目为字符型。

录入要求：保险费为进口货物运抵我国境内输入地点起卸前的保险费用，出口货物运至我国境内输出地点装载后的保险费用。保险费可按保险费总价或保险费率两种方式之一填报。

"保险费"项下第一栏为"保险费标记"栏。

当按照保险费率申报时，"保险费标记"栏选择填报"1 - 率"；按照保险费总价申报时，"保险费标记"栏选择填报"3 - 总价"。

编码规则："1 - 率"/"3 - 总价"。保险费/率 项目类型：

（二）"保险费/率"栏

项目类型：该申报项目为选填项。"保险费标志"、"保险费/率"和"保险费币制"共同填报；该项目为数值型。

录入要求：保险费填报进口货物运抵我国境内输入地点起卸前的保险费用，出口货物运至我国境内输出地点装载后的保险费用。保险费可按保险费总价或保险 费率两种方式之一填报。"保险费/率"为"保险费"项下第二栏。

当"保险费标志"为"1－率"，在本栏填报保险费率；

当"保险费标志"为"3－总价"，在本栏填报保险费总价。

该项目数据类型为数字型，最多支持录入 19 位，19 位中小数点后最多支持录入 5 位。

（三）"保险费币制"栏

项目类型：该申报项目为选填项。"保险费标志"、"保险费/率"和"保险费币制"共 同填报。该项目为字符型。

录入要求：填报进口货物运抵我国境内输入地点起卸前的保险费用，出口货物运至我 国境内输出地点装载后的保险费用。保险费可按保险费总价或保险费率两种方式之一 填报。

"保险费币制"为"保险费"项下第三栏。

当"保险费标志"为"3－总价"，本栏按海关规定的《货币代码表》录入相 应的币 种代码；

当"保险费标志"为"1－率"，本栏无需填报。

编码规则：保险费币制代码由 3 位英文字母构成。例如：美元代码为"USD 美元"。 参数引用《货币代码表》。

28 栏　杂费

（一）"杂费标志"栏

项目类型：该申报项目为选填项。"杂费标志"、"杂费/率"和"杂费币制"共同填 报。该项目为字符型。

录入要求：杂费填报成交价格以外的、按照《中华人民共和国进出口关税条例》相关 规定应计入完税价格或应从完税价格中扣除的费用。可按杂费总价或杂费 率两种方式之 一填报。"杂费标志"为"杂费"项下第一栏。当按照杂费率申报时，"杂费标志"栏选择 填报"1－率"；当按照杂费总价 申报时，"杂费标志"栏选择填报"3－杂费总价"。

编码规则："1－率"/"杂费标志"

（二）"杂费/率"栏

项目类型：该申报项目为选填项。"杂费标志"、"杂费/率"和"杂费币制"共同填 报。该项目为字符型。

录入要求：杂费填报成交价格以外的、按照《中华人民共和国进出口关税条例》相关 规定应计入完税价格或应从完税价格中扣除的费用。可按杂费总价或杂费 率两种方式之 一填报。

杂费/率"为"杂费"项下第二栏。

当"杂费标志"为"1－率"，在本栏填报杂费率；当"杂费标志"为"3 杂费总 价"，在本栏填报杂费总价。该项目最多支持录入 19 位，19 位中小数点后最多支持录入 5 位。

注意事项：应计入完税价格的杂费填报为正值或正率，应从完税价格中扣除的杂费填 报为负值或负率。

编码规则：数值。

（三）"杂费币制"栏

项目类型：该申报项目为选填项。"杂费标志"、"杂费/率"和"杂费币制"共同填报。该项目为字符型。

录入要求：杂费填报成交价格以外的、按照《中华人民共和国进出口关税条例》相关规定应计入完税价格或应从完税价格中扣除的费用。可按杂费总价或杂费 率两种方式之一填报。

"杂费币制"为"杂费"项下第三栏。

当"杂费标志"为"3－杂费总价"，本栏按海关规定的《货币代码表》录入相应的币种代码；

当"杂费标志"为"1－率"，本栏无需填报。

编码规则：保险费币制代码由 3 位英文字母构成。例如：美元代码为"USD 美元"。参数引用《货币代码表》。

29 栏　随附单证及编号

（一）"随附单证代码"栏

项目类型：该申报项目为有条件必填项。监管证件有要求时必填。该项目为字符型。

录入要求：除进（出）口许可证、两用物项和技术进（出）口许可证、两用物项和技术出口许可证（定向）、纺织品临时出口许可证、出口许可证（加工贸易 出口许可证（边境小额贸易）以外的其他进出口许可证件或监管证件，按海关规定的《监管证件代码表》选择填报相应证件代码。

注意事项：

1. 加工贸易内销征税报关单，"随附单证代码"栏填报"c"。

2. 一般贸易进出口货物"随附单证代码"栏填报"Y"。海关特殊监管区域和保税监管场所内销货物申请适用优惠税率的，有关货物进出海关特殊监管区域和保税监管场所以及内销时，"随附单证代码"栏按照上述一般贸易要求填报。向香港或者澳门特别行政区出口用于生产香港 CEPA 或者澳门 CEPA 项下货物的原材料时，"随附单证代码"栏按照上述一般贸易要求填报。

3. 各优惠贸易协定项下，免提交原产地证据文件的小金额进口货物"随附单证代码"栏填报"Y"。

编码规则：参数引用《监管证件代码表》。

（二）"随附单证编号"栏

项目类型：该申报项目为有条件必填项。监管证件有要求时必填。该项目为字符型。

录入要求：除进（出）口许可证、两用物项和技术进（出）口许可证、两用物项和技术出口许可证（定向）纺织品临时出口许可证、出口许可证（加工贸易 出口许可证（边境小额贸易）以外的其他进出口许可证件或监管证件，填报证件编号。

注意事项：

1. 加工贸易内销征税报关单，随附单证编号栏填报海关审核通过的内销征税联系单号。

　　一般贸易进出口货物，只能使用原产地证书申请享受协定税率或者特惠税率（以下统称优惠税率）的（无原产地声明模式），在"随附单证编号"栏填报"＜优惠贸易协定代码＞"和"原产地证书编号"。可以使用原产地证书或者原产地声明申请享受优惠税率的（有原产地声明模式）"随附单证编号"栏填报"＜优惠贸易协定代码＞"、"C"（凭原产地证书申报）或"D"（凭原产地声明申报），以及"原产地证书编号（或者原产地声明序列号）"。一份报关单对应一份原产地证书或原产地声明。

　　各优惠贸易协定代码如下：
　　"01"为"亚太贸易协定"；
　　"02"为"中国—东盟自贸协定"；
　　"03"为"内地与香港紧密经贸关系安排"（香港CEPA）；
　　"04"为"内地与澳门紧密经贸关系安排"（澳门CEPA）；
　　"06"为"台湾农产品零关税措施"；
　　"07"为"中国—巴基斯坦自贸协定"；
　　"08"为"中国—智利自贸协定"；
　　"10"为"中国—新西兰自贸协定"；
　　"11"为"中国—新加坡自贸协定"；
　　"12"为"中国—秘鲁自贸协定"；
　　"13"为"最不发达国家特别优惠关税待遇"；
　　"14"为"海峡两岸经济合作框架协议（ECFA）"；
　　"15"为"中国—哥斯达黎加自贸协定"；
　　"16"为"中国—冰岛自贸协定"；
　　"17"为"中国—瑞士自贸协定"；
　　"18"为"中国—澳大利亚自贸协定"；
　　"19"为"中国—韩国自贸协定"；
　　"20"为"中国—格鲁吉亚自贸协定"。

　　海关特殊监管区域和保税监管场所内销货物申请适用优惠税率的，有关货物进出海关特殊监管区域和保税监管场所以及内销时，已通过原产地电子信息交换系统实现电子联网的优惠贸易协定项下货物报关单，按照上述一般贸易要求填报；未实现电子联网的优惠贸易协定项下货物报关单，"随附单证代码"栏填报"Y"，"随附单证编号"栏填报"＜优惠贸易协定代码＞"和"原产地证据文件备案号"。"原产地证据文件备案号"为进出口货物的收发货物人或者其代理人录入原产地证据文件电子信息后，系统自动生成的号码。

　　向香港或者澳门特别行政区出口用于生产香港CEPA或者澳门CEPA项下货物的原材料时，按照上述一般贸易填报要求填制报关单，香港或澳门生产厂商在香港工贸署或者澳门经济局登记备案的有关备案号填报在"关联备案"栏。

　　"单证对应关系表"中填报报关单上的申报商品项与原产地证书（原产地声明）上的商品项之间的对应关系。报关单上的商品序号与原产地证书（原产地声明）上的项目编号应一一对应，不要求顺序对应。同一批次进口货物可以在同一报关单中申报，不享受优惠税率的货物序号不填报在"单证对应关系表"中。

2. 各优惠贸易协定项下，免提交原产地证据文件的小金额进口货物"随附单证编号"栏填报"＜优惠贸易协定代码＞XJE00000"，"单证对应关系表"享惠报关单项号按实际填报，对应单证项号与享惠报关单项号相同。

编码规则：该项目最多支持例如 32 字符。

30 栏　标记唛码及备注

用于填报标记唛码、备注说明和集装箱号等于进出口货物有关的文字或数字。

（一）"标记唛码"栏

俗称运输标志，在进出口货物报关单上标记唛码专指货物的运输标志。

录入要求：标记唛码中除图形以外的文字、数字，无标记唛码的填报 N/M。

（二）"备注"栏

备注是指除按报关单固定栏目申报进出口货物的有关情况外，需要补充说明的事项。

录入要求：

1. 填报受外商投资企业委托代理其进口投资设备、物品的进出口企业名称。

2. 与本报关单有关联关系的，同时在业务管理规范方面又要求填报的备案号，填报在电子数据报关单中"关联备案"栏。

保税间流转货物、加工贸易结转货物及凭《征免税证明》转内销货物，其对应的备案号填报在"关联备案"栏。

减免税货物结转进口（转入），"关联备案"栏填报本次减免税货物结转所申请的《中华人民共和国海关进口减免税货物结转联系函》的编号。

减免税货物结转出口（转出），"关联备案"栏填报与其相对应的进口（转入）报关单"备案号"栏中《征免税证明》的编号。

3. 与本报关单有关联关系的，同时在业务管理规范方面又要求填报的报关单号，填报在电子数据报关单中"关联报关单"栏。

保税间流转、加工贸易结转类的报关单，应先办理进口报关，并将进口报关单号填入出口报关单的"关联报关单"栏。

办理进口货物直接退运手续的，除另有规定外，应先填制出口报关单，再填制进口报关单，并将出口报关单号填报在进口报关单的"关联报关单"栏。

减免税货物结转出口（转出），应先办理进口报关，并将进口（转入）报关单号填入出口（转出）报关单的"关联报关单"栏。

4. 办理进口货物直接退运手续的，填报"＜ZT"＋"海关审核联系单号或者《海关责令进口货物直接退运通知书》编号"＋"＞"。办理固体废物直接退运手续的，填报"固体废物，直接退运表 XX 号/责令直接退运通知书 XX 号"。

5. 保税监管场所进出货物，在"保税/监管场所"栏填报本保税监管场所编码（保税物流中心（B 型）填报本中心的国内地区代码），其中涉及货物在保税监管场所间流转的，在本栏填报对方保税监管场所代码。

6. 涉及加工贸易货物销毁处置的，填报海关加工贸易货物销毁处置申报表编号。

（三）"集装箱规格"栏

项目类型：该申报项目为有条件必填项。申报使用集装箱装载进出口货物的情况时为必填。该项目为字符型。

录入要求：使用集装箱装载进出口商品的，在填报集装箱号后，在本栏按照《集装箱规格代码表》选择填报集装箱规格。例如：装载商品的集装箱规格为"普通2＊标准箱（L），在本栏下拉菜单选择"11普通2＊标准箱（L）。

编码规则：参数引用《集装箱规格代码表》。

（四）"集装箱号"栏

项目类型：该申报项目为有条件必填项。申报使用集装箱装载进出口货物的情况时为必填。该项目为字符型。

录入要求：使用集装箱装载进出口货物时，需填报集装箱体信息，包括集装箱号、集装箱规格和集装箱商品项号关系，集装箱号根据集装箱体上标示的全球唯一编号进行填报。一份报关单有多个集装箱的，则在本栏分别录入集装箱号。

注意事项：该项目应为11位字符。

编码规则：集装箱号码规则。

31栏　项号

录入要求：分两行填报。第一行填报报关单中的商品顺序编号；第二行填报备案序号，专用于加工贸易及保税、减免税等已备案、审批的货物，填报该项货物在《加工贸易手册》或《征免税证明》等备案、审批单证中的顺序编号。有关优惠贸易协定项下报关单填制要求按照海关总署相关规定执行。

注意事项：

1. 深加工结转货物，分别按照《加工贸易手册》中的进口料件项号和出口成品项号填报。

2. 料件结转货物（包括料件、制成品和未完成品折料），出口报关单按照转出《加工贸易手册》中进口料件的项号填报；进口报关单按照转进《加工贸易手册》中进口料件的项号填报。

3. 料件复出货物（包括料件、边角料），出口报关单按照《加工贸易手册》中进口料件的项号填报；如边角料对应一个以上料件项号时，填报主要料件项号。料件退换货物（包括料件、不包括未完成品），进出口报关单按照《加工贸易手册》中进口料件的项号填报。

4. 成品退换货物，退运进境报关单和复运出境报关单按照《加工贸易手册》原出口成品的项号填报。

5. 加工贸易料件转内销货物（以及按料件办理进口手续的转内销制成品、残次品、未完成品）填制进口报关单，填报《加工贸易手册》进口料件的项号；加工贸易边角料、副产品内销，填报《加工贸易手册》中对应的进口料件项号。如边角料或副产品对应一个以上料件项号时，填报主要料件项号。

6. 加工贸易成品凭《征免税证明》转为减免税货物进口的，应先办理进口报关手续。进口报关单填报《征免税证明》中的项号，出口报关单填报《加工贸易手册》原出口成品项号，进、出口报关单货物数量应一致。

7. 加工贸易货物销毁，填报《加工贸易手册》中相应的进口料件项号。

8. 加工贸易副产品退运出口、结转出口，填报《加工贸易手册》中新增成品的出口项号。

9. 经海关批准实行加工贸易联网监管的企业，按海关联网监管要求，企业需申报报关清单的，应在向海关申报进出口（包括形式进出口）报关单前，向海关申报"清单"。一份报关清单对应一份报关单，报关单上的商品由报关清单归并而得。加工贸易电子账册报关单中项号、品名、规格等栏目的填制规范比照《加工贸易手册》。

32 栏　商品编号

项目类型：该申报项目为必填项。该项目为字符型。

录入要求：填报由 10 位数字组成的商品编号。前 8 位为《中华人民共和国进出口税则》和《中华人民共和国海关统计商品目录》确定的编码；9、10 位为监管附加编号。

编码规则：参数引用《中华人民共和国进出口税则》和《中华人民共和国海关统计商品目录》

33 栏　商品名称及规格型号

（一）"商品名称"栏

项目类型：该申报项目为必填项。该项目为字符型。

录入要求：

1. 商品名称应据实填报，并与进出口货物收发货人或受委托的报关企业所提交的合同、发票等相关单证相符。

2. 商品名称应当规范，以能满足海关归类、审价及许可证件管理要求为准，可参照《中华人民共和国海关进出口商品规范申报目录》、《中华人民共和国海关进出口货物报关单填制规范》中对商品名称的要求进行填报。该项目最多支持录入 255 位字符。

编码规则：自由文本。

（二）"规格型号"栏

项目类型：该申报项目为必填项。该项目为字符型。

录入要求：

1. 规格型号应据实填报，并与进出口货物收发货人或受委托的报关企业所提交的合同、发票等相关单证相符。

2. 规格型号应当足够详细，以能满足海关归类、审价及许可证件管理要求 为准，可参照《中华人民共和国海关进出口商品规范申报目录》《中华人民 共和国海关进出口货物报关单填制规范》中对规格型号的要求进行填报。

3. 品牌类型。品牌类型为必填项目。可选择"无品牌"、"境内自主品牌"、"境 内收购品牌"、境外品牌〔贴牌生产 y、"境外品牌（其他 y 如实填报。其 中，"境内自主品牌"是指由境内企业自主开发、拥有自主知识产权的品牌；晓境内收购品牌"是指境内企业收购的原境外品牌；"境外品牌（贴牌生产 y 是指境内企业代工贴牌生产中使用的境外品牌；"境外品牌（其他）"是指除代工贴牌生产以外使用的境外品牌。

4. 出口享惠情况。出口享惠情况为出口报关单必填项目。可选择"出口货物 在最终目的国（地区）不享受优惠关税"、"出口货物在最终目的国（地区）享受优惠关税"、"出口货物不能确定在最终目的国（地区）享受优惠关税"如实填报。进口货物报关单免于填报该申报项。该项目数据类型为字符型，最多支持录入 255 位。

编码规则：自由文本。规格型号应当足够详细，以能满足海关归类、审价及许可证件管理要求为准，可参照《中华人民共和国海关进出口商品规范申报目录)《中华人民共和国海关进出口货物报关单填制规范》中对规格型号的要求 进行填报。

34 栏　数量及单位

（一）"成交数量"栏

项目类型：该申报项目为必填项。该项目为数值型。

录入要求：填报货物实际成交的数量。该项目最多支持录入 19 位，19 位中小数点后最多支持录入 5 位

编码规则：数值。

（二）"成交计量单位"栏

项目类型：该申报项目为必填项。该项目为字符型

录入要求：通过下拉菜单选择货物实际成交所用的计量单位。例如：成交单位为"台则通过下拉菜单选择"001 台"。

注意事项：

1. 已备案的加工贸易及保税货物，成交计量单位必须与《加工贸易手册》中同项号下货物的计量单位一致，加工贸易边角料和副产品内销、边角料复出口，填报其报验状态的计量单位。

2. 优惠贸易协定项下进出口商品的成交计量单位必须与原产地证书上对应商品的计量单位一致。编码规则：参数引用《计量单位代码表》。

（三）"法定第一数量"栏

项目类型：该申报项目为必填项。该项目为数值型。

录入要求：进出口货物按《中华人民共和国海关统计商品目录》中确定的法定第一计量单位，填报对应的法定第一数量。

1. 法定计量单位为"千克"的按数量填报，特殊情况下填报要求如下：

① 装入可重复使用的包装容器的货物，应按货物扣除包装容器后的重量填报，如罐装同位素、罐装氧气及类似品等。

② 使用不可分割包装材料和包装容器的货物，按货物的净重填报（即包括内层直接包装的净重重量），如采用供零售包装的罐头、药品及类似品等。

③ 按照商业惯例以公量重计价的商品，按公量重填报，如未脱脂羊毛、羊毛条等。

④ 采用以毛重作为净重计价的货物，可按毛重填报，如粮食、饲料等大宗散装货物。

⑤ 采用零售包装的酒类、饮料、化妆品，按照液体/乳状/膏状/粉状部分的重量填报。

2. 成套设备、减免税货物如需分批进口，货物实际进口时，按照实际报验状态确定数量。

3. 具有完整品或制成品基本特征的不完整品、未制成品，根据《商品名称及编码协调制度》归类规则按完整品归类的，按照构成完整品的实际数量填报。

4. 已备案的加工贸易及保税货物，成交计量单位必须与《加工贸易手册》中同项号

下货物的计量单位一致，加工贸易边角料和副产品内销、边角料复出口，填报其报验状态的计量单位。

5. 优惠贸易协定项下进出口商品的成交计量单位必须与原产地证书上对应商品的计量单位一致。

6. 法定计量单位为立方米的气体货物，折算成标准状况（即摄氏零度及 1 个标准大气压）下的体积进行填报。

该项目最多支持录入 19 位数字，19 位中小数点后最多支持录入 5 位。

编码规则：数值。

"法定第一数量单位"栏

项目类型：该申报项目为系统返填项。该项目为字符型

录入要求：进出口货物按海关通关系统《商品综合分类表》中确定的法定第一计量单位，自动返填计量单位

"法定第二数量"栏

项目类型：该申报项目为条件必填项。凡列明有法定第二计量单位的必填。该项目为数值型。

录入要求：凡列明有法定第二计量单位的，按照法定第二计量单位填报对应的数量。

无法定第二计量单位的无需录入。该项目最多支持录入 19 位数字 19 位中小数点后最多支持录入 5 位。

编码规则：数值。

"法定第二计量单位"栏

项目类型：该申报项目为系统返填项。

录入要求：进出口货物按海关通关系统《商品综合分类表》中确定的法定第二计量单位，自动返填计量单位。

35 栏　单价/总价/币制

（一）"单价"栏

项目类型：该申报项目为必填项。该项目为数值型。

录入要求：填报同一项号下进出口货物实际成交的商品单位价格。无实际成交价格的填报单位货值。该项目最多支持录入 19 位数字，19 位中小数点后最多支持录入 4 位。

注意事项：录入成交数量、成交单位、总价后，单价会自动生成。例如：某进口商品录入成交数量 1000，成交单位为千克（代码 035），总价 10000，单价则会自动生成 10。

编码规则：数值。

（二）"总价"栏

项目类型：该申报项目为必填项。该项目为数值型。

录入要求：填报同一项号下进出口货物实际成交的商品总价格。无实际成交价格的，填报货值。该项目最多支持录入 19 位，19 位中小数点后最多支持录入 2 位。

注意事项：录入成交数量、成交单位、单价后，总价会自动生成。例如：某进口商品录入成交数量 1000，成交单位为千克（代码 035），单价 10，总价则会自动生成 10000。

编码规则：数值。

（三）"币制"栏

项目类型：该申报项目为必填项。该项目为数值型。

录入要求：根据进出口贸易合同和发票中的币种，对照海关规定的《货币代码表》选择相应的货币名称及代码填报，如《货币代码表》中无实际成交币种，需将实际成交货币按申报日外汇折算率折算成《货币代码表》列名的货币填报。录入时可在本栏下拉菜单中选择币制或按《货币代码表》录入相应的币制代码。

注意事项：原报关《货币代码表》和原报检《货币代码表》采用 3 位数字，新修订的《货币代码表》采用 3 位子目。例如币制为美元，"币制"应录入"USD"，而非原报关代码"502"或原报检代码"840"

编码规则：参数引用《货币代码表》。

36 栏　原产国（地区）

项目类型：该申报项目为必填项。该项目为字符型。

录入要求：原产国（地区）依据《中华人民共和国进出口货物原产地条例》、《中华人民共和国海关关于执行〈非优惠原产地规则中实质性改变标准〉的规定》以及海关总署关于各项优惠贸易协定原产地管理规章规定的原产地确定标准，按海关规定的《国别（地区）代码表》选择填报相应的国家（地区）名称及代码。例如：某进口货物的原产国为"美国"，可在本栏下拉菜单中 选择"USA 美国"或录入"USA"，栏目自动生成"USA 美国"。

注意事项：同一批进出口货物的原产地不同的，分别填报原产国（地区）。进出口货物原产国（地区）无法确定的，填报"ZZZ 国（地）别不详"

37 栏　最终目的国（地区）

项目类型：该申报项目为必填项。该项目为字符型。

录入要求：最终目的国（地区）按海关规定的《国别（地区）代码表》选择填报已知 的进出口货物的最终实际消费、使用或进一步加工制造国家（地区）

注意事项：不经过第三国（地区）转运的直接运输货物，以运抵国（地区）为最终目的国（地区）经过第三国（地区）转运的货物，以最后运往国（地区）为最终目的国（地区同一批进出口货物的最终目的国（地区）不同的，分别填报最终目的国（地区）进出口货物不能确定最终目的国（地区）时，以尽可能预知的最后运往国（地区）为最终目的国（地区）。

编码规则：最终目的国（地区）代码由 3 位英文字母构成。例如：美国代码为"USA 美国"。参数引用《国别（地区）代码表》

38 栏　境内目的地/境内货源地

项目类型：该申报项目为必填项。该项目为字符型。

录入要求：进口填报"境内目的地代码"和"目的地代码"，出口填报"境内货源地代码"和"产地代码"。境内目的地填报已知的进口货物在国内的消费、使用地或最终运抵地，其中最终运抵地为最终使用单位所在的地区。境内货源地填报出口货物在国内的产地或原始发货地。按海关规定的《国内地区代 码表》选择填报相应的国内地区名称及代码，并根据《中华人民共和国行政区划代码表》选择填报对应的县级行政区名称及代码。

无下属区县级行 政区的，可选择填报地市级行政区。

注意事项：

1. 最终使用单位难以确定的，填报货物进口时预知的最终收货单位所在地。

2. 出口货物产地难以确定的，填报最早发运该出口货物的单位所在地。

3. 海关特殊监管区域、保税物流中心（B 型）与境外之间的进出境货物，境内目的地/境内货源地填报本海关特殊监管区域、保税物流中心（B 型）所 对应的国内地区名称及代码。

4. 进口货物需同时在"境内目的地代码"和"目的地代码"两个栏目录入相应的国内地区和县级行政区名称及代码；出口货物需同时在"境内货源地代 码"和"产地代码"两个栏目录入相应的国内地区和县级行政区名称及代码。例如：某批货物的境内目的地是广州市花都区。在"境内目的地代码"栏下 拉菜单选择"44019 广州其他"，或按海关规定的《国内地区代码表》录入"44019"，栏目自动生成"44019 广州其他"。同时"目的地代码"栏下拉菜单选择"440100 广东省广州市"，或根据《中华人民共和国行政区划代码表》录入"440114"，栏目自动生成"广州市花都区"。

编码规则：境内目的地/境内货源地代码由 5 位数字组成，目的地/产地代码由 6 位 数字组成。参数引用《国内地区代码表》和《中华人民共和国行政区划代码表》

39 栏　征免

项目类型：该申报项目为选填项。该项目为字符型。

录入要求：按照海关核发的《征免税证明》或有关政策规定，对报关单所列每项商品选择海关规定的《征减免税方式代码表》中相应的征减免税方式填报。

加工贸易货物报关单根据《加工贸易手册》中备案的征免规定填报；《加工贸易手册》中备案的征免规定为"保金"或"保函"的，填报"全免"。

代码	名称	代码	名称
1	照章征税	5	随征免性质
2	折半征税	6	保证金
3	全免	7	保函
4	特案		

40 栏　特殊关系确认

项目类型：该申报项目为选填项。该项目为字符型。

录入要求：根据《中华人民共和国海关审定进出口货物完税价格办法》（以下简称《审价办法》）第十六条，填报确认进出口行为中买卖双方是否存在特殊关系，有下列情形之一的，应当认为买卖双方存在特殊关系，应在下拉菜单中选择"1 - 是"，反之则选择"0 - 否"：

1. 买卖双方为同一家族成员的。

2. 买卖双方互为商业上的高级职员或者董事的。

3. 一方直接或者间接地受另一方控制的。

4. 买卖双方都直接或者间接地受第三方控制的。

5. 买卖双方共同直接或者间接地控制第三方的。

6. 一方直接或者间接地拥有、控制或者持有对方5%以上（含5%）公开发行的有表决权的股票或者股份的。

7. 一方是另一方的雇员、高级职员或者董事的。

8. 买卖双方是同一合伙的成员的。买卖双方在经营上相互有联系，一方是另一方的独家代理、独家经销或者独家受让人，如果符合前款的规定，也应当视为存在特殊关系。

注意事项：

1. 出口货物免予填报，加工贸易及保税监管货物（内销保税货物除外）免予填报。

2. 点击"其他事项确认"按钮打开本项目。编码规则："1－是"／"0－否"。

41 栏　价格影响确认

项目类型：该申报项目为选填项。该项目为字符型。

录入要求：根据《审价办法》第十七条，填报确认纳税义务人是否可以证明特殊关系未对进口货物的成交价格产生影响，纳税义务人能证明其成交价格与同时或者大约同时发生的下列任何一款价格相近的，应视为特殊关系未对成交价格产生影响，在下拉菜单中选择"0－否"，反之则选择"1－是"：

1. 向境内无特殊关系的买方出售的相同或者类似进口货物的成交价格。

2. 按照《审价办法》第二十三条的规定所确定的相同或者类似进口货物的完税价格。

3. 按照《审价办法》第二十五条的规定所确定的相同或者类似进口货物的完税价格。

注意事项：

1. 出口货物免予填报，加工贸易及保税监管货物〔内销保税货物除外）免予填报。

2. 点击"其他事项确认"按钮打开本项目。

编码规则："1－是"／"0－否"。

42 栏　支付特许权使用费确认

项目类型：该申报项目为选填项。该项目为字符型。

录入要求：根据《审价办法》第十一条和第十三条，填报确认买方是否存在向卖方或者有关方直接或者间接支付与进口货物有关的特许权使用费，且未包括在进口货物的实付、应付价格中。通过下拉菜单方式选择填报。买方存在需向卖方或者有关方直接或者间接支付特许权使用费，且未包含在进口货物实付、应付价格中，并且符合《审价办法》第十三条的，选择"1－是"。

买方存在需向卖方或者有关方直接或者间接支付特许权使用费，且未包含在进口货物实付、应付价格中，但纳税义务人无法确认是否符合《审价办法》第十三条的，选择"1－是"。

买方存在需向卖方或者有关方直接或者间接支付特许权使用费且未包含在实付、应付价格中，纳税义务人根据《审价办法》第十三条，可以确认需支付的特许权使用费与进口货物无关的，选择"0－否"。买方不存在向卖方或者有关方直接或者间接支付特许权使用费的，或者特许权使用费已经包含在进口货物实付、应付价格中的，选择

"0 - 否"。

注意事项：

1. 出口货物免予填报，加工贸易及保税监管货物（内销保税货物除外）免予 填报。

2. 点击"其他事项确认"按钮打开本项目

编码规则："1 - 是" /"0 - 否"。

43 栏　自报自缴

进出口企业、单位采用"自主申报、自行缴税"（自报自缴）模式向海关申报时，填报"是"；反之则填报"否"。

44 栏　申报单位

项目类型：该申报项目为系统返填项。该项目为字符型。

录入要求：自理报关的，填报进出口企业的名称及编码；委托代理报关的，填报报关企业名称及编码。编码填报 18 位法人和其他组织统一社会信用代码。报关人员填报在海关备案的姓名、编码、电话，并加盖申报单位印章。

注意事项：该项目内容系统返填，不可修改。

编码规则：系统返填。

45 栏　海关批注及签章

供海关作业时签注。

相关用语的含义：

报关单录入凭单：指申报单位按报关单的格式填写的凭单，用作报关单预录入的依据。该凭单的编号规则由申报单位自行决定。

预录入报关单：指预录入单位按照申报单位填写的报关单凭单录入、打印由申报单位向海关申报，海关尚未接受申报的报关单。

报关单证明联：指海关在核实货物实际进出境后按报关单格式提供的，用作进出口货物收发货人向国税、外汇管理部门办理退税和外汇核销手续的证明文件。

本规范所述尖括号（＜＞）、逗号（，）、连接符（－）、冒号（：）等标点符号及数字，填报时都必须使用非中文状态下的半角字符。

第三节　任务模块

在外贸业务中，考虑到实际装运时货物数量可能变动，外贸单证员一般只在报关委托书上盖章，而不填写详细内容，详细内容由报关员报关时填写。报关委托书正反两面都印有内容，现需要单证员李望完成的工作任务包括：

任务 1：认真审核商业发票、装箱单和订舱单等单证

任务 2：填制报关委托书

代理报关委托书

编号：□□□□□□□□□□□：

　　我单位现（A. 逐票√　B. 长期）委托贵公司代理等通关事宜。（A. 填单申报√
B. 辅助查验　C. 垫缴税款　D. 办理海关证明联√　E. 审批手册　F. 核销手册
G. 申办减免税手续　H. 其他）详见《委托报关协议》。我单位保证遵守《海关法》
和国家有关法规，保证所提供的情况真实、完整、单货相符。否则，愿承担相关法律
责任。

　　本委托书有效期自签字之日起至 2019 年 9 月 16 日止。

委托方（盖章）：醴陵鹏兴瓷厂
法定代表人或其授权签署《代理报关委托书》的人（签字）
年　　　月　　　日

委托报关协议

为明确委托报关具体事项和各自责任，双方经平等协商签定协议如下：

委托方	醴陵鹏兴瓷厂	被委托方	深圳市康海国际货运代理有限公司	
主要货物名称	日用陶瓷	*报关单编码	No.	
HS 编码	69111010.00	收到单证日期	2019 年 8 月 16 日	
货物总价	U. S. D6480.00	收到单证情况	合同□√	发票□√
出口日期	2019 年 8 月 15 日		装箱清单□√	提（运）单□√
提单号	CSZC02160497		加工贸易手册□	许可证作□
贸易方式	一般贸易		其他	
原产地/货源地	中国	报关收费	人民币：	240.00 元
其他要求：		承诺说明：		
背面所列通用条款是本协议不可分割的一部分，对本协议的签署构成了对背面通用条款的同意。		背面所列通用条款是本协议不可分割的一部分，对本协议的签署构成了对背面通用条款的同意。		
委托方业务签章：		被委托方业务签章：		
经办人签章：李望 联系电话：　　　　　　　2019 年 8 月 16 日		经办报关员签章： 联系电话：　　　　　　　2019 年 3 月 16 日		

（白联：海关留存。黄联：被委托方留存。红联：委托方留存）　　　　中国报关协会监制

第四节 任务拓展模块

能力实训项目1：缮制报关单并办理报关手续

上接项目五，根据青岛联江公司 LC163 信用证的要求，出口门把手和水平仪到日本大阪。2019 年 6 月 16 日，单证员刘燕备齐商业发票和装箱单等资料，填写报关委托书以及出口货物报关单，向青岛海关办理出口报关手续。

1. 商业发票。

QINGDAO LIANJIANG CO.，LTD.

No. 2 Taiping St. Qingdao，China

Tel：0166 – 532 – 8391926   Fax：0166 – 532 – 8391928

COMMERCIAL INVOICE

TO:	Taka Co.，Ltd. 16-15,Aza shinbo，Ohzaz Yamaya，Osaka，Japan Tel: 0161-665-39-3163 Fax: 0161-665-29-3163		INVOICE NO.:	LJ16071
			INVOICE DATE:	Jun.10,2019
			S/C NO.:	2016072
			S/C DATE:	May 9,2019
FROM:	Qingdao ,China	**TO:**		Osaka , Japan

Marks and Numbers	Number and kind of package Description of goods	Quantity	Unit Price	Amount
			FOB Qingdao	
N/M	(1)Door Handle 　Article No.DH5010 　Article No.DH5020 　PACKED IN 450 CARTONS OF 20 EACH (2) Spirit Level 　Article No.19161 　Article No.19163 　PACKED IN 392 CARTONS OF 60 EACH	4500 pairs 4500 pairs 8820 pcs 14700 pcs	USD8.80/pair USD8.50/pair USD2.00/pc USD2.20/pc	USD39600.00 USD38250.00 USD17640.00 USD32340.00
	Total:			**USD167830.00**

SAY TOTAL：U. S. DOLLARS ONE HUNDRED TWENTY SEVEN THOUSAND EIGHT HUNDRED THIRTY ONLY

QINGDAO LIANJIANG CO.，LTD.

* * *

2. 装箱单。

QINGDAO LIANJIANG CO.，LTD.

No. 2 Taiping St. Qingdao，China

Tel：0166－532－8391926　　Fax：0166－532－8391928

PACKING LIST

TO:	Taka Co.，Ltd. 16-15, Aza shinbo, Ohzaz Yamaya, Osaka, Japan Tel: 0161-665-39-3163 Fax: 0161-665-29-3163		INVOICE NO.:	LJ16071
			INVOICE DATE:	Jun. 10, 2019
			S/C NO.:	2016072
			S/C DATE:	May 9, 2019
FROM:	Qingdao ,China	TO:	Osaka, Japan	

Marks and Numbers	Number and kind of package Description of goods	Quantity	PACKAGE	G.W	N.W	Meas.
N/M	(1)Door Handle 　Article No.DH5010 　Article No.DH5020 　PACKED IN 450 CARTONS OF 20 　EACH (2) Spirit Level 　Article No.19161 　Article No.191　63 　PACKED IN 392 CARTONS OF 60 　EACH	4500 pairs 4500 pairs 8820 pcs 14700 pcs	225CTNS 225CTNS 147CTNS 245CTNS	4162.5KGS 4160KGS 2352KGS 4165KGS	3937.5KGS 3825KGS 2216KGS 3920KGS	16.325M^3 16.325M^3 3.467M^3 18.816M^3
	Total:		842CTNS	14729.5KGS	16887.5KGS	51.933M^3

SAY TOTAL：EIGHT HUNDRED AND FORTY TWO CARTONS ONLY

3. 其他信息。

（1）出境货物通关单编号：163456789000。

（2）青岛联江公司经营代码：5201166356。

（3）商品编码：门把手（金属制）83024100；水平仪：90153000。

（4）运输工具：YONG YUE，VOY. NO. 067E。

（5）原产地证明编号：CCPIT2016061111。

能力实训项目2：缮制报关单并办理报关手续

上接项目五，根据深圳普瑞珂出口有限公司出口竹地板，装船期是2019年8月20日。2019年8月10日单证员李红备齐商业发票和装箱单等资料，填写报关委托书以及出口货物报关单，向上海海关办理出口报关业务。

1. 商业发票。

Prima Construction Materials Co. , Ltd

Add：1401Room，38building，Chuangye Gardern，Baoan District，Shenzhen China

Tel：0166－755－32076630　　Fax：0166－755－32076630

COMMERCIAL INVOICE

To：CONSTRUCTION MOUDULAR SPECIALIST

POSTAL：16 HARVEY RD. , SHENTON PK, WA 6016 AUSTRALIA

Contract No. : CBF160724		No. : PR－20161620		
L/C No. : DC 16724		Date：AUG 22，2019		
From：SHENZHEN		To：FREMENTLE		
Marks&Nos. No	Description of Goods	Quantity	Unit Price	Amount
	BAMBOO FLOORING		CIF FREMENTLE	
CMS FREMENTLE CBF160724 NO. : 1－109	CARBONISED BAMBOO FLOORING	100SQM	$ 20. 00	$ 2,000. 00
	STRAND WOVEN BAMBOO FLOOR－ING DECKING	100SQM	$ 39. 50	$ 3,950. 00
TOTAL		EXW PRICE		$ 5,950. 00
		LCL CHARGE		$ 450. 00
		INSURANCE COST		$ 60. 00
		FREIGHT		$ 380. 00
		CIFVALUE		$ 6,480. 00

Prima Construction Materials Co. , Ltd

黄柯

2. 装箱单。

PENGXING IMP&EXP COMPANY

LILING PENGXING CERAMIC FACTORY
WUSHI JIASHU LILING HUNAN CHINA
TEL：86－731－23384199　　FAX：86－731－23384298

PACKING LIST

To:	CONSTRUCTION MOUDULAR SPECIALIST POSTAL: 16 HARVEY RD., SHENTON PK, WA 6016 AUSTRALIA			Date	AUG 22，2019
				Invoice No. :	PR－20191620
From:	SHANGHAI, CHINA		To:		FREMENTLE, CANADA

Item No.	Description of goods	Quantity（CTN）	G. W（KGS）	N. W（KGS）	Meas.（CBM）
CMS FREMENTLE CBF16072 NO.：1－109	BAMBOO FLOORING CARBONISED BAM－BOO FLOORING	55CTNS	1600KGS	1519KGS	2CEM
	STRANDWOVEN BAMBOO FLOORIN－G DECKING	54CTNS	1528KGS	1500KGS	2CBM
	Total：	109 CTNS	3168KGS	3019KGS	4CBM

ALL PACKED IN CARTONS SAY ONE HUNDRED AND NINE（109CTNS）CARTONS ONLY

3. 其他信息。
（1）深圳普瑞玛出口有限公司经营单位代码。
（2）出口海运提单编号：LLLFMT3821018。
（3）出境货物通关单编号。
（4）熏蒸证号码：331602216023407。
（5）运输工具名称：MOL INTEGRITY，VOY. NO. 102W。
能力实训项目3：缮制报关单并办理报关手续
上接项目，根据江西出口有限公司第 DOCMTN55163 号信用证的要求，2019 年 10 月 20 日，报关员张小兰根据商业发票、装箱单以及相关信息缮制报关单，办理报关手续。

1. 商业发票。

JIANGXI INTERNATIONAL IMP. & EXP. CORP.

8TH FLOOR FOREIGN TRADER BUILDING
200 ZHANQIAN ROAD, NANCHANG BUILDING
COMMERCIAL INVOICE

TO:	NICHIMEN CORPORATION 2－2 NAKANOSHINA 3－CHOME, KITA－KU NAGOYA, 632－8620, JAPAN		INVOICE NO. :	16AO－P001
			INVOICE DATE:	MAR. 10, 2019
			S/C NO. :	J515
			S/CDATE:	
			L/C NO. :	DCMTN55163
			L/C DATE:	FEB. 16, 2019
From:	SHANGHAI	to:	NAGOYA	

Marks and Numbers	Number and kind of package Description of goods	Quantity	Unit Price CIF NAGOYA	Amount CIF NAGOYA
J－515 NAGOYA PKG. NO. 1－166	100PCT COTTON GREIGE PRINT CLOTH ART. NO.3042 FIRST QUALITY SIZE: 30×30 68×68 50" EXPORT PACKING IN 166 SEAWORTHY BALES OF 1600 EACH THIS IS TO CERTIFY THAT THE GOODS IS CHINESE ORIGIN	199,200YDS	CIF NAGOYA USD 0. 32/YD	USD63,744. 00
	Total:	199, 200YDS		USD63,744. 00

SAY TOTAL：U. S. DOLLARS SIXTY THREE THOUSAND SEVEN HUNDRED AND FORTY FOUR ONLY

JIANGXI INTERNATIONAL IMP. & EXP. CORP.

XXX

2. 装箱单。

JIANGXI INTERNATIONAL IMP. & EXP. CORP.

8TH FLOOR FOREIGN TRADER BUILDING
200 ZHANQIAN ROAD，NANCHANG BUILDING

PACKING LIST

TO：	NICHIMEN CORPORATION 2 – 2 NAKANOSHINA 3 – CHOME，KITA – KU NAGOYA，632 – 8620，JAPAN	INVOICE NO.：	16AO – P001
		INVOICE DATE：	MAR. 10，2019
		S/C NO.：	J515
		S/C DATE：	
		L/C NO.：	DCMTN55163
		L/C DATE：	FEB. 16，2019
From：	SHANGHAI	to：	NAGOYA

Marks and Numbers	Number and kind of package Description of goods	Quantity	PACKAGE	G. W	N. W	Meas.
J – 515 NAGOYA PKG. NO. 1 – 166	100PCT COTTON GREIGE PRINT CLOTH ART. NO. 3042 FIRST QUALITY SIZE：30 × 30 68 × 68 50" EXPORT PACKING IN 166 SEAWORTHY BALES OF 1600 EACH	199，200YDS	166 BALES	23406KGS	23074KGS	53.618M^3
Total：		199，200YDS	166BALES	23406KGS	23074KGS	53.618M^3

SAY TOTAL：ONE HUNDRED AND SIXTY SIX BALES ONLY

JIANGXI INTERNATIONAL IMP. & EXP. CORP.

XXX

3. 其他信息。

（1）江西出口有限公司的经营单位代码。

（2）出口海运提单号码：MSCU42014737。

（3）运输工具名称：MSC SARAH V. 6A。

（4）商品编码（HS 编码）：学生归类查找该出口商品的编码。

（5）出境货物通关单编号。

第五节　学习导航

一、参考资料

[1] 中国报关协会报关员职业资格考试教材，报关员资格全国统一考试教材，中国海关出版社 2016.

[2] 郑俊田，刘文丽，徐晨，报关员资格考试考前辅导教材 [M]．北京：对外经济贸易大学出版社，2009.

二、自主学习平台

[1] http：//www. customs. gov. cn/publish/portal0/

[2] http：//www. exam8. com/zige/baoguanyuan/

[3] 福步外贸论坛。

[4] 报关实务国家教学资源库。

第一节　项目描述与目标

一、项目描述

◆开篇业务引入

根据"DC HMN214479"号信用证的要求,中国湖南某外贸公司"LILING PENGXING CERAMIC FACTORY WUSHI JIASHU LILING HUNAN, CHINA"出口一批货物给加拿大进口商"ELBY GIFTS INC. 879 INDUSTRIEL BOIS DES FILION, QUEBEC, J6Z 4T3, CANADA"。由 COSCO 中国远洋运输（集团）总公司承运该笔业务,公司业务员李某根据 L/C 规定"FULL SET OF CLEAN MULTIMODAL TRANSPORT DOCUMENT PLUS 2 N/N COPIES, MADE TO THE ORDER OF HSBC BANK CANADA, SHOWING ON BOARD NOTATION, MARKED FREIGHT PREPAID, AND NOTIFY APPLICANT (STATING FULL NAME AND ADDRESS)",以及双方签订的外销合同、已缮制好的商业发票出具海运提单,多式联运提单亦可接受。

◆项目预期目标

掌握海运提单的作用与分类,了解海运提单缮制中应注意的事项;通过对信用证项下装运条款的认真解读,结合该项目提供的商业发票等相关单据,掌握海运提单的缮制。

表7-1　项目预期目标

目标类型	运输单据的缮制
知识目标	熟悉海运提单的作用、分类
	了解运输单据的必要填写栏目
能力目标	能根据信用证及托运资料缮制运输单据
职业素质目标	海运业务操作能力
	与工厂、货代的沟通协调能力

◆项目实施条件

1. 组织学生参观货代公司或港口堆场。
2. 学生能够在实训室对该项目进行分组讨论并实施。
3. 指导教师熟悉贸易政策,具备扎实的外贸业务基础。

第二节　知识模块

一、海运提单的定义

海运提单（Marine Bill of Lading，B/L）简称提单，是货物的承运人或其代理人收到货物后，签发给托运人证明货物表面状况良好的一种证件。提单是托运人凭以向银行办理议付、结汇的主要单据之一，并在运输费用的结算和对外索赔中起到重要作用。

二、海运提单的作用

1. 提单是承运人或其代理人签发的货物收据（Receipt for the goods），证明承运人或其代理人已按提单所载内容收到货物。

2. 提单是一种货物所有权的凭证。提单代表货物，掌握了提单就掌握了货物。提单合法持有人有权凭提单在目的港向承运人提货。

3. 提单是托运人与承运人之间所订立的运输契约的证明（Evidence of contract of carriage）。承运人和托运人之间有关运输的条件，双方的权利和义务，责任与豁免都以提单作为合约凭证，它是处理承运人与货方运输方面的争议、纠纷的法律依据。

三、海运提单的种类

海运提单的种类很多，格式也不尽相同，但基本内容大致相同。以海运方式为主的几种不同提单如下：

1. 清洁已装船提单（clean Shipped On board B/L，clean Shipped B/L）。

提单上必须以文字表明货物已装船，且提单上还需记载已装船日期。提单签发时未加注任何货损或包装不良之类批注。

UCP600 规定：银行只接受清洁已装船运输单据。

2. 备运提单（Received for Shipment B/L）。

提单上只说明货物已经收到，暂代存入码头仓库，准备装船。承运人先签发提单，待船到港后再装船。此种提单虽列有承运船名，该船是否如期到达船公司并不负责。所以，备运提单实际上等于货运收据，而不构成运输契约。目前集装箱使用的提单和联合运输提单多属于备运提单。为满足银行只接受已装船提单的要求，这类提单需加"已装船批注（Laden on Board vessel）"。

3. 指示提单（Order B/L）。

在提单收货人一栏带有"凭指示（To Order）"的字样。这种提单通过指示人的背书而转让、流通，银行一般接受指示提单作为议付的凭证。在实务中，指示提单被广泛采用。

4. 记名提单（Straight B/L）。

提单收货人是指明特定的，提单收货人一栏填上具体的收货人。

记名提单又叫直交式提单，收货人可以不凭正本提单只需证明自己的收货人身份便可以提货，但不能转让提单。此类提单只在运送价值较高的货物或展品时使用。

5. 不记名提单（Open B/L）。

提单的收货人一栏表示"货交寺票人（To Bearer）"。这种提单无需证明收货人身份就可以提货，风险很大。提单一旦丢失，货物很容易被人提走。

6. 多式或联合运输提单（Multimodal or Combined Transport Bill of Lading，CTB/L）。

国际多式联运（International Multimodal Transport）是一种利用集装箱进行联运的运输方式，它通过采用海、陆、空等两种以上的运输手段，完成国际间的货物运输，从而打破了过去海、铁、公、空等单一运输方式互不连贯的传统做法。

国际多式联运能集中发挥各种运输方式的优势，使国际货物运输既快捷又安全，同时它简化了手续，减少了中间环节，加快了货运速度，降低了运输成本，并提高了货运质量，为实现"门到门"运输创造了有利条件。

多式联运提单指货物由海上、内河、铁路、公路、航空等两种或多种运输方式进行联合运输而签的适用于全程运输的提单。

目前我国使用的多式联合运输提单往往具有如下功能：

（1）有适用于不同方式的联合运输——陆海陆联合运输、海空联运、海铁联运等。

例如，联运承运人的责任是从接收货物起至交付货物为止，其接收货物地点可能是集装箱码头、内陆堆场、工厂或仓库、集装箱货运站等，因此在联运提单上印有货物收妥或接管的地点（Place of Receipt）。由于多式联运提单是在多式联运经营人收到货物后签发的，收货地不同，经营人签发的地点、时间也不同，承担的责任也就不同。另外，在提单上还印有最终交付货物的内陆交货地（Place of Delivery）。

（2）在多式联运中有海运方式。

例如：提单中还印有装货港（Port of Loading）、卸货港（Port of Discharge）和船名（Ocean Vessel）。

因此，在多式联合运输提单上通常包括六个运输项目：

① Pre-carriage（前段运输可以是铁路、公路或内河水运）

② Place of receipt（收货地点）

③ Port of loading（装运港，海运）

④ Ocean Vessel（船名）

⑤ Port of Discharge（卸货港）

⑥ Place of delivery（内陆交货地，陆运）

（3）多式联运提单还适于我国港口单一运输直达各国港口的集装箱运输。

例如：联合运输提单上包括三个项目：

①Container No.（集装箱号）

②Seal No.（铅封号）

③注意集装箱运输应在这种提单上加注"已装船批注"：

a. 装船日期。

b. 船名。

c. 承运人签字。

四、海运提单正反面内容

各国海运提单的格式不一，但其内容大致有正面内容和背面条款组成。

1. 正面内容。

（1）承运人或其代理人印定的文字声明。

表明提单（Bill of Lading）字样。

船公司名称（Name of the Shipping Company）。

承运人收到表面状况良好的货物。并已装船，将运往目的港卸货。

船方对在提单上所装货物的重量、数量、价值等内容不负责核对，概不知悉。

对托运人、收货人等在提单正面印定的条款表示接受。

承运人或其代理人为证明以上各个内容，签发正本提单，凭其中一份提货，其余各份即行失效。

（2）由托运人及承运人或其代理人填写的部分。包括：

提单号（B/L No.）

托运人（Shipper）

收货人（Consignee）与背书（Endorsement）

被通知人（Notify party）

船名（Name of Vessel）

装运港（Port of Loading）

卸货港（Port of Discharge）

唛头（Marks & Numbers）

大小写件数和包装种类（Number and Kind of Packages&In words）

货名（Description of Goods）

毛重（Gross Weight）

尺码（Measurements）

运费（Freight and Charges）

运费预付和到付地点（Prepaid at&Freight Payable at、

正本提单份数（Number of Original Bs/L）

提单签发地点及日期（Place and Date of Issue）

承运人签字（Signed for the Carrier）

2. 背面条款。

船公司通常在其背面印有承运人的责任、权利、义务的豁免，是托运人和承运人处理争议时的依据。承运人收到提单，如不表示异议，即被认为对此印定条款同意接受。

UPC600 第 20 条规定：载有承运条款和条件，或提示承运条款和条件参见别处（简式/背面空白的提单），银行将不予审核承运条款和条件的内容。

BILL OF LADING

1）SHIPPER	10）B/L NO.
2）CONSIGNEE	**C O S C O** 中国远洋运输（集团）总公司 CHINA OCEAN SHIPPING（GROUP）CO.
3）NOTIFY PARTY	
4）PLACE OF RECEIPT　　5）OCEAN VESSEL	
6）VOYAGE NO.　　7）PORT OF LOADING	ORIGINAL COMBINED TRANPORT BILL OF LADING
8）PORT OF DISCHARGE　　9）PLACE OF DELIVERY	

11）MARKS	12）NOS. &KINDS OF PKGS	13）DESCRIPTION OF GOODS	14）G. W.（kg）	15）MEAS（m³）

16）TOTAL NUMBER OF CONTAINERS OR PACKAGES（IN WORDS）

FREIGHT & CHARGES	REVENUE TONS	RATE	PER	PREPAID	COLLECT
PREPAID AT	PAYABLE AT	17）PLACE AND DATE OF ISSUE			
TOTAL PREPAID	18）NUMBER OF ORIGINAL B（S）L				
LOADING ON BOARD THE VESSEL 19）DATE	20）BY				

图7-1　海运提单样本

五、海运提单的缮制项目

1. 提单号（B/L No. ）。

（1）填写内容：

提单号码位于提单右上角。提单上必须注明承运人及代理人规定的提单号，以便核查和便于工作联系，否则提单无效。

（2）实例：

B/L No.：CDE567420

2. 托运人（Shipper）。

（1）填写内容：

在信用证项下，托运人一般为受益人。以托收支付方式成交的，托收的委托人为托运人。

（2）实例：

Shipper：

　　HUNAN TEXTILE IMP & EXP CORP.

　　4E WUYI RD. ，CHANGSHA，CHINA

3. 收货人（Consignee）与背书（Endorsement）。

● 收货人（Consignee）

（1）填写内容：

提单的收货人又称"抬头人"。提单的抬头决定了海运提单的性质和货权的归属。所以，信用证项下的提单必须严格按照信用证规定的提单条款缮制。

一般信用证支付方式多使用指示式抬头。这种抬头的特征是有"凭指示"（To Order）字样。指示式收货人将收货人以广义的形式表示出来，掩饰了具体的收货人的名称、地址，使单据可以背书转让、流通。

指示式的抬头人又分为两种：不记名指示式（To order）和记名指示式（To order of ××Bank/shipper）。

● 不记名指示式（To order）

"To order"（凭指示或称空白抬头）没有具体的收货人名称。常见信用证规定为："Full set of…B/L made out to order endorsed in blank/blank endorsed"字样。"信用证要求提单空白抬头、空白背书"。

（2）实例1：

①提单正面收货人一栏填：To order

②背面由背书人签章并注明背书的日期：

B. T. I Co. （背书人签章）

Mar. 16，2004

③此种提单由托运人在提单背面进行背书后，即可转让。由被转让人持单向船公司提货。

● 记名指示式抬头（To order of ××Bank/Shipper）

"To order o××Bank/Shipper"（凭银行或托运人指示）。由银行或托运人背书转让，记名指示中的记名人有权控制和转让提单。信用证一般规定为"... B/L made out to order of ××Bank/Shipper endorsed in blank/blank endorsed"。

（3）实例2：

①单正面收货人一栏填：To order of ××Bank/Shipper

②背面由银行或托运人签章并注明背书的日期：

××Bank/××Co. （银行或托运人签章）

Mar. 16，2004.

③此种提单由银行/托运人在提单背面进行背书后，即可转让。由被转让人持单向船公司提货。

● 背书（Endorsement）

（1）填写内容：

背书分为记名背书（Endorsement in full）和空白背书（Endorsement in blank）两种：

▶记名背书：在提单的背面先写上被背书人的名称，同时再由背书人签署并盖章，并注明背书的日期。例如："...B/L made out to order deliver to/endorsed to A. B. C Co."

▶不记名背书：只在背面有托运人签章即可。

（2）实例：

①提单正面填：To order

②背面由背书人做记名背书，提单记名背书的指示文句中不用"Pay"而用"Deliver"。

Deliver to/Endorsed to A. B. C Co.

③背书人签章并注明背书的日期

J. M. L Co.　（签章）

Mar. 16. 20

4. 被通知人（Notify Party）。

（1）填写内容：

指货物到达目的港时船方发送到货通知的对象。其职责是及时地接受船方发出的到货通知，并将该通知转告真实的收货人。被通知人无权提货。"被通知人栏目"是对指示提单方法的一个补充，在提单抬头人不是收货人时，减少了船方通知提货、报关的麻烦。因此，在空白指示提单和银行及托运人指示提单时，此栏必须详细将被通知人的名称、地址写清楚，否则船方就无法与收货人联系，收货人也不能及时报关提货，甚至会因超过海关规定申报时间而被没收货物。此栏在信用证方式下按规定填写。有时为进口方或买方代理。

（2）实例1：

信用证条款为"Full set of B/L .. notify applicant"，应在此栏中将开证申请人的全称及地址填上。

（3）实例2：

信用证条款为"Full set of B/L…notify our forwarding agent：M. K Co. addressed to 60 Green RD. ，London U. K. "应在此栏中将货代 M K Co. 的全称及地址填上。

5. 船名（Name of Vessel）。

（1）填写内容：

按实际所装运的船只名称填写。

（2）实例：

Name of Vessel：S. S Taishan V. 108

6. 装运港（Port of Loading）。

（1）填写内容：

填实际装运港口的具体名称，不能笼统填写"Chinese Port"字样。

（2）实例：

Port of Loading：Qingdao

7. 卸货港（Port of Discharge）。

（1）填写内容：

填实际货物卸下的港口。如经转船，则应填上转运港字样。

（2）实例：

from Qingdao to Rotterdam w/t HongKong.

注意事项：

①卸货港和装运港一样不能填笼统名称，如"European Main Ports（欧洲主要口岸）"，应填具体卸货港。

实例：Port of Discharge：Antwerp.

如果在国际上有重名港口的，还要加注国名和地区名来区别。

②如来证列明几个卸货港的，如"Hamburg/Rotterdam"提单只能填一个具体卸货港的名称。

③货物经转（Transshipment），如：货物从青岛装运，在中国香港转船再运至德国汉堡，可有以下填法：

a. 在提单中印有装货港（Port of Loading）、卸货港（Port of Discharge）和最终目的港（Final Destination）栏目，应分别在装货港栏内填"青岛（Qingdao）"，卸货港栏内填"香港（HongKong）"，在最终目的港栏内填"汉堡（Hamburg）"。

b. 在提单中只有卸货港栏，没有最终目的港栏目，则在卸货港栏内填"汉堡（Hamburg）"，再加注转船港名称：如"Hamburg With Transshipment at HongKong 或 Hamburg W/T HongKong（在 HongKong 转船）"。

c. 如有印就的转船港（Port of Transshipment）栏目，则直接将"中国香港（HongKong）"填入转船港栏即可。有关转运事项，请参见"转船提单"。

d. 如果信用证中规定卸货港后有"In transit to×××"，则表明货物自卸货港卸货后，经转运或陆运至其他目的地或邻国，尤其在卖方不负责转口时，不能在卸货港栏内后加填转船港的港名，应另在货名栏下方的空白处或在唛头处加注"In transit to×××"。

（3）实例：来证规定："Marseilles in transit to Genoa"，具体做法是：

①卸货港栏 Marseilles。

②货名栏下方的空白处或在唛头处加注：In transit to Genoa。

注意："In transit to×××"一般不能填在卸货港后。因为卖方只负责将货运至该卸货港，以后的转运由买方负责。

8. 唛头（Marks&Numbers）。

（1）填写内容：

按发票缮制。

（2）实例：

Marks&Numbers

N/M（没有唛头）

9. 大小写件数和包装种类（Number and Kind of Packages& In words）。

（1）填写内容：

应填写数量和计量单位，与唛头中件号的累计数相符。大写是用英文打出包装及数量，必须大小写一致。

（2）实例：

小写（In figures）：240 cartons.

大写（In words）：（Say Two Hundred and Forty Cartons Only）

小写（In figures）：350 cases.

大写（In words）：（Say Three Hundred and Fifty Cases Only）

10. 货名（Description of Goods）。

（1）填写内容：

提单列明的货名仅是信用证规定装运的货物名称，应与商业发票及其他单据一致。如信用证规定品名繁多，允许提单打出货物的统称表示商品的名称。

（2）实例：

Description of Goods

T-SHIRT

11. 毛重（Gross Weight）。

（1）填写内容：

应与发票一致，一般以千克为计算单位，毛重指包括包装材料在内的货物重量。如果一次装运的货物中有几种不同的包装材料或完全不同的货物，那么应先分别计算并将合计的毛重填在这一栏目中。

（2）实例：

Gross Weight

163.56KGS

12. 尺码（Measurements）。

（1）填写内容：

与发票一致，小数点后保留三位数，以立方米为计算单位，应填一批货的尺码总数。总尺码不仅包括各件货物尺码之和，还应包括件与件之间堆放时的合理空间所占的体积。因此总尺码数等于各种货物的尺码之和。

（2）实例：

Measurements

6CBMS

13. 运费（Freight and Charges）。

（1）填写内容：

除非信用证中明确规定提单中表明运费的计算与数额，否则提单中不填运费的数额为好。

（2）实例：

①在以 CIF 或 CFR 成交的价格术语中，支付的运费为卖方，一般卖方在交货前把运费付清，计入 CIF 或 CFR 价格中。因此应根据信用证的规定，选择"Freight Prepaid（运费预付）"或"Freight Paid（运费已付）"。银行将接受以戳记或以其他方式清楚表明运费预付或已付的词语。

②价格术语为 FOB 或 FAS 时，运费由买方支付，此时应填"Freight Collect（运费到付）"或"Payable at destination（运费在目的港支付）"。

14. 运费预付和到付地点（Prepaid at &Freight Payable at）。

（1）填写内容：

在提单相应栏目中填实际运费预付和到付的地点。

（2）实例：

Prepaid at：Qingdao

Freight Payable at：New York

15. 正本提单份数（Number of Original Bs/L）。

（1）填写内容：

按照 UCP600 规定，运输单据必须注明所出具的正本的份数。正本提单的份数按信用证的要求应在本栏中用大写（如 THREE，TWO）等注明。向银行提供信用证规定的全套正本提单的份数，可使收货人凭正本提单提货。UCP600 第 17 条 a 款规定：凡信用证规定的每一种单据必须至少提交一份正本。对正副本提单的要求，一般在信用证中有规定，出口商应按要求提供。

（2）实例：

"Full set of B/L in triplicate with two non-negotiable Bs/L"（三份正本两份副本）

注意事项：

①注明"第一正本（First Original）""第二正本（Second Original）""第三正本（Third Original）""正本（Original）""第二份（Duplicate）""第三份（Triplicate）"等类似表述的运输单据都是正本。提单不一定非要注明"正本（Original）"字样才能被接受为正本提单。

②提单有正本（original）和副本（non-negotiable B/L）之分。正本提单可交银行议付，并流通转让，副本则不行。每份正本提单的份数效力相同，凭其中一份提货后，其余各份失效。

16. 提单签发地点及日期（Place and Date of Issue）。

（1）填写内容：

地点应为装运地点。日期应不迟于信用证或合同规定的最迟装运日期，该日期将视为装运日期。如果提交的是预先印就"已装运于船"的提单（a pre-printed "Shipped on board" bill of lading），提单的出具日期即视为装运日，除非提单带有加注日期的单独装船批注（a separate dated on board notation），此时，该装船批注的日期即视为装运日，而不论该批注日期是在提单签发日期之前还是之后。

（2）实例：

Place and Date of Issue

QINGDAO，SEPT. 25，2019

17. 承运人签字（Signed for the Carrier）。

（1）填写内容：

正本提单必须有承运人（carrier）或其代理人、船长（master）或其代理人的签字或印章方能生效。

根据 UCP600 规定：

①承运人（船长、船东、多式运输营运人）签署或证实时，须分别按实际情况标明其真实身份，代理需要表明被代理人身份。例如船长签署提单，则船长的签字必须表明"船长"身份。在此情况下，不必标明船长的姓名。

②代理人代表承运人（船长、船东、多式运输营运人）签署时，必须标明他所代表的委托人名称及身份，即分别按实际情况注明代理人是代表某承运人/船长签署或证实。如果由代理人代表船长签署提单，在此情况下，不必标明船长的姓名。

（2）实例 1：承运人签字

提单上部：COSCO

提单签署处：COSCO（签署）

As Carrier/Signed on behalf of COSCO

（3）实例 2：代理人签字

提单上部：COSCO

提单签署处：Sino trans（签署）

As agent for（on behalf of）the Carrier：COSCO

（4）实例 3：船长签字

提单上部：Pacific Ocean Shipping Company

提单签署处：Johnson（签署）

As Master/Signed on behalf of Pacific Ocean Shipping Company

第三节　任务模块

在该项目中，业务员李某应完成的工作任务包括：

任务 1：认真审核信用证中的装运条款。

任务 2：认真审核商业发票。

任务 3：根据要求缮制海运提单。

1. "DC HMN214479" 号信用证部分条款。

DC NO：　　　　　　　　　　DC HMN214479

DATE OF ISSUE：　　　　　　190620

APPLICABLE RULES：　　　　UCP LATEST VERSION

EXPIRY DATE AND PLACE：　190903 IN COUNTRY OF BENEFICIARY

APPLICANT：　　　　　　　ELBY GIFTS INC. 879 INDUSTRIEL

　　　　　　　　　　　　　BOIS DES FILION，QUEBEC，J6Z 4T3，CANADA

BENEFICIARY：   LILING PENGXING CERAMIC FACTORY
                                       WUSHI JIASHU LILING HUNAN，CHINA
AMOUNT：   USD27,010.40
PCT CR AMT TOLERANCE：   10/10
AVAILABLE WITH/BY：   ANY BANK BY NEGOTIATION
DRAFTS AT：   AT SIGHT FOR FULL INVOICE VALUE
DRAWEE：   ISSUING BANK
PARTIAL SHIPMENTS：   ALLOWED
TRANSHIPMENT：   ALLOWED
LOADING PORT/DEPART AIRPORT：SHENZHEN，CHINA
DISCHARGE PORT/DEST AIRPORT：PRINCE RUPERT，BC
FINAL DEST/DELIVERY/TRNSP TO：BOIS DES FILION，CANADA
LATEST DATE OF SHIPMENT：   190819
GOODS：   CERAMIC CUPS AND BOWLS AS PER SC NO.：CB161039
                                       CIF PRINCE RUPERT，BC
                                       V23－234   U.S.D 4.05/SET
                                       V23－234F   U.S.D 4.05/SET
                                       V23－235   U.S.D 2.40/SET
                                       V23－236   U.S.D 2.10/SET
                                       ALL PACKED IN CARTONS.
DOCUMENTS REQUIRED：   + ORIGINAL SIGNED COMMERCIAL INVOICE PLUS
                                       THREE COPIES.
                                       + FULL SET OF CLEAN MULTIMODAL TRANSPORT
                                       DOCUMENT PLUS 2 N/N COPIES, MADE TO THE
                                       ORDER OF HSBC BANK CANADA, SHOWING ON
                                       BOARD NOTATION, MARKED FREIGHT PREPAID,
                                       AND NOTIFY APPLICANT (STATING FULL NAME
                                       AND ADDRESS).

2. 商业发票。

PENGXING IMP&EXP COMPANY

LILING PENGXING CERAMIC FACTORY
WUSHI JIASHU LILING HUNAN CHINA
TEL：86 − 731 − 23384199   FAX：86 − 731 − 23384298

COMMERCIAL INVOICE

TO：	ELBY GIFTS INC. 879 INDUSTRIEL BOIS DES FILION QUEBEC，J6Z 4T3，CANADA		Invoice No. ：	PX16IVN1039
			Invoice Date：	AUG 16，2019
			S/C No. ：	S/C NO. ：CB161039
			S/C Date：	JUL 5，2019
From：	SHENZHEN，CHINA	TO：	PRINCE RUPERT，BC，CANADA	
Letter of Credit No. ：	DC HMN214479	Issued By：	HSBC BANK，MONTREAL CANADA	
Marks and Numbers	Description of goods	Quantity CTN	Unit Price U. S. D/set	Amount U. S. D
ELBY	CERAMIC CUPS AND BOWLS	CIF PRINCE RUPERT，BC		
S/C NO. ：CB161039	V23 − 234	228	4. 05	3 693. 60
NO：1 − 1589	V23 − 234F	228	4. 05	3 693. 60
	V23 − 235	190	2. 40	3 648. 00
	V23 − 236	189	2. 10	3 175. 20
	V23 − 237	186	1. 95	2 901. 60
	V23 − 238	190	2. 04	3 100. 80
	36 − 062	191	2. 30	3 514. 40
	36 − 063	187	2. 16	3 171. 52
	Total：	1 589		26 898. 72

Say Total：U. S DOLLARSTWENTY SIX THOUSAND EIGHT HUNDRED AND NINETY EIGHT AND CENTS SEVENTY TWO（USD26898. 72）ONLY

PENGXING IMP&EXP COMPANY
李望

据此，李望缮制了一份海运提单：

1. Shipper Insert Name, Address and Phone			许可证号	
LILING PENGXING CERAMIC FACTORY WUSHI JIASHU LILING HUNAN, CHINA			B/L No. COSFMT3821018	

远集装箱运输有限公司
COSCO CONTAINER LINES

TLX: 33057 COSCO CN
FAX: +86 (021) 65458984　ORIGINAL

2. Consignee Insert Name, Address and Phone

TO THE ORDER OF HSBC BANK CANADA

Port – to – Port or Combined Transport

BILL OF LADING

RECEIVED in external apparent good order and condition except as otherwise noted. The total number of packages or unites stuffed in the container, the description of the goods and the weights shown in this Bill of Lading are furnished by the Merchants, and which the carrier has no reasonable means of checking and is not a part of this Bill of Lading contract. The carrier has issued the number of Bills of Lading stated below, all of this tenor and date, one of the original Bills of Lading must be surrendered and endorsed or signed against the delivery of the shipment and whereupon any other original Bills of Lading shall be void. The Merchants agree to be bound by the terms and conditions of this Bill of Lading as if each had personally signed this Bill of Lading.

SEE clause 4 on the back of this Bill of Lading (Terms continued on the back hereof, please read carefully).

* Applicable Only When Document Used as a Combined Transport Bill of Lading.

3. Notify Party Insert Name, Address and Phone
　(It is agreed that no responsibility shall attach to the Carrier or his agents for failure to notify)

4. Combined Transport *	5. Combined Transport *
Pre – carriage by TRAIN NO.: 67589	Place of Receipt CHANGSHA
6. Ocean Vessel Voy. No.	7. Port of Loading
COSCO SEATTLE V. 0078E	YANTIAN, SHENZHEN, CHINA
8. Port of Discharge	9. Combined Transport *
PRINCE RUPERT, BC, CANADA	Place of DeliveryBOIS DES FILION, CANADA

Marks & Nos. Container / Seal	No. No. of Containers or Packages	Description of Goods (If Dangerous Goods, See Clause 20)	Gross Weight Kgs	Measurement
N/M	1589CTNS CONTAINER NO.: CBHU8150082/ B45171/40' HQ	SHIPPER'S LOAD & COUNT & SEAL 1X40'HQ (F. C. L) S. T. C CY/CY ONE THOUSAND FIVE HUNDRED AND EIGHTY NINE (1589CTNS) CARTONS OF CERAMIC CUPS AND BOWLS FOB SHENZHEN, CHINA THIS SHIPMENT CONTAINS NO SOLID WOOD PACKING MATERIALS.	17 654. 40KGS	68. 160CBM
		Description of Contents for Shipper's Use Only (Not part of This B/L Contract)		

10. Total Number of containers and/or packages (in words) SAY ONE (1) CONTAINER ONLY.

续表

11. Freight & Charges	Revenue Tons	Rate	Per	Prepaid	Collect
FREIGHT COLLECT	AS ARRANGED				

Ex. Rate	Prepaid at	Payable at	Place and date of issue
			SHENZHEN, CHINA AUG. 20, 2019
	Total Prepaid	No. of Original B (s) /L	Signed for the Carrier, COSCO CONTAINER LINES
		THREE	COSCO AS CARRIER XXX

第四节　任务拓展模块

能力实训项目1：海运提单业务操作

2019年7月25号，业务员李某通过审核"DC 16724"号信用证以及商业发票，缮制一份海运提单。

1."DC 16724"号信用证。

SEQUENCE OF TOTAL：	1/1
FORM OF DC：	IRREVOCABLE
DC NO：	DC 16724
DATE OF ISSUE：	190710
APPLICABLE RULES：	UCP 600
EXPIRY DATE AND PLACE：	190920 IN CHINA
APPLICANT：	CONSTRUCTION MOUDULAR SPECIALIST
POSTAL：	16 HARVEY RD., SHENTON PK, WA 6008
BENEFICIARY：	PRIMA CONSTRUCTION MATERIOLS CO., LTD 1401 ROOM, 38 BUILDING, CHUANGYE GARDEN BAOAN DISTRICT, SHENZHEN, CHINA
AMOUNT：	USD6,840.00
AVAILABLE WITH/BY：	ANY BANK BY NEGOTIATION
DRAFTS AT：	AT 30DAYS AFTER SIGHT
DRAWEE：	DRAWN ON US
PARTIAL SHIPMENTS：	ALLOWED
TRANSHIPMENT：	ALLOWED
LOADING PORT：	CHINA MAIN PORT
DISCHARGE PORT：	FREMENTLE, AUSTRALIA
LATEST DATE OF SHIPMENT：	190905
GOODS：	BAMBOO FLOORING

ITEM 1 100 SQM U. S. D20. 00/SQM

ITEM 1 100 SQM U. S. D39. 50/SQM

ALL PACKING IN SEA WORTHY CARTONS

CIF FREMENTLE AS PER PI NO. : BFF0610

DOCUMENTS REQUIRED:　+MANUALLY SIGNED COMMECIAL INVOICE 3 ORIGINALS PLUS THREE COPIES.

+ FULL SET (3/3) OF MARINE BILLS OF LADING, MADE OUT TO ORDER, MARKED FREIGHT PREPAID, AND NOTIFY APPLICANT (STATING FULL NAME AND ADDRESS).

+ INSURANCE POLICY OR CERTIFICATE IN TRIPLICATE, BLANK INDORSED, FOR THE INVOICE VALUE PLUS 10% COVERING ICC (A) RISK AND ICC (STRIKE). FROM WAREHOUSE TO WAREHOUSE AND I. O. P, PAYABLE AT FREMENTLE IN U. S. D

2. 商业发票。

Prima Construction Materials Co., Ltd
Add: 1401Room, 38building, Chuangye Gardern, Baoan District, Shenzhen China
Tel: 0086 – 755 – 32076630　　　Fax: 0086 – 755 – 32076630

COMMERCIAL INVOICE

Contract No. : CBF160724	No. : PR – 20160820
L/C No. : DC 16724	Date: AUG 22, 2016
From: SHENZHEN	To: FREMENTLE

Marks&Nos. No	Description of Goods	Quantity	Unit Price	Amount
	BAMBOO FLOORING		CIF FREMENTLE	
CMS FREMENTLE CBF160724 NO. : 1 – 109	CARBONISED BAMBOO FLOORING	100SQM	$ 20. 00	$ 2,000. 00
	STRAND WOVEN BAMBOO FLOOR – ING DECKING	100SQM	$ 39. 50	$ 3,950. 00
	TOTAL EXW PRICE			$ 5,950. 00
	LCL CHARGE			$ 450. 00
	INSURANCE			$ 60. 00
	FREIGHT			$ 380. 00
	CIF VALUE			$ 6,480. 00

3. 装运资料

B/L NO./：COS BB19020

船名及航次：CHANGHE V. 702

外包装：20 sea – worthy cartons

毛重：650.00KGS

据此，缮制海运提单：

Shipper			BILL OF LADING B/L No.	
Consignee			**COSCO** 中国远洋运输公司 CHINA OCEAN SHIPPING COMPANY ORIGINAL	
Notify Party				
* Pre carriage by	* Place of Receipt			
Ocean Vessel Voy. No.	Port of Loading			
Port of discharge	* Final destination		Freight payable at	Number original Bs/L
Marks and Numbers	Number and kind of packages；Description		Gross weight	Measurement m³
TOTAL PACKAGES （IN WORDS）				
Freight and charges				
			Place and date of issue	
			Signed for the Carrier	

* Applicable only when document used as a Through Bill of Loading

第五节　学习导航

一、参考资料

[1] 章安平. 外贸单证操作 [M]. 北京：高等教育出版社，2008.

[2] 刘启萍，周树玲. 外贸单证 [M]. 北京：对外经贸大学出版社，2008.

[3] 方士华，国际结算 [M]. 沈阳：东北财经大学出版社，2016.

[4] 吴轶群，国际商务单证操作 [M]. 青岛：中国海洋大学出版社，2018.

二、自主学习平台

[1] 全国外贸单证员考试中心。

[2] 外贸经理人微信公众号。

[3] 外贸单证课程国家教学资源库。

项目八
汇票制作业务

第一节 项目描述与目标

一、项目描述

◆ 开篇业务引入

根据第 L-16017 号信用证的要求，长沙鹏兴进出口有限公司于 2019 年 8 月 24 日完成装运取得了所有的单据后，缮制汇票通过银行向付款人收款。该项目任务具体由单证员李望负责。2019 年 8 月 26 日，单证员李望根据发票、装运资料和 L/C 相关内容缮制汇票。

◆ 项目预期目标

通过对信用证项下汇票条款的认真解读，介绍汇票的概念和汇票的种类，熟悉汇票的当事人及其关系，掌握汇票的内容。了解汇票在流通过程中的使用环节，具备缮制汇票的能力。

在项目实施过程中，通过学习汇票的缮制，了解汇票在国际结算中的重要性，逐渐培养审核、制单、归类等国际商务单证基本职业能力，亦培养独立操作业务和与银行等部门有效沟通的能力。

表 8-1 项目预期目标

目标类型	汇票的缮制
知识目标	熟悉汇票的内容和汇票的票据行为
	了解汇票在流通过程中使用环节
	掌握信用证结算和托收方式下汇票的制作
能力目标	能区分不同种类的汇票
	根据合同和信用证准确缮制汇票
职业素质目标	独立业务操作能力
	与银行沟通衔接能力

二、项目实施条件

1. 向学生提供商业汇票样单，指出汇票的必要项目和非必要项目。

2. 学生进行角色扮演展示汇票在流通过程中的使用环节。

3. 学生能够在实训室根据提供的业务资料使用计算机缮制汇票。

4. 指导教师掌握相关的国际贸易法律，具备扎实的外贸业务基础

第二节 知识模块

一、汇票的概念

汇票简称 BILL 或 DRAFT 或 BILL OF EXCHANGE。它是一人（即：出票人 DRAWER）向另一人（即：DRAWEE 受票人/付款人）签发的，要求该受票人立即或在一定时间或一个固定时期支付一定金额给某人或其指定人或来人（持票人 HOLDER）的无条件书面支付命令。

国际贸易中使用的汇票是出口商凭此向进口商要求付款的收款工具，也是付款的重要凭证。由于该汇票由出口商签发，属商业汇票，收汇方式为逆汇。商业汇票通常签发一套，一式两份，具有同等的法律效力，个别标明 FIRST OF EXCHANGE（1），FIRST OF EXCHANGE（2），付款人仅凭其中一份付一次款，先见到哪份付哪份，即"付一不付二"或"付二不付一"。在国际贸易实务中，托收或信用证方式都有可能使用汇票。在信用证方式下，除延期付款信用证不需要汇票外，其他情况下都可能使用，凡信用证中有"BY PAYMENT"字样的，就需要附有汇票。而托收方式下汇票则必不可少。

二、汇票的种类

1. 按有无附有货运单据，可分为光票和跟单汇票。

光票（CLEAN BILL）：光票是不附带货运单据的汇票。光票的流通完全依靠当事人的信用，即完全看出票人、付款人或背书人的资信。在国际贸易中，对少量货运，或收取保险费、运费等其他费用，可采用光票向对方收款。

跟单汇票（DOCUMENTARY BILL）：跟单汇票是附带货运单据的汇票，以承兑或付款作为交付单据的条件。除了有当事人的信用外，还有货物的保证。因此，在国际贸易中，这种汇票使用较为广泛。

2. 按付款时间，可分为即期汇票和远期汇票。

即期汇票（SIGHT BILL）：提示或见票时立即付款的汇票。

远期汇票（TIME BILL OR USANCE BILL）：在一定期限或特定日期付款的汇票。

3. 按出票人不同，可分为商业汇票和银行汇票。

商业汇票（TRADE BILL）：商业汇票是指出票人是商号、企业或个人。在国际贸易结算中，出口商用逆汇法，向国外进口商收取货款签发的汇票，即属商业汇票。

银行汇票（BANKER'S BILL）：银行汇票的出票人是银行。在国际结算中，银行汇票签发后，一般交汇款人，由汇款人寄交国外收款人向指定的付款银行取款。银行汇票一般为光票，不随附货运单据。

4. 按承兑人的不同，分为商业承兑汇票和银行承兑汇票。

商业承兑汇票（TRADER'S ACCEPTANCE BILL）：由工商企业或个人承兑的远期汇票。商业承兑汇票建立在商业信用的基础之上，出票人是工商企业或个人。

银行承兑汇票（BANKER'S ACCEPTANCE BILL）：由银行承兑的远期汇票。它是建立在银行信用基础上的，出票人是出口商，银行对汇票承兑后成了汇票主债务人，则出票人成为次债务人。

凭	信用证　　　第　　　号
Drawn under _____	L/C No.
日期	按　　　　息　　　　付款
Dated _____	Payable with interest@ _____ % per annum
号码	汇票金额　　　　　　　中国，上海　　年　月　日
No.：_____	Exchange for ▮▮▮ Shanghai，China
见票	日后（本 汇票之副本未付）
At _____	Sight of this FIRST of Exchange（Second of exchange being unpaid）
Pay to the order of _____或其指定人付金额	
The sum of	
To：	
	For

图 8 – 1　汇票空白样本

三、具体业务操作

（一）跟单 L/C 下汇票的缮制

1. 出票依据（Draw under…L/C No. …Dated）。

信用证项下的汇票需要列明出票条款即出票依据（Drawn under Clause）。出票条款表明汇票的起源。

（1）填写内容：

Drawn under	开证行名称、城市名、国名
L/C No.	信用证号码
Dated	开证日期

（2）实例：

Drawn under	Bank of America，New York
L/C No.	BOANY00158
Dated	Feb. 16，2017

2. 利息（Interest）。

信用证项下的汇票制作模板中一般会列出利息。通常填写的是合同或者信用证规定的利息率。一般情况下由银行填写。

3. 号码（No.）。

（1）填写内容：填写发票号码。让该业务中的发票和汇票建立关联。

（2）实例：

  No. HNCS001

4. 汇票金额（Exchange for（小写金额）／The sum of（大写金额））。

（1）填写内容：

①参照 L/C 的汇票条款分别填写小写金额和大写金额。

如果 L/C 规定：full invoice value 则填发票全额，V 汇 = V 发。

如果发票金额含佣金、折扣，则取净价填写（即不含佣金和折扣）。

CIF C5	USD 10,000.00	
LESSC5	USD 500.00	
	USD 9,500.00	V 汇 ＜ V 发

L/C 规定汇票金额按发票金额的一定百分比支付，例如议付金额按发票金额的 95% 支付。

$$V 汇 = V 发 * 95\%$$

②小写金额填货币代号和阿拉伯数字，小数点保留两位，第三位小数四舍五入，不得涂改。

③大写金额则填写在 "The sum of" 后面，用大写英语文字表示，并在文字金额后面加上 "ONLY"，以防止涂改。大小写必须保持一致。

a. 计价货币的英文全称；b. 大写汇票金额；c. 辅币，如 CENTS；d. 前 "SAY" ＋大写金额＋后 "ONLY"（整）。

（2）实例：Exchange for USD28,500.00

  The sum of SAY U. S. DOLLARS TWENTY EIGHT THOUSAND FIVE HUNDRED ONLY.

5. 出票地点及日期。

（1）填写内容：地点一般就印制在汇票上，无需填写。日期由银行填写。

日期一般参照提单日期填写，不要早于提单日期，但又不能超过信用证规定的交单期和有效期。提单日期 ≤ 汇票日期 ≤ 交单期和有效期。

（2）实例：Shanghai Jan. 5. 2016

6. 付款期限（at…sight of…）。

（1）填写内容：根据 L/C 上汇票条款所规定的付款期限填写，一般分为即期付款和远期付款两类。

（2）实例：

即期付款：At * * * sight of/ At …sight of ／ At－－－sight of

远期付款：见票后若干天付款：at 60 DAYS AFTER sight of，见票后 60 天。

    出票后若干天付款：at 60 DAYS DATE SIGHT

    提单后若干天付款：at 60 DAYS sight AFTER DATE OF B/L

7. 受款人（又称汇票抬头 Pay to the order of…）。

（1）填写内容：信用证项下，如办理议付，则填写议付行名称或填写受益人指定银行。限制议付的 L/C，该栏只能填限制议付银行的名称。

（2）实例：

pay to the order of BANK OF CHINA , HUNAN BRANCH

8. 付款人（又称受票人 To…）。

（1）填写内容：《UCP60C》规定信用证业务下汇票付款人应为开证行或其指定银行。

（2）实例：

To：BANK OF MONTREL，MONTREL，CANADA

9. 出票人（Drawer）。

（1）填写内容：一般是在汇票右下角打上受益人公司的名称及业务员姓名，多采用加盖受益人公司印章并手签的方式。

（2）实例：

HUNAN PROVINCIAL IMP & EXP CORP.

陈明

AUTHORIIED SIGNATURE

（二）托收项下汇票的缮制

托收项下汇票的缮制与信用证项下汇票的缮制大致相同，其区别的具体内容如下：

1. 出票依据（Draw under…L/C NO…Dated）。

（1）填写内容：托收项下的汇票只需在 Draw under 后填写 For collection，其他不填。

（2）实例：

Drawn underFor collection

2. 付款期限（at…sight of…）。

（1）填写内容：支付方式一般为 D/P 或者 D/A，填写在 AT 的前面，付款期限应填写在 AT 与 SIGHT 的中间。

（2）实例：

D/P At ＊＊＊ Sight　　　　即期付款交单

D/P At 60 DAYS Sight　　　60 天付款交单

3. 收款人（又称汇票抬头 Pay to the order of…）。

（1）填写内容：一般填写由出口商所委托的某家银行即托收行。

（2）实例：

Pay to the order ofHSBC，SHANGHAI BRANCH

4. 付款人（又称受票人 To…）。

（1）填写内容：托收项下汇票的付款人（Payer/Drawee）同样是在汇票的左下角"To"后面填写，填写的是进出口合同中的进口方名称和详细地址。

（2）实例：

TO：ABC TRADING CO.，LTD

　　　QUEEN AVE.，NO. 23，

　　　LOS ANGELES，U. S. A

第三节　任务模块

上接项目八，在取得装运单据后，单证员李望在此项目中应完成的工作任务包括：

任务 1：认真审核信用证中的汇票条款。

任务2：根据信用证、发票和装运资料等按要求缮制汇票。

提单上标注的装船日期为 AUG 24，2019

信用证如下：

SEQUENCE OF TOTAL	27：	1/1
FORM OF DC	40A：	IRREVOCABLE
DC NO	20：	DC HMN214479
DATE OF ISSUE	31C：	190720
APPLICABLE RULES	40E：	UCP LATEST VERSION
EXPIRY DATE AND PLACE	31D：	190919 IN COUNTRY OF BENEFICIARY
APPLICANT	50：	ELBY GIFTS INC. 879 INDUSTRIEL BOIS DES FILION, QUEBEC, J6Z 4T3, CANADA
BENEFICIARY	59：	LILING PENGXING CERAMIC FACTORY WUSHI JIASHU LILING HUNAN, CHINA
AMOUNT	32B：	USD27010,40
PCT0R AMT TOLERANCE	39A：	10/10
AVAILABLE WITH/BY	41D：	ANY BANK BY NEGOTIATION
DRAFTS AT	42C：	AT SIGHT FOR FULL INVOICE VALUE
DRAWEE	42A：	ISSUING BANK
PARTIAL SHIPMENTS	43P：	ALLOWED
TRANSHIPMENT	43T：	ALLOWED
PORTOF LOADING	44E：	SHENZHEN, CHINA
PORT OF DISCHARGE	44F：	PRINCE RUPERT, BC
LATEST DATE OF SHIPMENT	44D：	190905
DESCRIPTION OFGOODS OR SERVICES ALL PACKED IN CARTONS.	45A：	CERAMIC CUPS AND BOWLS AS PER S/C NO.：CB161039 CIF PRINCE RUPERT, BC
DOCUMENTS REQUIRED	46A：	+ ORIGINAL SIGNED INVOICE PLUS THREE COPIES.

+ FULL SET OF CLEAN MULTIMODAL TRANSPORT DOCUMENT PLUS 2 N/N COPIES, MADE TO THE ORDER OF HSBC BANK CANADA, SHOWING ON BOARD NOTATION, MARKED FREIGHT PREPAID, AND NOTIFY APPLICANT (STATING FULL NAME AND ADDRESS).

+INSURANCE POLICY OR CERTIFICATE BLANK INDORSED, FOR THE INVOICE VALUE PLUS 10% COVERING ALL RISKS AND S. R. CC. FROM WAREHOUSE TO WAREHOUSE.

+ ORIGINAL PACKING LIST PLUS 2 COPIES

+ GSP CERTIFICATE OF ORIGIN FORM A, IN ONE ORIGINAL PLUS 2 COPIES, INDICATING COUNTRY OF ORIGIN, COUNTERCHOPPED BY GOVERNMENT

AUTHORITIES OR EXPORTER'S STATMENT OF ORIGIN

+ SHIPPING NOTE INCLUDING SHIPPING MARKS, CTN NO., B/L NO., QUANTITY, VESSEL'S NAME, VOYAGE NO., SHOULD BE SENT TO THE ISSUING BANK ON THE DATE OF SHIPMENT.

ADDITIONAL CONDITIONS	47A:	+ BENEFICIARY'S DETAILS:

CTC: MILLER LEE

TEL: 86 - 731 - 2338 - 4199

FAX: 86 - 731 - 2338 - 4298

FOLLOWING CHARGES ARE FOR BENEFICIARY'S ACCOUNT:

1) REIMBURSEMENT / REMITTANCE CHARGES

2) DISCREPANCY FEE OF USD/CAD/EUR100 PLUS ALL RELEVANT CABLE CHARGES WILL BE DEDUCTED FROM EACH PRESENTATION OF DISCREPANT

DOCUMENTS UNDER THIS DC.

CHARGES	71B:	ALL BANKING CHARGES OUTSIDE COUNTRY OF ISSUE FOR ACCOUNT OF BENEFICIARY/EX-PORTER
PERIOD OF PRESENTATION	48:	WITHIN 15 DAYS AFTER THE DATE OF SHIPMENT BUT WITHIN THE VALIDITY OF THE CREDIT
CONFIRMATION INSTRUCTIONS	49:	WITHOUT
INFO TO PRESENTING BK	78:	+ UPON RECEIPT OF DOCUMENTS CONFORMING TO THE TERMS OF THIS CREDIT WE UNDERTAKE TO REIMBURSE YOU IN THE CURRENCY OF THIS CREDIT IN ACCORDANCE WITH YOUR INSTRUCTIONS, LESS CABLE CHARGES,

+ FORWARD DOCUMENTS IN ONE LOT BY COURIER AT BENEFICIARY'S EXPENSES TO

HSBC BANK CANADA, TRADE AND SUPPLY CHAIN, 5100 SHERBROOKE STREET EAST, SUITE 190, MONTREAL, QUEBEC, H1V 3R9 CANADA.

+ THE AMOUNT OF EACH DRAWING MUST BE ENDORSEDON THE REVERSE OF THIS DC BY THE NEGOTIATING/PRESENTING BANK.

发票如下：

PENGXING IMP&EXP COMPANY

LILING PENGXING CERAMIC FACTORY

WUSHI JIASHU LILING HUNAN CHINA

TEL：86-731-23384199   FAX：86-731-23384298

COMMERCIAL INVOICE

TO：	ELBY GIFTS INC. 879 INDUSTRIEL BOIS DES FILION QUEBEC, J6Z 4T3, CANADA		INVOICE NO. :	PX16IVN1039
			INVOICE DATE：	AUG 16，2019
			S/C NO. :	CB161039
			S/C DATE：	JUL 5，2019
FROM：	SHENZHEN, CHINA	TO：	PRINCE RPERT, BC, CANADA	
Letter of Credit No. :	DC HMN214479	Issued By：	HSBC BANK, MONTREAL CANADA	
Marks and Numbers	Number and kind of package	Quantity	Unit Price	Amount
Description of goods		U. S. D/set		
	Description of goods		CIF PRINCE RUPERT，BC	
	CERAMIC CUPS AND BOWLS			
ELBY		CTN	U. S. D	U. S. D
S/C NO. : CB161039	V23－234	228	4. 05	3 693.60
NO：1－1589	V23－234F	228	4. 05	3 693.60
	V23－235	190	2. 40	3 648.00
	V23－236	189	2. 10	3 175.20
	V23－237	186	1. 95	2 901.60
	V23－238	190	2. 04	3 100.80
	36－062	191	2. 30	3 514.40
	36－063	187	2. 16	3 171.52
	Total：	1 589 CTNS		U. S. D 26 898.72

Say Total：U. S DOLLARSTWENTY SIX THOUSAND EIGHT HUNDRED AND NINETY EIGHT AND CENTS SEVENTY TWO（USD26898.72）ONLY

PENGXING IMP&EXP COMPANY

李望

由于汇票条款中出现了溢短装条款"PCT 0R AMT TOLERANCE：10/10"，必须根据商业发票确定交货数量1589CTNS和金额USD26,898.72，据此，单证员李望缮制了一份汇票。

凭 Drawn under HSBC BANK CANADA	信用证 第 号 L/C No. DC HMN214479

日期 Dated JULY 20, 2019 . 按 息 付款 Payable with interest @ .... % per annual

号码 汇票金额 中国，长沙 年 月 日
No.：PX16IVN1039 Exchange for USD26,898.72 Shanghai, China AUG. 26, 2019

见票 日后（本 汇票之副本未付）

At ＊＊＊ Sight of this FIRST of Exchange（Second of exchange being unpaid）

Pay to the order of BANK OF CHINA, HUNAN BRANCH 或其指定人付金额

The sum of U.S. DOLLARS TWENTY SIX THOUSAND EIGHT HUNDRED NINETY EIGHT AND CENTS SEVENTY TWO ONLY.

To： HSBC BANK CANADA

TRADE AND SUPPLY CHAIN, 5100 SHERBROOKE STREET EAST,

SUITE 190, MONTREAL, QUEBEC, H1V 3R9 CANADA.

LILING PENGXING CERAMIC FACTORY
李望

第四节 任务拓展模块

能力实训项目1：信用证下汇票的缮制

上接项目八，根据JIANGSU I‑TOUCH BUSINESS SERVICE LTD 第0684160117426号信用证的要求，2019年9月24日，单证员彭婷装船完毕后根据信用证、商业发票和提单缮制汇票。

1. 信用证。

SEQUENCE OF TOTAL	27：	1/1
FORM OF DC.	40A：	IRREVOCABLE
DC. NO.	20：	0684160117426
DATE OF ISSUE	31C：	190825
APPLICABLE RULES	40E：	UCP LATEST VERSION
EXPIRY DATE AND PLACE	31D：	161024，CHINA
APPLICANT	50：	M/S. MEMORY STEEL CORPORATION
		73/A，LAL MOHAN SHAHA STREET
		（DHOLAIKHAL），DHAKA－1100.
		BANGLADESH.
BENEFICIARY	59：	JIANGSU I‑TOUCH BUSINESS SERVICE LTD,
		ROOM 117，JIANGSU EDIFICE

ZHANGJIAGANG FREE TRADE ZONE,
JIANGSU, CHINA   TEL: 86 - 516 - 56363783

AMOUNT	32B:	USD35000,00
AVAILABLE WITH/BY	41D:	ANY BANK IN CHINA BY NEGOTIATION
DRAFTS AT	42C:	AT SIGHT FOR FULL INVOICE VALUE
DRAWEE	42A:	DRAWN ON US
PARTIAL SHIPMENTS	43P:	ALLOWED
TRANSSHIPMENT	43T:	ALLOWED
PORTOF LOADING	44A:	ANY SEA PORT, CHINA
PORT OF DISCHARGE	44B:	CHITTAGONG SEA PORT, BANGLADESH
LATEST DATE OF SHIPMENT	44C:	191009
DESCRIPTION OFGOODS	45A:	201/2B SECONDARY GRADE STAINLESS STEEL SHEET OF WIDTH 1619MM THICKNESS 1MM TO 3MM, QTY: 25, 000KGS AT THE RATE OF USD1. 40/KG

FOR TOTAL AMOUNT OF USD35,000. 00 CFR CHITTAGONG, BANGLADESH. AS PER BENEFICIARY'S PROFORMA INVOICE NO. SK20160802 - 001 DATED AUG 2, 2016

DOCUMENTS REQUIRED   46A: +MANUALLY SIGNED COMMERCIAL INVOICE IN TRIPLICATE CERTIFYING MERCHANDISE TO BE OF CHINA ORIGIN AND INDICATING THAT THE GOODS ARE BEING IMPORTED AGAINST IRC NO. BA - 0171646, TI NO. 157 - 107 - 0161, VAT REGISTRATION NO. 9141093671.

+ FULL SET OF CLEAN 'SHIPPED ON BOARD' OCEAN BILL OF LADING SHOWING' FREIGHT PREPAID' MADE OUT TO ORDER AND BLANK INDORSED, NOTIFY APPLICANT.

+ PACKING LIST IN TRIPLICATE SHOWING GROSS WEIGHT, NET WEIGHT.

+ CERTIFICATE OF ORIGIN ISSUED AND LEGALED BY CCPIT

+ BENEFICIARY'S DECLARATION SHOULD CERTIFY THAT THE COUNTRY OF ORIGIN HAS BEEN PRINTED ON GOODS PACKING BAG.

+ BENEFICIARY SHOULD SEND A FAX OR BY COUR

IER TO L/C OPENING BANK WITHIN FIVE DAYS FROM THE OF SHIPMENT, ADVISING THE DATE OF SHIPMENT, VESSEL'S NAME, AMOUNT OF BILL AND L/C NO. AND A COPY OF THIS FAX SHOULD ACCOMPANY THE SHIPPING DOCUMENTS.

+SHIPMENT BY ISRAELI LINER IS PROHIBITED AND A

CERTIFICATE TO THIS EFFECT ISSUED BY THE SHIPPING COMPANY MUST ACCOMPANY THE ORIGINAL DOCUMENTS.

CHARGES 71B: ALL FOREIGN BANK CHARGES ARE FOR THE ACCOUNT OF THE BENEFICIARY.

PERIOD OF PRESENTATION 48: 15 DAYS FROM SHIPMENT DATE BUT WITHIN VALIDITY OF THE CREDIT

2. 其他信息。

发票号码：67080 – 9

提单日期：SEP. 16，2019

Bill of Exchange

凭 Drawn under	信用证 第 号 L/C No.		
日期 Dated	按 息 付款 Payable with interest @ _____ % per annual		
号码 No.：	汇票金额 Exchange for _____	中国，上海 年 月 日 Shanghai, China	
见票 At _____ Sight of this FIRST of Exchange（Second of exchange being unpaid）	日后（本汇票之副本未付）		
Pay to the order of _____ 或其指定人付金额			
The sum of			
To：			
For.			

能力实训项目 2：托收下汇票的缮制

上接项目八，根据合同的要求，2019 年 10 月 18 日，单证员王丹装船完毕后根据合同、商业发票和提单相关信息缮制汇票。

1. 合同信息。

合同卖方：GUANGDONG JIAMEI TRADING CO.，LTD

合同买方：G. KLEEYE GMBH，GERMANY

支付方式：D/P AT SIGHT

托收银行：BANK OF CONSTUCTION，GUANGZHOU BRANCH

合同金额：EUR70，800.00

2. 其他信息。

发票号码：GDJM2016045

提单日期：OCT. 17，2019

Bill of Exchange

凭 Drawn under _____	信用证 第 号 L/C No.	
日期 Dated _____	按 息 付款 Payable with interest @ _____ % per annual	
号码 No. : _____	汇票金额 Exchange for	中国，上海 年 月 日 Shanghai，China
见票 At _____ Sight of this FIRST of Exchange（Second of exchange being unpaid）	日后（本汇票之副本未付）	
Pay to the order of _____ 或其指定人付金额		
The sum of		
To:		
	For.	

第五节 学习导航

一、参考资料

[1] 章安平. 外贸单证操作［M］. 北京：高等教育出版社，2008.

[2] 刘启萍，周树玲. 外贸单证［M］. 北京：对外经贸大学出版社，2008.

[3] 方士华，国际结算［M］. 沈阳：东北财经大学出版社，2016.

[4] 吴轶群，国际商务单证操作［M］. 青岛：中国海洋大学出版社，2018.

二、自主学习平台

[1] 全国外贸单证员考试中心。

[2] 外贸经理人微信公众号。

[3] 外贸单证课程国家教学资源库。

◆项目预期目标

通过对信用证项下装运通知条款、受益人证明条款及船公司证明条款的认真解读，结合该项目提供的商业发票等相关单据，并介绍几种主要的附属单据背景知识，使同学们了解附属单据的使用场合及制作要领。

在项目实施过程中，通过对三种单据制作任务的分解，在分工与合作中逐渐培养审核、制单、归类等国际商务单证基本职业能力，亦培养独立操作业务和与其他业务或政府部门有效沟通的能力。

表9-1　项目预期目标

目标类型	其他单据的制作
知识目标	熟悉货运单据与其他单据的衔接
	掌握几种重要的其他单据的制作
能力目标	能根据贸易术语及信用证要求有效制作其他单据
	能备齐全套单据
职业素质目标	独立业务操作能力
	与国外客户及船公司的沟通衔接能力

◆项目实施条件

1. 学生能够在实训室对该项目进行分组讨论并实施。

2. 指导教师具备扎实的外贸业务基础。

◆开篇业务引入

根据第 DC HMN214479 号信用证的要求，长沙鹏兴进出口有限公司在完成货物的装运并取得提单后还需出具装运通知及受益人证明，同时信用证还要求一份船公司证明作为议付单据，这类单据统称为其他单据或附属单据。该项目任务具体由单证员李望负责。

2019 年 8 月 25 日，单证员李望根据 L/C 规定"+SHIPPING NOTE INCLUDING SHIP-PING MARKS, CTN NO., B/L NO., QUANTITY, VESSEL'S NAME, VOYAGE NO., SHOULD BE SENT TO THE ISSUING BANK ON THE DATE OF SHIPMENT."等条款，以及缮制好的商业发票及装运资料等，制作三种其他单据。

第一节　其他单据的制作

一、其他单据的含义及使用场合

在国际贸易中，卖方应在发货完毕后按合同或信用证要求提供相关单据，这是卖方在国际贸易中应该履行的基础业务之一，同时也是卖方安全收汇的前提之一。卖方除应在提供基本结汇单证如商业发票、运输单据等之外，在某些特定的情况下，往往还要根据买方、进口国海关的要求，提供如装箱单、受益人证明、装运通知、船公司证明等一些常见的辅助性结汇单据，这些单据对于出口商安全结汇都是必不可少的。

二、其他单据的主要范围

（一）受益人证明（Beneficiary's Certificate）

受益人证明亦称受益人声明（Beneficiary's Statement/Declaration），是由受益人签发的证实某件事实的单据，它是信用证支付方式下买方要求的常见单据之一。

1. 受益人证明的种类。

（1）寄单证明（Beneficiary's Certificate for Dispatch of Documents）。

（2）寄样证明（Beneficiary's Certificate for Dispatch of Shipment Sample）。

（3）包装和标签证明（Packing & Label Certificate）。

2. 受益人证明的基本内容。

受益人证明的内容一般包括：单据名称、出证日期与地点、抬头人、事由、证明文句、受益人名称及签章等，具体如下：

（1）单据名称。这种单据的名称因所证明的事项不同而略异，可能是寄单证明、寄样证明（船样、样卡和码样等）、取样证明、证明货物产地、品质、唛头、包装和标签情况、电抄形式的装运通知、证明产品生产过程、证明商品也已检验、环保人方面的证明（非童工、非狱工制造）等。

（2）出证日期和地点。单据一般都应在规定的时间内做出，并列明出证地点。

（3）证明上通常会显示发票号、合同号或信用证号以表明与其他单据的关系。

（4）受益人证明应明确列明抬头人。

（5）证明的内容严格与合同或信用证规定相符。

（6）因属于证明性质，按有关规定证明人（受益人）必须签字。

3. 受益人证明的应用。

（1）买方为了某种原因如转口货物等，要求在限定时间内先直接邮寄必要的单据以便及时提货、通关或再另转口。买方为了确保卖方能按时寄单，在信用证条款中明确此要求并由受益人出具已寄送单据的证明，此即为寄单证明。

（2）买方为预先取得装运的货样，要求寄样的寄样证明。

（3）要求受益人在限定时间内将装运情况通知买方而出具的证明。

（4）买方要求单据由买方所属国的领事签证，但出口所在地又无该国领事而出具的证明。

（5）要求卖方执行某些行为而出具相应的证明。

（二）装运通知（Shipping Advice/Note）

装运通知或称装船证明（Shipping Statement 或 Shipping Declaration），即按信用证或合同规定出口方在订妥舱位或货物装船后向买方发出的通知，以便对方办理保险或准备提货、租仓等。其目的在于让进口商做好筹措资金、付款和接货准备，如成交条件 FOB/FCA、CFR/CPT 等还需要向进口国保险公司发出该通知以便其为进口商办理货物保险手续，出口装船通知应按合同或信用证规定的时间发出，通知客人发货的细节，包括船名、航班次、开船日、预计抵港日、货物及数量、金额、包装件数、唛头、目的港代理人等。接收通知的一般是进口方，也有的是进口方指定的保险公司。该通知副本（Copy of Telex/Fax）常作为向银行交单议付的单据之一，在进口方派船接货的交易条件下，进口商实现使船、货衔接也会向出口方发出有关通知。

装船通知一般以英文信函的格式制作，也可根据业务需要自拟，但内容一定要符合信用证的规定，一般只提供一份正本，以电报的形式通知，副本则随其他单据交银行议付。

装运通知的内容主要包括：收件人名称和地址；合同号和信用证号、货名、数量、金额；船名、航次；开航日期；提单号码及出单日期等。

注意：出单日期不能超过信用证规定的日期，如装船后 2 天内（within two days after shipping）。如果信用证规定 IMMEDIATELY AFTER SHIPMENT（装船后立即通知），立视为在提单后 3 天之内。

（三）船公司证明（Certificate of Shipping Co.，）

船公司证明为几类单据的统称，根据实际业务的需要通常有以下几种：

1. 船龄证明（Certificate of Age of Vessel/Certificate of Vessel's Age）。

有些国家/地区来证规定装载货物的船舶的船龄不得超过 15 年，受益人必须要求船代或船公司出具载货船只的船龄证明书（Certificate to evidence the ship is not over 15 years old 或 is under 15 years of age），这样的要求主要目的在于禁止使用老龄船，保护货物运输安全。

2. 船籍证明（Certificate of Registry）。

它用于证明船舶所属国籍，指的是证明船舶的国籍、船籍港及船舶所有权等的一种书面文书。一般的船籍证书的有效期为 10 年，自登记之日算起。有效期满，船舶所有人持原船籍证书到原登记机关换发新的船级证书。根据我国《海商法》及船舶登记规则的规定，船舶经登记并取得船舶国籍证书后，才有权悬挂我国国旗在海上航行。由此可见，船籍证书属于法律登记性质，船舶不得具有双重国籍。进口商要求出口商提供船籍证明一般是因为一些政治原因，如巴基斯坦银行开来的信用证会要求出口商提供载货船舶的船籍不属于印度的证明，阿拉伯国家银行开来的信用证会要求出口商提供载货船舶的船籍不属于以色列的证明。

3. 船级证明（Confirmation of Class）。

有的信用证规定提供不同国家的船级社证明，对这样的要求我们通常应予以满足。

世界上比较著名的船级社，有英国劳合级社（LD）、德国劳埃德船级社（GL）、挪威船级社（DNV）、法国船级局（BV）、日本海事协会（NK）、美国航运局（ABS）、中国船级社（China Classification Society）等。中国船级社是中华人民共和国交通部所属的船舶检验局。船级证书除了记载船舶的主要技术性能外，还绘制出相应的船级符号，各国船级社对船级符号的规定不同。中国船级社的船级符号为 ZC。劳合社的船级符号为 LR，标志100A1，100A 表示该船的船体和机器设备是根据劳氏规范和规定建造的，1 表示船舶的装备如船锚、锚链和绳索等处于良好和有效的状态。

4. 黑名单证明（Black List Certificate）。

证明运送货物的船舶不在黑名单之列和保险公司不在黑名单之列，由船舶公司和保险公司出具。典型的是阿拉伯国家所要求的抵制以色列证明（CERTIFICATE OF BOYCOTT ISRAEL）。其通常规定为：THE VESSEL CARRYING THE GOODS IS NOT ISRAELI AND WILL NOT CALL ON ANY ISRAELI PORTS WHILE CARRYING THE GOODS AND THAT THE VESSEL IS NOT BANNED ENTRY TO THE PORT OF THE ARAB STATES FOR ANY REASONS WHATEVER UNDER LAW AND THE LAWS AND REGULATIONS OF SUCH SATES ALLOWED.（船上所装货物为非以色列原产，船不经停任何以色列港口，船只可依法自由进入阿拉伯国家法律和规则所容许进出的港口。）

（四）运输和航行证明

1. 航程证明（Certificate of Itinerary）。

它主要说明航程中船舶停靠的港口，一些阿拉伯国家开来的信用证中，往往要求在提单上随附声明一份，明确船籍、船名、船东及途中所经港口顺序，出口方须按要求签发此类证明并按证明中所述行驶、操作船舶。

2. 转船证明书（Certificate of Transshipment）。

出口方出具转船证明书，说明出口货物将在中途转船且已联系妥当，并由托运人负责将有关转船事项通知收货人。

3. 货装具名船舶证明。

如信用证要求"A CERTIFICATE FROM THE SHIPPING COMPANY OR ITS AGENT STATING THAT GOODS ARE SHIPPED BY COSCO"，意思是要求出口方提供由船公司或其代理出具的货装中国远洋集装箱运输有限公司的证明。

4. 船长收据（Captain's Receipt）。

船长收据是指船长收到随船带交给收货人单据时的收单证明。船长收据的内容一般是：收到单据的种类、分数，并声明在船舶到达目的港后交给指定人。有的信用证规定，样品或单据副本交载货船只的船长代交进口商，并提供船长收据，若委托船长带去而未取得船长收据将影响出口商收汇，常见于近洋运输。如今随着航空快递业的发展，现在船长收据已基本不用。此外，船证还包括进港证明、运费已交收据、港口费用单（Port Charges Documents）、装卸准备就绪通知书和装卸时间事实记录等，由于政治原因，巴基斯坦和印度不允许悬挂对方国旗的船舶靠岸，巴基斯坦港口还不接受来自南非、韩国、以色列和中国台湾的船舶，若要求出具相应证明的，出口方必须提供。

　　5. 关于 SMC、DOC 和 SOLAS。

　　这几个缩略语近年来常出现在信用证的要求中，SMC（Safety Management Certificate 船舶安全管理证书）和 DOC（Documents of Compliance 安全符合证书，也有人称其为船/港保安符合证书）是按照国际安全管理规则（ISM）的规定，载货船舶应在船上拥有的必要证书。我国海事局按 ISM 的规章发给船公司 DOC，船舶则可获 SMC，如果船公司没有相应证书则无法按信用证要求来出具此类证明。信用证中的一般要求是："THE CARRYING VESSEL SHOULD COMPLY WITH PROVISIONS OF THE（ISM）CODE WHICH NECESSITATES THAT SUCH VESSEL MUST HAVE ON BOARD, COPIES OF THE TWO（WMC AND DOC）VALID CERTIFICATES AND COPIES OF SUCH CERTIFICATE MUST BE PRESENTED WITH THE ORIGINAL DOCUMENTS."也可体现为"Certificate issued, signed and stamped by the owner/carrier/master of the carrying vessel holds valid ISM certificate and ISPS（International Shipping and Port Security Safety Code,《国际船舶和港口设施保安规则》）"；SOLAS 指的是《1974 年国际海上人命安全公约》（简称 SOLAS 公约），公约规定，船舶应持有"安全管理证书"正本，其船名与国籍证书一致，所载公司名称与"符合证明"中的公司名称一致。

三、几种主要的附属单据制作

（一）受益人证明的缮制

　　1. 单据名称（Name of Documents）。

　　单据名称位于单据正上方，可根据信用证要求确定具体名称。一般标明"Beneficiary's Certificate（受益人证明）""Beneficiary's Statement（受益人声明）或 Beneficiary's Declaration（受益人申明）"等。

　　2. 出证日期与地点（Date and Place of Issue）。

　　按照实际签发日期与地点填写。地点一般即受益人所在地点；日期一般与提单日期相同或者稍晚，但不能迟于交单期和证效期。

　　3. 抬头人（To）。

　　按信用证的要求填写开证申请人的名称，如无特别规定，也可填写笼统的抬头，如"TO WHOM IT MAY CONCERN"或"DAER SIRS"。

　　4. 交易参考号号码（Ref No.）。

　　一般填写信用证号，非信用证支付方式下则填写发票号或合同号。有些信用证规定除汇票和发票外，其他单据都不能显示信用证号码，则不可填写信用证号码。

5. 证明内容（Content of Certificate）。

此项内容必须与信用证要求的内容严格相符。通常以"We hereby certify that ⋯" "This is to certify that ⋯"等常见句型开头，然后按照信用证中的受益人证明条款要求照抄，但有时根据实际情况也应作相应修改，如信用证要求受益人寄单据则提供寄单证明；若信用证要求受益人寄货样则提供寄样证明。

6. 受益人名称及签章（Signature）。

该栏一般填写卖方或受益人（如出口公司）的名称，由法人代表或经办人签字盖章。受益人证明一般不分正副本。若来证要求正本，可在单据名称的正下方打上"Origin"字样。证明的右下方必须由受益人即出口公司签章，才能生效。

（二）装运通知的缮制

1. 单据名称（Name of Documents）。

主要体现为 Shipping/Shipment Advice，Advice of shipment 等，也有人将其称为 Shipping Statement/Declaration/Note，简称（S/A，S/N）。如果信用证有具体要求，应严格按照信用证要求缮制。

2. 抬头（To）。

该栏一般为提货人，即信用证开证申请人或合同的买方，有时在 CFR 术语下要求将装运通知同时寄给进口方及保险公司以保证业务衔接，此时则需做成两个抬头，并注明详细地址、如电话或传真号。

3. 合同号或信用证号（Contract No./L/C No.）。

如信用证项下应注明信用证号及合同号；非信用证方式则注明合同或订单号。

4. 品名（Description of Goods）。

一般只需列明品名品牌即可。

5. 数量（Quantity）。

填写货物的外包装数量及包装单位，如有规定也可以同时填写内包装数量。

6. 船名及航次号（Vessel's Name & Voyage No.）。

应填写载货船只的船名及航次。

7. 预计开航日（ETD）。

如果知道确切的开航日期，则应填写实际开航日，否则填写提单签发日。

8. 预计到港日期（ETA）。

填写船舶预计到达目的港的时间，以便对方做好提货准备。

9. 提单号（B/L No.）。

填写签发的海运提单的提单号码。

10. 日期（Date）。

填写缮制装运通知的日期，该日期应严格按照信用证规定的日期填写，否则单证不符。常见的有以下三种表达方式：以小时为准（Within 24/48 Hours）；装船后立即通知（Immediately after shipment），此时应视为提单后 3 天内发出；以天为准（Within 2 Days After Shipment Date），假如提单日为 4 月 10 日，则装运通知最晚不能超过 11 日午夜 12 点发出。

11. 签署（Signature）。

此处一般可以不签署，若信用证要求，一般缮制卖方或受益人的名称。

（三）船公司证明的缮制

1. 单据名称（Name of Documents）。

该栏应严格按照信用证要求填制相应的单据名称。

2. 抬头（To）。

一般都笼统缮制"TO WHOM IT MAY CONCERN"（致启者）。

3. 出证地址和日期（Date And Place of Issue）。

一般应为提单的签发地址和日期。

4. 船名及航次号（Vessel's Name & Voyage No.）。

填写承担本次运输的船名及航次号。

5. 提单号（B/L No.）。

填写本次运输的海运提单的提单号。

6. 证明内容（Content of Certificate）。

严格按照信用证条款的要求，根据实际情况缮制，如证明船籍、船龄或船级等内容，格式与受益人证明类似。

7. 签章（Signature）。

该类单据必须签章，且签章人与提单签发人一致，一般为船公司或多式联运经营人及其代理等。

第二节　装运通知等典型业务演示

上接项目八，根据信用证要求，受益人在取得货运单据之后应立即制作装运通知及受益人证明并在规定时间内发出。据此，鹏兴公司单证员李望在此项目中的工作任务包括：

任务 1：认真审核信用证中的装运通知及受益人证明款。

任务 2：准备制作单据要用的相关装运资料。

任务 3：制作装运通知并及时发送。

任务 4：制作受益人证明。

据此已知的装运资料，李望制作了装运通知及受益人证明：

PENGXING IMP&EXP COMPANY

LILING PENGXING CERAMIC FACTORY
WUSHI JIASHU LILING HUNAN CHINA
TEL：86 – 731 – 23384199   FAX：86 – 731 – 23384298

SHIPPING NOTE

To：ELBY GIFTS INC.   **Date**：AUG. 24，2019

879 INDUSTRIEL BOIS DES FILION QUEBEC，

J6Z 4T3，CANADA

From：SHENZHEN，CHINA   **To**：PRINCE RUPERT，BC，CANADA

DEAR SIRS，

WE HEREBY INFORM YOU THAT ALL OF THE CARGO UNDER THE L/C MENTIONED HAVE BEEN
SHIPPED. THE DETAILS ARE AS FOLLOWS，

C/I NO. &DATE：	PX12IVN1039，AUG. 16，2019
B/L NO. &DATE：	B/L NO. ：AUG. 24 2019，SHENZHEN，CHINA
VESSEL &VOY. ：	COSCO SEATTLE V. 0078E
QUANTITY：	1589 CARTONS
MARKS：	ELBY S/C NO. ：CB121039 NO：1 – 1589

PENGXING IMP&EXP COMPANY

李望

PENGXING IMP&EXP COMPANY

LILING PENGXING CERAMIC FACTORY
WUSHI JIASHU LILING HUNAN CHINA
TEL：86 – 731 – 23384199　　　FAX：86 – 731 – 23384298

BENEFICIARY'S CERTIFICATE

To：ELBY GIFTS INC.　　　　　　　Date：AUG. 26, 2019

879 INDUSTRIEL BOIS DES FILION QUEBEC，

J6Z 4T3, CANADA

From：SHENZHEN, CHINA　　　　　To：PRINCE RUPERT, BC, CANADA

DEAR SIRS,

WE HEREBY INFORM YOU THAT ALL OF THE CARGO UNDER THE L/C MENTIONED HAVE BEEN SHIPPED. THE DETAILS ARE AS FOLLOWS,

PENGXING IMP&EXP COMPANY

李望

第三节　装运通知等拓展业务操作

能力实训项目 1：根据上海淼睿进出口有限公司第 0684160117426 号信用证的要求，2016 年 9 月 24 日，单证员彭婷根据信用证的要求，备齐相关装运资料完成三个任务。

1. 信用证。

SEQUENCE OF TOTAL	27：	1/1
FORM OF DC.	40A：	IRREVOCABLE
DC. NO.	20：	0684160117426
DATE OF ISSUE	31C：	190825
APPLICABLE RULES	40E：	UCP LATEST VERSION
EXPIRY DATE AND PLACE	31D：	191024, CHINA
APPLICANT	50：	M/S. MEMORY STEEL CORPORATION
		73/A, LAL MOHAN SHAHA STREET
		(DHOLAIKHAL), DHAKA – 1100.
		BANGLADESH.
BENEFICIARY	59：	JIANGSU I – TOUCH BUSINESS SERVICE LTD,
		ROOM 117, JIANGSU EDIFICE
		ZHANGJIAGANG FREE TRADE ZONE,
		JIANGSU, CHINA TEL：86 – 512 – 56363783
AMOUNT	32B：	USD35000,00

AVAILABLE WITH/BY	41D：	ANY BANK IN CHINA BY NEGOTIATION
DRAFTS AT	42C：	AT SIGHT FOR FULL INVOICE VALUE
DRAWEE	42A：	DRAWN ON US
PARTIAL SHIPMENTS	43P：	ALLOWED
TRANSSHIPMENT	43T：	ALLOWED
PORT OF LOADING	44A：	ANY SEA PORT, CHINA
PORT OF DISCHARGE	44B：	CHITTAGONG SEA PORT, BANGLADESH
LATEST DATE OF SHIPMENT	44C：	191009
DESCRIPTION OF GOODS	45A：	201/2B SECONDARY GRADE STAINLESS STEEL SHEET OF WIDTH 1219MM THICKNESS 1MM TO 3MM, QTY：25,000KGS AT THE RATE OF USD1.40/KG FOR TOTAL AMOUNT OF USD35,000.00 CFR CHITTAGONG, BANGLADESH. AS PER BENEFICIARY'S PROFORMA INVOICE NO. SK20160802-001 DATED AUG 2, 2016
DOCUMENTS REQUIRED	46A：	+ MANUALLY SIGNED COMMERCIAL INVOICE IN TRIPLICATE CERTIFYING MERCHANDISE TO BE OF CHINA ORIGIN AND INDICATING THAT THE GOODS ARE BEING IMPORTED AGAINST IRC NO. BA-0171646, TI NO. 157-107 -0121, VAT REGISTRATION NO. 9141093671. + FULL SET OF CLEAN "SHIPPED ON BOARD" OCEANBILLOFLADINGSHOWING "FREIGHT PREPAID" MADE OUT TO ORDER AND BLANK INDORSED, NOTIFY APPLICANT. + PACKING LIST IN TRIPLICATE SHOWING GROSS WEIGHT, NET WEIGHT. + CERTIFICATEOFORIGINISSUEDAND LEGALED BY CCPIT + BENEFICIARY'S DECLARATION SHOULD CERTIFY THAT THE COUNTRY OF ORIGIN HAS BEEN PRINTED ON GOODS PACKING BAG. + BENEFICIARY SHOULD SEND A FAX OR BY COURIER TO L/C OPENING BANK WITHIN FIVE DAYS FROM THE OF SHIPMENT, ADVISING THE DATE OF SHIPMENT,

VESSEL'S NAME, AMOUNT OF BILL AND L/C NO. AND A COPY OF THIS FAX SHOULD ACCOMPANY THE SHIPPING DOCUMENTS.

+ SHIPMENT BY ISRAELI LINER IS PROHIBITED AND ACERTIFICATE TO THIS EFFECT ISSUED BY THE SHIPPING COMPANY MUST ACCOMPANY THE ORIGINAL DOCUMENTS.

ADDITIONAL CONDITIONS	47A:	ALL SHIPPING DOCUMENTS MUST SHOWING THE L/C NO. AND S/C NO.
PERIOD OF PRESENTATION	48:	15 DAYS FROM SHIPMENT DATE BUT WITHIN VALIDITY OF THE CREDIT

2. 商业发票。

Jiangsu I - Touch Business Service Ltd.

Add：Room117, Jinggang Edifice Zhangjiagang Free Trade Zone, Jiangsu Province, China

Tel：0086 - 512 - 56363783 Fax：0086 - 512 - 56366780

COMMERCIAL INVOICE

To：M/S. MEMORY STEEL CORPORATION73/A, LAL MOHAN SHAHA STREET（DHOLAIKHAL）, DHAKA - 1100. BANGLANDESH

Contract No. ：C20160807	No. ：67080 - 9
L/C No. ：0684160117426	Date：SEP. 16, 2019
From：SHANGHAI, CHINA	To：CHITTAGONG, BANGLANDESH

Marks	Description of Goods Size （mm）	Quantity （G. W/KG）	Unit Price （USD/KG）	Amount
	STAINLESS STEEL SHEET		CFR CHITTAGONG	
N/M	201/2B SECONDARY GRADE			
	1. 2 * 1,219 * 2,438	5,728. 00	1. 400,0	7,806. 40
	1. 5 * 1,219 * 2,438	3,315. 20	1. 400,0	4,547. 20
	2. 0 * 1,219 * 2,438	11,894. 00	1. 400,0	16,282. 00
	1,219MM OR MORE THICKNESS 1MM TO 3MM			
	3. 0 * 1,219 * 2,438	4,663. 70	1. 400,0	6,364. 40
	TOTAL：	25,600. 90		35,000. 00

SAY U. S. DOLLARS THIRTY FIVE THOUSAND ONLY

WE HEREBY CERTIFY THAT ABOVE MERCHANDISE TO BE OF CHINA ORIGIN AND ARE BEING IMPORTED AGAINST IRC NO. BA – 0171646，TI NO. 157 – 107 – 0121，VAT REGISTRATION NO. 9141093671 AND L. C. A. NO. 101804 UNDER H. S. CODE NO. 721933. 00，721934. 00

Jiangsu I – Touch Business Service Ltd.
彭婷

3. 装运资料。

DATE OF SHIPMENT：2016 – 9 – 24

VESSEL VOYAGE：ZU. S. A. V. 66W

根据上述资料完成下面几个实训项目：

任务 1：装运通知制作。

任务 2：受益人证明制作。

任务 3：船公司证明制作。

第四节　学习导航

一、参考资料

[1] 章安平. 外贸单证操作［M］. 北京：高等教育出版社，2008.

[2] 刘启萍，周树玲. 外贸单证［M］. 北京：对外经贸大学出版社，2008.

[3] 方士华，国际结算［M］. 沈阳：东北财经大学出版社，2016.

[4] 吴轶群，国际商务单证操作［M］. 青岛：中国海洋大学出版社，2018.

二、自主学习平台

[1] 全国外贸单证员考试中心。

[2] 外贸经理人微信公众号。

[3] 外贸单证课程国家教学资源库。

项目十
进口信用证业务办理

第一节　项目描述与目标

一、项目描述

◆开篇业务引入

根据第 CB161039 号合同的要求，进口方 ELBY GIFTS INC. 需要于 2019 年 8 月 5 日之前向出口方长沙鹏兴进出口有限公司开出不可撤销即期信用证，且该信用证的有效期关装运日后的 15 天。2019 年 7 月 15 日，进口方公司单证员根据第 CB161039 号合同，填写开证申请书并办理申请开证手续。在收到出口方的改证函后，结合自身改证需求，填写改证申请书并办理申请改证手续。

◆项目预期目标

信用证是当今国际贸易中的核心支付工具，也是我国进口业务中最主要的支付方式之一。在进口业务中，信用证申请书是企业自行缮制的一项重要文件，也是信用证的前身，进口商科学、缜密地设置相关条款并填写开证申请书，对于降低进口风险，有效履行合同非常关键。而当信用证受到受益人提出的改证申请后，也应当综合权衡，填写改证申请书并通过开证行办理改证手续。本项目通过介绍开证申请书和改证申请书的填制，引导学生熟悉开证和改证申请书的格式及内容，重点训练学生掌握开证和改证申请书的填制要点，并最终能独立完成开证和改证申请书的填写，掌握开证和改证手续的操作流程。

在项目实施过程中，有效训练学生对合同条款和信用证结构的理解和掌握，培养学生操作进口结汇业务的职业能力，亦培养其独立操作业务和与开证行有效沟通的能力。

表 10-1　项目预期目标

目标类型	申请开立和修改信用证
知识目标	掌握开证申请书和改证申请书的填写要求
	熟悉申请开证和改证的业务操作流程
能力目标	能根据合同，正确填写开证申请书并办理申请开证手续
	能根据出口商的改证函或进口商的改证需求，填写改正申请书并办理申请改证手续
职业素质目标	独立业务操作能力
	与银行沟通衔接能力

二、项目实施条件

1. 教师演示工作项目和归纳技能要点。
2. 学生能够在实训室对该项目进行分组讨论并实施。

第二节　知识模块

一、开证申请书的使用

进出口双方在合同明确以信用证方式结算后，即由进口方向有关银行申请开立信用证。开证申请是进口信用证业务的第一个环节，进口方应在合同规定的时间或在规定的装船前一定时间内申请开证，并填制开证申请书。

开证申请书（Application Form）是进口方作为开证申请人委托开证行开出的以出口方为受益人的信用证申请文件，一般根据贸易合同中的商品条款、支付条款等主要条款填制，申请人填制后与合同副本一并提交银行，供银行参考、核对。但信用证一经开立则独立于合同，因而在填写开证申请书时应审慎查核合同的主要条款，并将其列入申请书中。开证行在接受开证申请并开出信用证后即成为第一性付款人，而开证申请书也成为开证申请人与开证行的合约，具有法律效力。目前常见的做法是由开证行事先将空白的开证申请书印就，再由开证申请人直接填制。

IRREVOCABLE DOCUMENTARYCREDIT APPLICATION

To：	Date：
□Issue by airmail □With brief advice by teletransmission □Issue by express delivery □Issue by teletransmission（which shall be the operative instrument）	Credit No. Date and place of expiry
Applicant	Beneficiary（Full name and address）
Advising Bank	Amount
Partial shipments □allowed □not allowed	Transshipment □allowed □not allowed	Credit available with By □sight payment □acceptance □negotiation □deferred payment at against the documents detailed herein □and beneficiary's draft（s）for _____ % of invoice value at _____ sight drawn on
Loading on board/dispatch/taking in charge at/from not later than For transportation To：	
FOB CFR CIF □or other terms	

Documents required：（marked with X）

1. （　）Signed commercial invoice in _____ copies indicating L/C No. and Contract No.
2. （　）Full set of clean on board Bills of Lading made out To order and blank endorsed, marked "freight ［　］ To collect /［　］ prepaid ［　］ showing freight amount" notifying _____ .

   （　）Airway bills/cargo receipt/copy of railway bills issued by _____ showing "freight ［　］ To collect/ ［　］ prepaid ［　］ indicating freight amount" and consigned To _____ .
3. （　）Insurance Policy/Certificate in _____ copies for _____ % of the invoice value showing claims payable in _____ _____ in currency of the draft, blank endorsed, covering All Risks, War Risks and _____ .
4. （　）Packing List/Weight Memo in _____ copies indicating quantity, gross and weights of each package.
5. （　）Certificate of Quantity/Weight in _____ copies issued by _____ .
6. （　）Certificate of Quality in _____ copies issued by ［　］ manufacturer/［　］ public recognized surveyor _____ .
7. （　）Certificate of Origin in _____ copies.
8. （　）Beneficiary's certified copy of fax / telex dispatched To the applicant within _____ days after shipment advising L/C No. , name of vessel, date of shipment, name, quantity, weight and value of goods.

Other documents, if any

Description of goods：

Additional instructions：

1. （　）All banking charges outside the opening bank are for beneficiary's account.
2. （　）Documents must be presented within _____ days after date of issuance of the transport documents but within the validity of this credit.
3. （　）Third party as shipper is not acceptable, Short Form/Blank back B/L is not acceptable.
4. （　）Both quantity and credit amount _____ % more or less are allowed.
5. （　）All documents must be sent To issuing bank by courier/speed post in one lot.

   （　）Other terms, if any

图 10-1   开证申请书样本

二、申请开立信用证的流程

申请开立信用证的流程一般包括：填写开证申请书、开证申请人承诺书、提交有关合同的副本及附件、支付开证保证金、支付开证手续费等环节。

开证申请人承诺书

××银行：

我公司已办妥一切进口手续，现请贵行按我公司开证申请书内容（见背面英文）开出不可撤销跟单信用证，为此我公司承担有关责任如下：

一、我公司同意贵行依照国际商会第 600 号出版物《跟单信用证统一惯例》办理该信用证项下一切事宜，并同意承担由此产生的一切责任。

二、我公司保证按时向贵行支付该证项下的货款、手续费、利息及一切费用等（包括国外受益人拒绝承担的有关银行费用）所需的外汇和人民币资金。

三、我公司保证在贵行单到通知书中规定的期限之内通知贵行办理对外付款/承兑，否则贵行可认为我公司已接受单据，同意付款/承兑。

四、我公司保证在单证表面相符的条件下办理有关付款/承兑手续。如因单证有不符之处而拒绝付款/承兑，我公司保证在贵行单到通知书中规定的日期之前将全套单据如数退还贵行并附书面拒付理由，由贵行按国际惯例确定能否对外拒付。如贵行确定我公司所提拒付理由不成立，或虽然拒付理由成立，但我公司未能退回全套单据，或拒付单据退到贵行已超过单到通知书中规定的期限，贵行有权主动办理对外付款/承兑，并从我公司账户中扣款。

五、该信用证及其项下业务往来函电及单据如因邮、电或其他方式传递过程中发生遗失、延误、错漏，贵行当不负责。

六、该信用证如需修改，由我公司向贵行提出书面申请，由贵行根据具体情况确定能否办理修改。我公司确认所有修改当由信用证受益人接受时才能生效。

七、我公司在收到贵行开出的信用证、修改书副本后，保证及时与原申请书核对，如有不符之处，保证在接到副本之日起，两个工作日内通知贵行。如未通知，当视为正确无误。

八、如因申请书字迹不清或词意含混而引起的一切后果由我公司负责。

开证申请人

（签字盖章）

年　月　日

三、信用证修改书的使用

出口商在收到信用证后经审核发现证约不符或有些不能接受或无法办到的条款，可按合同规定并结合自身需要向进口商及开证行提出修改信用证。同时，进口商因一些形势或情况的变化，也可以对信用证提出修改。

（一）信用证修改的常见场合

1. 出口方（受益人）要求修改信用证。

（1）由于信用证内容与合同不符。

（2）信用证中某些条款受益人无法办到，如软条款。

（3）货源或船期等出现问题，要求展期。

2. 进口方（开证申请人）要求展期。

（1）受国际市场行情变化需临时改变交货期或调整货物价格。

（2）由于进口国政策发生变化必须增加进口许可证等官方单据。

（3）由于政治等方面原因导致进出口风险增加而要求加投战争险等。

3. 开证行印制信用证时出现的文字错误或或传递上造成的错误必须修正。

（二）信用证修改的注意事项（根据 UCP 600 规定）

1. 需要修改的条款应一次性向对方提出，避免多次修改。

2. 任何条款的修改都必须取得当事人的同意后才能生效。对信用证修改内容的接受或拒绝有两种表示形式：

受益人明确作出接受或拒绝该信用证修改的通知；受益人以实际行动表示接受或拒绝。如受益人虽没明确表示接受修改但单据是按修改后的条款制作并提示则认为实际接受修改。

3. 对于信用证修改书的条款要么全部接受，要么全部拒绝。部分接受视为拒绝接受修改。

4. 信用证的修改书必须由原通知行通知方可生效；当事人直接寄送视为无效修改。

编号　No.：

信用证修改申请书
APPLICATION FOR AMENDMENT
TO DOCUMENTARY CREDIT

致 To：　光大银行湖南省分行　银行 Bank

信用证编号 L/C No.：　LCD6600201000165　开证日期 Issuing date：　181025

受益人 Beneficiary：　AGILENT TECHNOLOGIES MALAYSIA（SALES）PTE LTD

有效期 Expiry date：　190215

装运期 latest shipment date：　190202

金额 Amount：　USD235,000.00

请将上述信用证以□ 电讯□ 信函方式做如下修改：

Please amend the above credit by□ SWIFT or by□ AIRMAIL as follows：

最迟装运期展至 The latest shipment date extended To _____（mm）/ _____（dd）/ _____（yy）

有效期展至 The expiry date extended To _____（mm）/ _____（dd）/ _____（yy）

金额增加/减少 Increase/Decrease the amount by _____ 到 To

其他 Other terms：　Please amend 46A "+ AIR WAYBILL SHOWING 'FREIGHT PREPAID' NOTIFYING APPLICANT INDICATING FREIGHT AMOUNT AND CONSIGNED TO APPLICANT IN THREE ORIGINALS." To "+ AIR WAYBILL SHOWING 'FREIGHT PREPAID' NOTIFYING APPLICANT INDICATING FREIGHT AMOUNT AND CONSIGNED TO APPLICANT IN 1 ORIGINAL & 2 COPIES."

银行费用 Banking charges by：　受益人负担 Beneficiary，□申请人负担 Applicant。

信用证其他各项条款保持不变。

All other terms and conditions of the L/C remain unchanged.

除本申请书另有约定外，申请人和银行间的权利义务仍按原申请书（编号_____）执行。

Except as otherwise expressly stated herein, the right（s）and obligation（s）between the Applicant and the Issuing bank are still subject To the application（No. _____）.

申请人（公章）

（Stampand）Signature of Applicant

_____ 月（mm）_____ 日（dd）_____ 年（yy）

图 10-2　信用证修改申请书样本

四、开证申请书的填制操作

1. 申请书抬头（TO）。

（1）填写内容：

银行印制的申请书上事先都会印就开证银行的名称、地址，银行的 SWIFT CODE、TELEX NO 等也可同时显示。

（2）实例：

TO：HSBC BANK CANADA

2. 申请开证日期（DATE）。

（1）填写内容：

在申请书右上角填写实际申请日期。

（2）实例：

Date：July 15，2019

3. 信用证开立方式。

（1）填写内容：

在相对应的方式前打"×"。开证方式多为电开（BY TELETRANSMISSION），也可以是信开（BY AIRMAIL）、快递（BY EXPRESS）或简电（WITH BRIEF ADVICE BY TELE-TRANSMISSION）开立。SWIFT 形式信用证即为电开本，在 ISSUE BY TELETRANSMIS-SION 前打"×"。如果信用证是保兑或可转让的，应在此加注有关字样。

注意：根据银行开证申请书填写操作习惯，在正确选择项前要打"×"，而不是打"√"。

（2）实例：

（×）ISSUE BY TELETRANSMISSION

4. 信用证号码（L/C NUMBER）。

填写内容：此栏由银行填写。

5. 开证申请人（APPLICANT）。

（1）填写内容：

本栏目填写开证申请人，即进口合同买方的全称及详细地址，有的要求注明联系电话、传真号码等。

（2）实例：

APPLICANT：ELBY GIFTS INC. 879 INDUSTRIEL

BOIS DES FILION，QUEBEC，J6Z 4T3，CANADA

6. 受益人（BENEFICIARY）。

（1）填写内容：

本栏目填写受益人，即进口合同卖方的全称及详细地址。

（2）实例：

BENEFICIARY：PENGXING IMP&EXP COMPANY

LILING PENGXING CERAMIC FACTORY

WUSHI JIASHU LILING HUNAN，CHINA

7. 通知行（ADVISING BANK）。

（1）填写内容：

本栏目填写通知行名称、地址和 SWIFT 号码，若卖方没有提供，则由开证行指定。

（2）实例：

ADVISING BANK：BANK OF CHINA

8. 信用证金额（AMOUNT）。

（1）填写内容：

本栏目填写信用证金额的大小写，即分别用数字和文字两种形式表示，并且表明币制。如果允许有一定比率的上下浮动，要在信用证中明确表示出来。

（2）实例：

AMOUNT：USD27,010.40

SAY：U.S. DOLLARS TWENTY SEVEN THOUSAND AND TEN CENTS FORTY ONLY.

9. 到期日期和地点（DATE AND PLACE OF EXPIRY）。

（1）填写内容：

本栏目填写信用证的有效期及到期地点。到期地点一般情况下在受益人所在国，信用证有效期一般是最迟装运日期加交单期限。

（2）实例：

DATE AND PLACE OF EXPIRY：SEP.19，2016 IN COUNTRY OF BENEFICIARY

10. 分批装运（PARTIAL SHIPMENT）、转运（TRANSHIPMENT）。

（1）填写内容：

根据合同的实际规定打"×"进行选择。

（2）实例：

PARTIAL SHIPMENT：（×）ALLOWED

TRANSHIPMENT：（×）ALLOWED

11. 装运港/地（Loading on board/dispatch/taking in charge at/from）、目的港/地（For transportation To），最迟装运日期（DATE OF SHIPMENT）。

（1）填写内容：

按实际情况填写，如允许有转运地/港，也应清楚标明，一般在目的港后加"VIA"和转运港/地。

（2）实例：

Loading on board/dispatch/taking in charge at/from：SHENZHEN，CHINA

not later than SEP.5，2019

For transportation To：PRINCE RUPERT，BC

12. 指定银行和付款方式（CREDIT AVAILABLE WITH/BY）。

（1）填写内容：

填写指定的银行，并选择对应的付款方式。在所提供的即期（SIGHT PAYMENT）、承兑（ACCEPTANCE）、议付（NEGOTIATION）和延期付款（DEFERRED PAYMENT）四种信用证有效兑付方式中选择与合同要求一致的类型。

（2）实例：

CREDIT AVAILABLE WITHHSBC BANK CANADA

BY（×）NEGOTIATION

13．汇票条款（BENEFICIARY'S DRAFT）。

（1）填写内容：

若需要出具汇票，则本栏目填写汇票金额。具体金额应根据合同规定填写为：发票金额的一定百分比；发票金额的100%（全部货款都用信用证支付）；如部分信用证，部分托收时按信用证下的金额比例填写。

付款期限可根据实际填写即期或远期，如属远期则必须填写具体的天数。信用证条件下的付款人通常是开证行，也可能是开证行指定的另外一家银行。

（2）实例：

beneficiary's draft（s）for 100 % of invoice value

at ＊＊＊＊ sight

drawn onISSUING BANK

14．所需单据条款（DOCUMENTS REQUIRED）。

（1）填写内容：

根据合同的要求或实际需要选择所需提供的单据，在所需单据前画"×"进行标识。

各银行提供的申请书中已印就的单据条款通常为十几条，从上至下一般为发票、运输单据（提单、空运单、铁路运输单据及运输备忘录等）、保险单、装箱单、质量证书、装运通知和受益人证明等，最后一条是OTHER DOCUMENTS，IF ANY（其他单据）。如要求提交超过上述所列范围的单据就可以在此栏填写，比如有的合同要求出具CERTIFICATE OF BLACK LIST（黑名单证明）等。

申请人填制这部分内容时应依据合同规定，不能随意增加或减少。选中某单据后对该单据的具体要求（如一式几份、要否签字、正副本的份数、单据中应标明的内容等）也应如实填写，如申请书印制好的要求不完整应在其后予以补足。

（2）实例：

Documents required：(marked with X)

1．（×）Signed commercial invoice in ___3___ copies indicating L/C No. and Contract No.

2．（×）Full set of clean on board Bills of Lading made out To order and blank endorsed, marked "freight [X] To collect / [ ] prepaid [ ] showing freight amount" notifying _____APPLICANT_____ .

（ ）Airway bills/cargo receipt/copy of railway bills issued by _____showing "freight [ ] To collect/ [ ] prepaid [ ] indicating freight amount" and consigned To _____.

3．（ ）Insurance Policy/Certificate in _____ copies for _____% of the invoice value showing claims payable in _____ in currency of the draft, blank endorsed, covering All Risks, War Risks and _____ _____.

4．（ ）Packing List/Weight Memo in _____ copies indicating quantity, gross and weights of each package.

5．（ ）Certificate of Quantity/Weight in _____ copies issued by _____.

---

15. 商品描述（DESCRIPTION OF GOODS）。

（1）填写内容：

所有内容（品名、规格、包装、单价、唛头）都必须与合同内容相一致，价格条款里附带"AS PER INCOTERMS 2010"、数量条款中规定"MORE OR LESS"或"ABOUT"、使用某种特定包装物等特殊要求必须清楚列明。

（2）实例：

DESCRIPTION OFGOODS：

CERAMIC CUPS AND BOWLS AS PER S/C NO.：CB161039 CIF PRINCE RUPERT，BC ALL PACKED IN CARTONS.

16. 附加指示（ADDITIONAL INSTRUCTIONS）。

（1）填写内容：

该栏通常体现为以下一些条款：

+ ALL DOCUMENTS MUST INDICATE CONTRACT NUMBER（所有单据加列合同号码）。

+ ALL BANKING CHARGES OUTSIDE THE OPENING BANK ARE FOR BENEFICIARY'S ACCOUNT（所有开证行以外的银行费用由受益人承担）。

+ BOTH QUANTITY AND AMOUNT FOR EACH ITEM % MORE OR LESS ALLOWED（每项数量与金额允许 %增减）。

+ THIRD PARTY AS SHIPPER IS NOT ACCEPTABLE（第三方作为托运人是不能接受的）。

+ DOCUMENTS MUST BE PRESNTED WITHIN xxx DAYS AFTER THE DATE OF ISSUANCE OF THE TRANSPORT DOCUMENTS BUT WITHIN THE VALIDITY OF THIS CREDIT（单据必须在提单日后 xxx 天送达银行并且不超过信用证有效期）。

+ SHORT FORM/BLANK BACK/CLAUSED/CHARTER PARTY B/L IS UNACCEPTABLE（银行不接受略式/不清洁/租船提单）。

+ ALL DOCMENTS TO BE FORWARDED IN ONE COVER，UNLESS OTHERWISE STATED ABOVE（除非有相反规定，所有单据应一次提交）。

+ PREPAID FREIGHT DRAWN IN EXCESS OF L/C AMOUNT IS ACCEPTABLE AGAINST PRESENTATION OF ORIGINAL CHARGES VOUCHER ISSUED BY SHIPPING CO./AIR LINE OR ITS AGENT（银行接受凭船公司/航空公司或其代理人签发的正本运费收据索要超过信用证金额的预付运费）。

+ DOCUMENT ISSUED PRIOR TO THE DATE OF ISSUANCE OF CREDIT NOT ACCEPTABLE（不接受早于开证日出具的单据）。

如需要已印就的上述条款，可在条款前打"×"，对合同涉及但未印就的条款还可以做补充填写。

（2）实例：

Additional instructions：

1. （×）All banking charges outside the opening bank are for beneficiary's account.

2. （×）Documents must be presented within ___15___ days after date of issuance of the transport documents but within the validity of this credit.

3. （ ）Third party as shipper is not acceptable, Short Form/Blank back B/L is not acceptable.

---

17. 签章。

填写内容：授权人名称、签章、电话、传真等内容。

五、改证申请书的填制操作

1. 申请书抬头（TO）。

（1）填写内容：

开证银行的名称和地址，银行的 SWIFT CODE、TELEX NO 等也可同时显示。

（2）实例：

TO：HSBC BANK CANADA

2. 信用证号码（L/C No.）。

（1）填写内容：

申请修改的信用证号码。

（2）实例：

L/C No.：DC HMN214479

3. 开证日期（Issuing date）。

（1）填写内容：

申请修改的信用证开证日期。

（2）实例：

Issuing date：160720

4. 受益人（Beneficiary）。

（1）填写内容：

申请修改的信用证的受益人。

（2）实例：

Beneficiary：PENGXING IMP&EXP COMPANY LILING PENGXING CERAMIC FACTORY WUSHI JIASHU LILING HUNAN，CHINA

5. 信用证的有效期（Expiry date）。

（1）填写内容：

申请修改的信用证的有效期。

（2）实例：

Expiry date：190919

6. 最迟装运日（latest shipment date）。

（1）填写内容：

申请修改的信用证的最迟装运日。

（2）实例：

latest shipment date：190905

7. 信用证金额（Amount）。

（1）填写内容：

申请修改的信用证可使用的最高限额。

（2）实例：

Amount：USD27,010.40

8. 信用证修改书的传递方式。

（1）填写内容：

本栏目可选择 SWIFT 系统或者航空挂号信（AIRMAIL）的方式，在对应的项目前选择。

（2）实例：

Please amend the above credit by ?? SWIFT or by ?? AIRMAIL as follows

9. 信用证申请修改的具体条款。

（1）填写内容：

逐一列出需要修改的信用证条款。如：最迟装运日从×年×月×日延展至×年×月×日，信用证的有效期从×年×月×日延展至×年×月×日，信用证的金额从×增加至×等等。

（2）实例：

The latest shipment date extended To ___09___（mm）/ ___15___（dd）/ ___2019___（yy）

The expiry date extended To ___09___（mm）/ ___29___（dd）/ ___2019___（yy）

Increase the amount by ___USD27,010.40___ To ___USD28,000.00___

Other terms：___Please amend 43P "PARTIAL SHIPMENTS：NOT ALLOWED" To "PARTIAL SHIPMENTS：ALLOWED"___

10. 改证申请人的签章（Signature of Applicant）。

（1）填写内容：

改证申请人签章

（2）实例：

（Stampand）Signature of Applicant

Mary

11. 改证申请的日期（date）。

（1）填写内容：

改正申请书的填制日期。

（2）实例：

___07___（mm）___22___日（dd）___2019___年（yy）

第三节　任务模块

在该项目中单证员应完成的工作任务：

1. 根据第 CB161039 号合同填写开证申请书并向银行办理申请开证手续。

CONTRACT

Contract No.：CB161039   Date：JUL 5，2019

THE SELLER：PENGXING IMP&EXP COMPANY

LILING PENGXING CERAMIC FACTOR

WUSHI JIASHU LILING HUNAN，CHINA

TEL：86 – 731 – 23384199   FAX：86 – 731 – 23384298

THE BUYER：ELBY GIFTS INC.

879 INDUSTRIEL BOIS DES FILION

QUEBEC，J6Z 4T3，CANADA

TEL：514 – 420 – 0282   FAX：514 – 420 – 0322

This Contract is made by and between the Buyer and Seller，whereby the Buyer agrees To buy and the Selleragrees To sell the under mentioned goods on the terms and conditions stated below：

Description of Goods，Specifications，	Quantity (set)	Unit Price (U. S. D/set)	Amount (U. S. D)
Ceramic Cups and Bowls		C. I. F Prince Rupert	
V23 – 234	916	4. 05	3 693. 60
V23 – 234F	916	4. 05	3 693. 60
V23 – 235	1 520	2. 40	3 648. 00
V23 – 236	1 516	2. 10	3 175. 20
V23 – 237	1 488	1. 95	2 901. 60
V23 – 2348	1 520	2. 04	3 100. 80
36 – 062	1 528	2. 30	3 514. 40
36 – 063	1 496	2. 16	3 171. 52
As per the P/I No.：CCB23 – 36			
Total	10 888		26 898. 72

Say Total：U. S DOLLARS TWENTY SIX THOUSAND EIGHT HUNDRED AND NINETY EIGHT AND CENTS SEVENTY TWO（USD26898. 72）ONLY.

PACKING：4 sets packed in a carton（V 23 – 234/V23 – 234F），8 sets packed in a carton for others.

TRANSPORT DETAILS：the goods should shipped on or before：5th Sep，2019，from Shenzhen，China To Prince Rupert

Canada，transshipment and partial shipment are all allowed.

INSURANCE：To be effected by the Seller for 110% of invoice value covering all risks and S. R. C. C as per C. I. C of PICC dated 01/01/1981.

PAYMENT: By irrevocable documentary letter of credit at sight, reaching the seller not later than Aug 5, 2016 and remain valid for negotiation in China for 15 days after shipment.

DOCUMENTS:

+ Signed commercial invoice one original and three copies.

+ Full set of clean on board ocean Bill of Lading made To order of issuing bank.

+ Packing List one original and two copies.

+ Insurance policy endorsed in blank.

+ GSP Form A certified bygovernment authority.

INSPECTION: Quality /Quantity/Weight Discrepancy and Claim: In case the quality and /or quantity/weight are found by the Buyer not To conform with the contract after arrival of the goods at the final destination, the Buyer may lodge a claim against the seller supported by a survey report issued by an inspection organization agreed upon by both parties with the exception of those claims for which the insurance company and /or the shipping company are To be held responsible. Claim for quality discrepancy should be filed by the Buyer within 60 days after arrival of the goods at the final destination while for quantity / weight discrepancy claim should be filed by the Buyer within 30 days after arrival of the goods at the final destination.

FORCE MAJEURE: The Seller shall not be held responsible for failure or delay in delivery of the entire or portion of the goods under this contract in consequence of any Force Major incidents.

ARBITRATION: All disputes in connection with this Contract or the execution thereof shall be settled through friendly negotiations. If no settlement can be reached, the case shall then be submitted To the Foreign Trade Arbitration Commission of the China Council for the Promotion of International Trade, Beijing, for settlement by arbitration in accordance with the Commission's Provisional Rules of Procedure. The award rendered by the Commission shall be final and binding on both parties. The arbitration expenses shall be borne by the losing party unless otherwise award by the arbitration organization.

Signed by:

THE SELLER:	**THE BUYER**:
PENGXING IMP&EXP COMPANY	ELBY GIFTS INC.
LILING PENGXING CERAMIC FACTORY	
李 望	**Camp Wolf**

IRREVOCABLE DOCUMENTARY CREDIT APPLICATION

To: HSBC BANK CANADA	Date: Jul. 15, 2019

☐Issue by airmail ☐With brief advice by teletransmission ☐Issue by express delivery (×) Issue by teletransmission (which shall be the operative instrument)	Credit No. Sep. 19,2019 IN COUNTRY OF Date and place of expiry BENEFICIARY
Applicant ELBY GIFTS INC. 879 INDUSTRIEL BOIS DES FILION, QUEBEC, J6Z 4T3, CANADA	Beneficiary (Full name and address) PENGXING IMP&EXP COMPANY LILING PENGXING CERAMIC FACTORY WUSHI JIASHU LILING HUNAN, CHINA
Advising Bank	Amount USD27,010. 40 SAY: U. S. DOLLARS TWENTY SEVEN THOUSAND AND TEN CENTS FORTY ONLY.

Partial shipments (×) allowed ☐not allowed	Transshipment (×) allowed ☐not allowed	Credit available with ANY BANK
Loading on board/dispatch/taking in charge at/from SHENZHEN, CHINA not later than For transportation To:		By ☐sight payment ☐acceptance (×) negotiation ☐deferred payment at against the documents detailed herein (×) and beneficiary's draft (s) for __100__ % of invoice
FOB CFR CIF ☐or other terms		value at _____ * * * * _____ sight drawn on ISSUING BANK

Documents required: (marked with X)

1. (×) Signed commercial invoice in __4__ copies indicating L/C No. and Contract No.
2. (×) Full set of clean on board Bills of Lading made out To order and blank endorsed, marked "freight [ ] To collect /[ ]pre-paid[ ] showing freight amount" notifying __APPLICANT (STATING FULL NAME AND ADDRESS)__.
   ( ) Airway bills/cargo receipt/copy of railway bills issued by _____showing "freight [ ] To collect/ [ ] prepaid [ ] indicating freight amount" and consigned To _____.
3. (×) Insurance Policy/Certificate in __3__ copies for __110__ % of the invoice value showing claims payable in __CANADA__ in currency of the draft, blank endorsed, covering All Risks, War Risks and __S. R. C. C.__ .
4. (×) Packing List/Weight Memo in __3__ copies indicating quantity, gross and weights of each package.
5. ( ) Certificate of Quantity/Weight in _____ copies issued by _____.
6. ( ) Certificate of Quality in _____ copies issued by[ ]manufacturer/[ ]public recognized surveyor _____.
7. (×) Certificate of Origin in __3__ copies.
8. ( ) Beneficiary's certified copy of fax / telex dispatched To the applicant within _____ days after shipment advising L/C No., name of vessel, date of shipment, name, quantity, weight and value of goods.

(×) Other documents, if any
SHIPPING NOTE INCLUDING SHIPPING MARKS, CTN NO. , B/L NO. , QUANTITY , VESSELS NAME, VOYAGE NO. , SHOULD BE SENT TO THE ISSUING BANK ON THE DATE OF SHIPMENT

Description of goods:
CERAMIC CUPS AND BOWLS AS PER S/C NO. : CB161039 CIF PRINCE RUPERT, BC
ALL PACKED IN CARTONS.

Additional instructions:
1. (×) All banking charges outside the opening bank are for beneficiary's account.
2. (×) Documents must be presented within _____ days after date of issuance of the transport documents but within the validity of this credit.
3. ( ) Third party as shipper is not acceptable, Short Form/Blank back B/L is not acceptable.
4. (×) Both quantity and credit amount _____% more or less are allowed.
5. (×) All documents must be sent To issuing bank by courier/speed post in one lot.
   ( ) Other terms, if any

2. 根据长沙鹏兴公司的改证函填写改证申请书并办理申请改证手续。

改证函如下：

Dear sirs，

We here have received your L/C No. DC HMN214479 for Contract No. CB161039. After checking，we would request you to make the following amendments：

（1）The latest date of shipment should be extended to Sep 15，2019.

（2）The L/C's expiry date should extended to Sep 29，2019.

（3）Increase the amount to U. S. D28，000.00

（4）Partial shipment is allowed.

Yours truly

No. ：

APPLICATION FOR AMENDMENT

TO DOCUMENTARY CREDIT

To：　HSBC BANK CANADA

L/C No. ：　DC HMN214479　　Issuing date：190720

Beneficiary：　PENGXING IMP&EXP COMPANY LILING PENGXING CERAMIC FACTORY WUSHI JIASHU LILING HUNAN，CHINA

Expiry date：　160919

latest shipment date：　160905

Amount：　USD27，010.40

Please amend the above credit by□　SWIFT or by□　AIRMAIL as follows：

The latest shipment date extended To　09　（mm）/　15　（dd）/　2019　（yy）

The expiry date extended To　09　（mm）/　29　（dd）/　2019　（yy）

Increase the amount by　USD27，010.40　To　USD28，000.00

Other terms：　Please amend 43P "PARTIAL SHIPMENTS：NOT ALLOWED" To " + PARTIAL SHIP-MENTS：ALLOWED"

Banking charges by：Beneficiary，□Applicant 。

All other terms and conditions of the L/C remain unchanged.

Except as otherwise expressly stated herein，the right（s）and obligation（s）between the Applicant and the Issuing bank are still subject To the application（No. _____）.

（Stampand）Signature of Applicant

07　（mm）22 日（dd）2019 年（yy）

第四节　任务拓展模块

能力实训项目 1：填写开证申请书和开证申请书

进口商 M/S. MEMORY STEEL CORPORATION 根据第 SSW0803 号合同，2019 年 8 月 20 日，业务员 John Lee 填写了开证申请书并办理申请开证手续。

SALESCONTRACT

Contract   No. : SSW0803

Date: AUG 15, 2019

THE SELLER: JIANGSU I – TOUCH BUSINESS SERVICE LTD,

　　　　　　ROOM 117, JIANGSU EDIFICE

　　　　　　ZHANGJIAGANG FREE TRADE ZONE,

　　　　　　JIANGSU, CHINA TEL: 86 – 516 – 56363783

THE BUYER: M/S. MEMORY STEEL CORPORATION

　　　　　　73/A, LAL MOHAN SHAHA STREET

　　　　　　(DHOLAIKHAL), DHAKA – 1100.

　　　　　　BANGLADESH.

This Contract is made by and between the Buyer and Seller, whereby the Buyer agrees To buy and the Seller agrees To sell the under mentioned goods on the terms and conditions stated below:

Description of Goods, Specifications,	Quantity (set)	Unit Price (U. S. D/set)	Amount (U. S. D)
		C. F. R	CHITTAGONG
201/2B SECONDARY GRADE STAINLESS	1.2 * 1619 * 2438	1.40	7 806.40
STEEL SHEET OF WIDTH1619MM OR MORE	1.5 * 1619 * 2438	1.40	4 547.20
THICKNESS 1MM TO 3MM, QTY: 25,	2.0 * 1619 * 2438	1.40	16 282.00
000KGS AT THE RATE OF USD1.40/KG. AS	3.0 * 1619 * 2438	1.40	6 364.40
PER BENEFICIARY'S PROFORMA INVOIVE			
NO. SK20160802 – 001 DATED AUG 2, 2016			35 000.00
Total			

Say Total: U. S DOLLARS THIRTY FIVE THOUSAND ONLY.

PACKING: Standard export packing on pallets.

TRANSPORT DETAILS: the goods should shipped before: 9th Oct, 2019, from any Chinese port To Chittagong Bangladesh,

transsshipment and partial shipment are allowed.

PAYMENT: By sight L/C and remain valid for negotiation in China for 15 days after shipment.

DOCUMENTS:

　+ Signed commercial invoice in triplicate, certifying the goods are of Chinese origin and being imported against IRC No. BA – 0171646, VAT Registration No. 9141093671..

　+ Full set (3/3) of clean on board ocean Bill of Lading made out To order of shipper and blank endorsed.

+ Packing List in triplicate.

+ Certificate of origin by CCPIT.

+ Beneficiary's Declaration certifying that the country of origin has been printed on goods packing bag.

INSPECTION: Quality /Quantity/Weight Discrepancy and Claim: In case the quality and /or quantity/weight are found by the Buyer not To conform with the contract after arrival of the goods at the final destination, the Buyer may lodge a claim against the seller supported by a survey report issued by an inspection organization agreed upon by both parties with the exception of those claims for which the insurance company and /or the shipping company are To be held responsible. Claim for quality discrepancy should be filed by the Buyer within 60 days after arrival of the goods at the final destination while for quantity / weight discrepancy claim should be filed by the Buyer within 30 days after arrival of the goods at the final destination.

FORCE MAJEURE: The Seller shall not be held responsible for failure or delay in delivery of the entire or portion of the goods under this contract in consequence of any Force Major incidents.

ARBITRATION: All disputes in connection with this Contract or the execution thereof shall be settled through friendly negotiations. If no settlement can be reached, the case shall then be submitted To the Foreign Trade Arbitration Commission of the China Council for the Promotion of International Trade, Beijing, for settlement by arbitration in accordance with the Commission's Provisional Rules of Procedure. The award rendered by the Commission shall be final and binding on both parties. The arbitration expenses shall be borne by the losing party unless otherwise award by the arbitration organization.

Signed by:

THE SELLER:	**THE BUYER**:
JIANGSU I – TOUCH BUSINESS	M/S. MEMORY STEEL
CORPORATION. SERVICE LTD	
彭　婷	John Lee

开证申请
IRREVOCABLE DOCUMENTARYCREDIT APPLICATION

To:	Date:
☐ Issue by airmail ☐With brief advice by teletransmission ☐ Issue by express delivery ☐ Issue by teletransmission (which shall be the operative instrument)	Credit No. Date and place of expiry
Applicant	Beneficiary (Full name and address)
Advising Bank	Amount

Partial shipments ( ) allowed ☐not allowed	Transshipment ( ) allowed ☐not allowed	Credit available with
Loading on board/dispatch/taking in charge at/from not later than For transportation To: ☐FOB ☐CFR ☐CIF ☐or other terms		By ☐sight payment ☐acceptance ☐negotiation ☐deferred payment at against the documents detailed herein ☐and beneficiary's draft (s) for _____% of invoice value at _____ sight drawn on ISSUING BANK

Documents required: (marked with X)

1. (   ) Signed commercial invoice in _____copies indicating L/C No. and Contract No.
2. (   ) Full set of clean on board Bills of Lading made out To order and blank endorsed, marked "freight 〔   〕To collect / 〔   〕 prepaid 〔   〕 showing freight amount" notifying _____.
   (   ) Airway bills/cargo receipt/copy of railway bills issued by _____ showing "freight 〔   〕 To collect/〔   〕prepaid 〔   〕 indicating freight amount" and consigned To _____.
3. (   ) Insurance Policy/Certificate in _____ copies for _____% of the invoice value showing claims payable in _____ in currency of the draft, blank endorsed, covering All Risks and _____.
4. (   ) Packing List/Weight Memo in _____ copies indicating quantity, gross and weights of each package.
5. (   ) Certificate of Quantity/Weight in _____ copies issued by _____.
6. (   ) Certificate of Quality in _____copies issued by 〔   〕 manufacturer/〔   〕 public recognized surveyor _____.
7. (   ) Certificate of Origin in _____copies.
8. (   ) Beneficiary's certified copy of fax / telex dispatched To the applicant within _____ days after shipment advising L/C No., name of vessel, date of shipment, name, quantity, weight and value of goods.
   (   ) Other documents, if any

Description of goods:

Additional instructions:

1. (   ) All banking charges outside the opening bank are for beneficiary's account.
2. (   ) Documents must be presented within _____days after date of issuance of the transport documents but within the validity of this credit.
3. (   ) Third party as shipper is not acceptable, Short Form/Blank back B/L is not acceptable.
4. (   ) Both quantity and credit amount _____% more or less are allowed.
5. (   ) All documents must be sent To issuing bank by courier/speed post in one lot.
   (   ) Other terms, if any

能力实训项目 2：改证申请书及手续办理

进口商 M/S. MEMORY STEEL CORPORATION 业务员 John Lee 根据出口商的改证函和本公司的需求，于 2019 年 8 月 27 日填写改证申请书并办理申请改证手续。

Dear sirs,

We here have received your L/C No. DC HMN214479 for Contract No. CB161039. After checking, we would request you to make the following amendments:

（1）The latest date of shipment should be extendedto Oct 09, 2019.

（2）The L/C's expiry date should extended to Sep 24, 2019, and should expiry in China.

（3）Transshipment is allowed.

（4）Our company correct name is JIANGSU I – TOUCH BUSINESS SERVICE LTD.

Yours truly

No. :

APPLICATION FOR AMENDMENT
TO DOCUMENTARY CREDIT

To： L/C No. ：　　　　　　　　　Issuing date：

Beneficiary：

Expiry date：

latest shipment date：

Amount：

Please amend the above credit by 　□SWIFT or by 　□AIRMAIL as follows：

1.

2.

3.

......

Other terms：

Banking charges by： 　□Beneficiary，　　□Applicant 。

All other terms and conditions of the L/C remain unchanged.

Except as otherwise expressly stated herein, the right（s）and obligation（s）between the Applicant and the Issuing bank are still subject To the application（No. _____）.

（Stampand）Signature of Applicant

_____（mm）_____（dd）_____（yy）

能力实训项目 3：填写开证申请书

进口商 CONSTRUCTION MOUDULAR SPECIALIST 根据第 BFF0606 号合同，2019 年 7 月 5 日，业务员 Rechard 填写了开证申请书并办理申请开证手续。

销售合同：

CONTRACT

No. : BFF0606   Date: JUL 1, 2019

THE SELLER: PRIMA CONSTRUCTION MATERIOLS CO. , LTD

            1401 ROOM, 38 BUILDING, CHUANGYE GARDEN

            BAOAN DISTRICT, SHENZHEN, CHINA

THE BUYER: CONSTRUCTION MOUDULAR SPECIALIST

            POSTAL: 16 HARVEY RD. ,

            SHENTON PK, WA 6008 AUSTRALIA

This Contract is made by and between the Buyer and Seller, whereby the Buyer agrees To buy and the Seller agrees To sell the under mentioned goods on the terms and conditions stated below:

Description of Goods, Specifications,	Quantity (SQM)	Unit Price (U. S. D/SQM)	Amount (U. S. D)
BAMBOO FLOORING		CIF FREMENTLE	
ITEM 1	100	20. 00	2 000. 00
ITEM 2	100	39. 50	3 950. 00
AS PER PI NO. : BFF0610			
Total	200		5 950. 00

Say Total: U. S DOLLARS FIFTY NINE HUNDRED AND FIFTY (USD5950) ONLY.

PACKING: ALL PACKING IN SEA WORTHY CARTONS.

TRANSPORT DETAILS: the goods should shipped on or before: 5th Sep, 2019, from Shenzhen, China To Frementle Australia, transshipment and partial shipment are all allowed.

INSURANCE: To be effected by the Seller for 110% of invoice value covering ICC (A) risk and ICC (War Risk) .

PAYMENT: By irrevocable documentary letter of credit at 30 days after sight, reaching the seller not later than Jul 30, 2019 and remain valid for negotiation in China for 15 days after shipment.

DOCUMENTS:

+ Signed commercial invoice three originals and three copies.

+ Full set of clean on board ocean Bill of Lading made To order.

+ Packing List three originals and two copies.

+ Insurance policy endorsed in blank and in triplicate.

+ Certificate of Origin in China issued by official authority.

开证申请
IRREVOCABLE DOCUMENTARYCREDIT APPLICATION

To：	Date：
☐ Issue by airmail ☐With brief advice by teletransmission ☐ Issue by express delivery ☐ Issue by teletransmission (which shall be the operative instrument)	Credit No. Date and place of expiry
Applicant	Beneficiary (Full name and address)
Advising Bank	Amount

Partial shipments ( ) allowed ☐not allowed	Transshipment ( ) allowed ☐not allowed	Credit available with
Loading on board/dispatch/taking in charge at/from not later than For transportation To：		By ☐sight payment ☐acceptance ☐negotiation ☐deferred payment at against the documents detailed herein ☐and beneficiary's draft (s) for _____ % of in-voice value at _____ sight drawn on ISSUING BANK
☐FOB ☐CFR ☐CIF ☐or other terms		

Documents required： (marked with X)

1. ( ) Signed commercial invoice in _____ copies indicating L/C No. and Contract No.
2. ( ) Full set of clean on board Bills of Lading made out To order and blank endorsed, marked "freight [ ]To collect / [ ] prepaid [ ] showing freight amount" notifying _____ .
   ( ) Airway bills/cargo receipt/copy of railway bills issued by _____showing "freight [ ] To collect/[ ]prepaid [ ] indicating freight amount" and consigned To _____ .
3. ( ) Insurance Policy/Certificate in _____ copies for _____% of the invoice value showing claims payable in _____ in currency of the draft, blank endorsed, covering All Risks and _____ .
4. ( ) Packing List/Weight Memo in _____ copies indicating quantity, gross and weights of each package.
5. ( ) Certificate of Quantity/Weight in _____ copies issued by _____ .
6. ( ) Certificate of Quality in _____ copies issued by [ ] manufacturer/[ ] public recognized surveyor _____ .
7. ( ) Certificate of Origin in _____ copies.
8. ( ) Beneficiary's certified copy of fax / telex dispatched To the applicant within _____ days after shipment advising L/C No. , name of vessel, date of shipment, name, quantity, weight and value of goods.
   ( ) Other documents, if any

Description of goods：

Additional instructions：

1. ( ) All banking charges outside the opening bank are for beneficiary's account.
2. ( ) Documents must be presented within _____ days after date of issuance of the transport documents but within the validity of this credit.
3. ( ) Third party as shipper is not acceptable, Short Form/Blank back B/L is not acceptable.
4. ( ) Both quantity and credit amount _____ % more or less are allowed.
5. ( ) All documents must be sent To issuing bank by courier/speed post in one lot.
   ( ) Other terms, if any

能力实训项目 4：改证申请书及手续办理

进口商 CONSTRUCTION MOUDULAR SPECIALIST 业务员 JACKY 根据出口商的改证函和本公司的需求，于 2019 年 7 月 16 日填写改证申请书并办理申请改证手续。

Dear sirs,

We here have received your L/C No. DC HMN214479 for Contract No. CB161039. After checking, we would request you to make the following amendments：

(1) The L/C'S total amount is USD6,840.00

(2) The L/C is at sight.

(3) The freight is prepaid.

(4) The PI NO. is BFF0610.

Yours truly

No. :

APPLICATION FOR AMENDMENT
TO DOCUMENTARY CREDIT

To： L/C No. ：   Issuing date：

Beneficiary：

Expiry date：

latest shipment date：

Amount：

Please amend the above credit by □SWIFT or by □AIRMAIL as follows：

1.

2.

3.

……

Other terms：

Banking charges by： □Beneficiary, □Applicant 。

All other terms and conditions of the L/C remain unchanged.

Except as otherwise expressly stated herein, the right (s) and obligation (s) between the Applicant and the Issuing bank are still subject To the application (No. _____).

(Stampand) Signature of Applicant

_____ (mm) _____ (dd) _____ (yy)

第五节　学习导航

一、参考资料

[1] 章安平. 外贸单证操作 [M]. 北京：高等教育出版社，2008.

[2] 刘启萍，周树玲. 外贸单证 [M]. 北京：对外经贸大学出版社，2008.

[3] 方士华，国际结算 [M]. 沈阳：东北财经大学出版社，2016.

[4] 吴轶群，国际商务单证操作 [M]. 青岛：中国海洋大学出版社，2018.

二、自主学习平台

[1] 全国外贸单证员考试中心。

[2] 外贸经理人微信公众号。

[3] 外贸单证课程国家教学资源库。

项目十一
跨境电商电子单证业务

第一节　项目描述与目标

一、项目描述

◆开篇业务引入

随着信息技术的发展和"互联网＋"时代的到来，跨境电子商务已成为当前对外贸易发展的一种新业态，外贸企业在利用展会等传统平台开发 B2B 市场的同时，也要充分利用跨境电商平台发展 B2C 和 C2C 等市场，长沙鹏兴进出口有限公司业务部通过阿里巴巴旗下的速卖通平台开始了跨境电商业务，将最新的马克杯系列产品直接销售到国外消费者手中，单证员李望也由此总结了跨境电商单证与传统外贸单证的区别。

◆项目预期目标

通过跨境电商中各类电子单证的学习，学生能理解跨境电商中三大单证的基本概念、特点，掌握跨境电商电子单证的使用，具备在跨境电商当中使用电子单证能力。

在项目实施过程中，通过对跨境电商中的电子单证的学习，了解电子单证在跨境电商实际操作中的重要性，逐渐培养跨境电商实务操作的能力。

表 11-1　项目预期目标

目标类型	熟练掌握跨境电商当中的电子单证
知识目标	熟悉跨境电商的各大单证概念和特点
	了解电子单证在跨境电商中如何使用
	掌握在跨境电商电子单证的缮制
能力目标	能区分不同种类的电子单证
	在跨境电商平台中准确缮制单证
职业素质目标	独立业务操作能力
	熟练使用跨境电商平台中电子单证

二、项目实施条件

1. 向学生提供三大电子单证样单，指出电子单证的必要项目和非必要项目。
2. 学生能够在跨境电商实训室根据提供的业务资料缮制相关电子单证。

3. 指导教师掌握核心的跨境电商平台的业务操作，具备一定的跨境电商理论。

第二节   知识模块

一、跨境电商单证知识背景

随着互联网消除信息不对称和世界扁平化、网络支付工具的流行，以及快递渠道的完善，网络贸易的全球化壁垒正被迅速推平。在经济危机的影响下，出于资金风险的考虑，以"集装箱"式大额交易为代表的传统外贸正在倾向于将大额采购转变为中小额采购，长期采购变为短期采购。在此背景下，互联网便捷的优势使网上小额批发或零售的井喷水到渠成。但是目前外贸电子商务的配套环境还不成熟，在支付、汇兑、物流、通关等方面还存在一定的不便。比如，按照以往的规定，电商通过快件、邮件方式销往国外的出口商品，不能办理结汇手续，也不能享受出口退税的鼓励政策。为适应跨境电子商务的发展态势，国家也出台了相应的政策，旨在规范、保护和推动跨境电子商务的健康、有序发展，从而有效解决跨境贸易电子商务出境商品出口退税和结汇问题。

其中海关总署 56 号公告中提到的跨境电商通关服务平台是为外贸企业进出口通关提供便利服务的系统平台。全国首个统一版海关总署跨境贸易电子商务通关服务平台在广东东莞正式上线运营。海关总署建设全国统一版的通关服务平台，意为统一报关流程。该平台所上传的数据可直接对接海关总署内部系统，节省报关时间，提升通关效率。跨境电子商务流程如图 11－1 所示，其中三单是指电商企业提供的报关单、支付企业提供的支付清单、物流企业提供的物流运单。"三单"数据确认无误后即可放行。

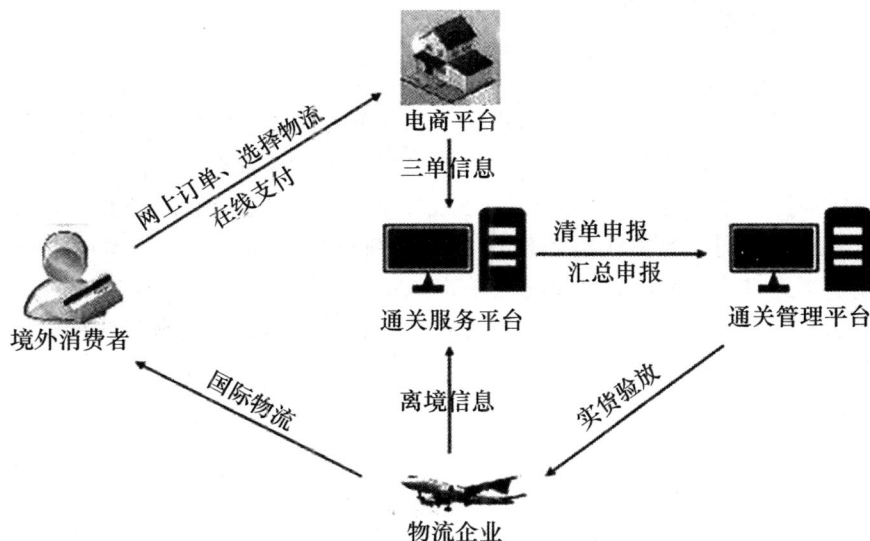

图 11－1   跨境电子商务业务流程图

除了跨境电商通关服务平台，目前还涌现出以下两种跨境电商服务平台：

（1）跨境电商公共服务平台，"公共服务"的含义具有双向性，一方面为各地政府的职能部门之间搭建公共信息平台；另一方面是服务于大众（主要是指外贸企业）。阳光化的外贸环节众多，涉及国检（检验检疫）、国税（纳税退税）、外管局（支付结汇）、商委或外经贸委（企业备案、数据统计）等政府职能部门及银行结汇等，传统外贸企业需一一对接。

（2）跨境电商综合服务平台，其"综合"的含义囊括了金融、通关、物流、退税、外汇等代理服务。跨境贸易的链条很长，涉及的操作环节众多，对于传统中小外贸企业和个人卖家来说难以吃透且工作量极其繁重。综合服务平台的出现可以一站式解决这部分人遇到的外贸问题，是真正服务于基层的平台。业内知名的综合服务平台有：阿里巴巴建设的一达通、大龙网建设的海通易达等。综上，跨境电商服务平台在降低外贸门槛、处理外贸问题、降低外贸风险等问题上为跨境电商的发展提供了便利和解决方案。但是由于服务平台建设不统一，服务内容有所差异，界面操作也不同，特别是对企业上传信息的要求和定义也各有不同。因此，有必要建立相应的电子单证基本信息描述规范，从而规范对相关信息的描述，促进跨境电商服务行业的健康发展。

跨境贸易电子商务一般进口模式：跨境电商企业通过事前备案，将企业信息、商品信息进行备案。当境内消费者成功支付订单后，跨境电商企业将订单信息发送至服务平台进行申报；支付企业将订单支付信息发送至服务平台进行申报；跨境物流企业在成功预订舱单信息后，将对应的跨境贸易相关的舱单信息（含运单信息）发送至服务平台进行申报。服务平台集齐三单信息后，自动生成清单供有报关报检资质的企业进行申报。清单经海关、检验检疫审核后，若无异常，则放行进入终端配送环节。

二、电子运单

1. 电子运单的概念。

电子运单，即将货运单抛弃传统的八联纸质运单的形式，而以一份电子数据的形式存在信息系统中，类似"E - TICKET"，即电子客票，这是实现电子物流的重要标志。电子运单具有操作便捷、数据准确、绿色环保等优点和功能，不仅能够提高运输公司的服务质量，更是能为运输公司、海关联检和代理企业节约不少成本，也符合节能减排政策。同时，更为航空货运进入互联网时代奠定了一定的技术基础。

电子运单的信息包括基本信息、货物（物品）信息、寄件方信息、收件方信息和承运方信息，电子运单信息模型见图 11 - 2。

```
                              电子运单信息
   ┌──────────┬──────────────┬──────────────┬──────────────┬──────────────┐
基本信息      货物(物品)信息    寄件方信息        收件方信息       承运方信息
```

基本信息	货物(物品)信息	机构信息（寄件方）	机构信息（收件方）	机构信息（承运方）
·单证号	·类型	·机构名称	·机构名称	·承运方名称
·日期	·品名	·机构代码(编号)	·机构代码(编号)	·承运方网址
·订单号	·英文说明	·税号	·税号	·承运方有务电话
·业务类型	·成分说明			·手机短信查询号码
·货物(物品)种类	·件数	寄件人信息	收件人信息	·收寄局
·货物(物品)重量	·单价重量	·国家(地区)名称	·国家(地区)名称	·收寄日期
·货物(物品)体积	·单价	·国家识别编号	·国家识别编号	
·包装类型	·产地	·城市	·城市	承运人信息
·包装类型代码	·货物(物品)英文	·寄件人姓名	·寄件人姓名	·收件员姓名
·保险金额	·说明	·寄件人地址	·寄件人地址	·收件员编号
·保价金额	·内件成分说明	·邮编	·邮编	·收个员电话
·包装费		·联系电话	·联系电话	·派件员姓名
·运费				·派件员编号
·其它费用				·派件员电话
·费用合计				

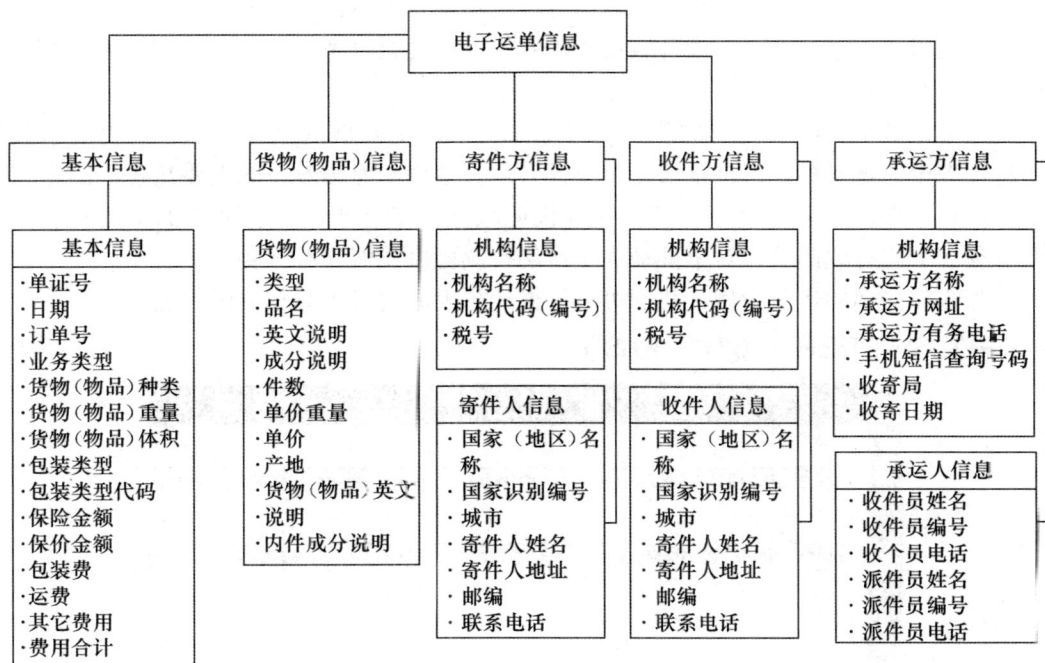

图 11-2　电子单证信息模型图

2. 电子运单的特点。

与纸制运单相比，电子运单具有以下特点：

（1）处理效率高。除人工填写外，纸制运单普遍采用针式打印机进行信息打印，打印速度一般在 500～700 张/小时之间。电子运单采用热敏条码打印机进行信息打印，打印速度在 2500～3600 张/小时之间，其打印效率比纸制运单快 2～5 倍。此外，电子运单的打印信息由对接的计算机信息系统自动转入，且无须打印服务协议，大大节省了信息录入时间，提升了快件处理效率。有快递公司反映，一个 50 人的揽收团队使用电子运单后可降低至 10 人，人力成本降低 5 倍以上。

（2）生产成本低。电子商务用户使用的电子运单一般宽为 100 毫米，长不超过 200 毫米，其规格尺寸仅为纸制运单的一半。相比纸制运单，电子运单的纸张用量整体减少 70%以上。目前，纸制运单的售价约为 0.19 元/张，电子运单的售价约为 0.09 元/张。以 2015年快递业务量 206 亿件、电子运单的用量占快递业务量 60%计算，仅电子运单的生产成本就节约了 12 亿元。再加上打印成本的减少，电子运单的整体生产成本比纸制运单降低60%～70%以上。

（3）环保效果好。电子运单不仅大幅减少了纸张原材料的消耗，而且也相应减少了制作过程中的碳排放量和有害物质的释放量。此外，标准还首次对电子运单的用纸和用胶的环保性能提出限制要求，更加有利于节能减排，更加有利于环境保护，符合国家生态文明建设和国家邮政局关于推进绿色邮政建设的战略部署。

（4）用户权益得以更好保障。针对电子运单使用过程中出现的纸张质量不合格、打印信息不统一、服务协议不明确等用户普遍关心的问题，标准都设定了相应的技术条款，从电子运单的纸张定量、保存期限、信息内容、提示信息等方面予以明确规定，既充分考虑了企业发展需要，推动企业转型升级提质增效，同时也充分考虑了用户使用需要，切实保护用户权益和用户信息安全。

由此可以看出，电子运单的应用是产业融合、市场发展的重要产物，是行业科技创新、科技进步的重要标志，也是快递企业提升运行效率、经营效益的重要途径。制定《快递电子运单》邮政行业标准，有利于提升快递服务质量和水平，有利于保护用户合法权益，有利于实施有效监管，对于推动快递市场持续健康发展具有重要意义。

以为联邦快递的运单为例，我们可以根据运单上的内容填写相关的信息

（一）SHIPPER（发件人资料）

1. SHIPPER'S UPS ACCOUNT NO.——发件人帐号，是 UPS 分给发件人的，例如：HK-UPS：0E2R89。

2. NAME OF SENDER：发件人名。

3. TELEPHONE NO：发件方的联络电话。

4. COMPANY NAME AND ADDRESS：发件人公司和地址（包括邮编及国家）。

（二）RECEIVER（收件人资料）

1. CONSIGNEE'S ACCOUNT NO：收件人帐号（UPS 到付帐号，一般到付件才需要填写此项）。

2. NAME OF CONTACT PERSON：收件人名。

3. TELEPHONE NO.：收件方联络电话。

4. COMPANY NAME AND ADDRESS：收件人公司、地址（包括邮编及国家）。

（三）PAYMENT OF CHARGES（付款选项）

1. BILL SHIPPING CHARGES TO：运费的支付。

（1）SHIPPER（S）：发件人付运费——CREDIT CARD：信用卡；CHEQUE：支票；CASH：现金。

（2）RECEIVER（R）：收件人付运费。

（3）THIRD PARTY：第三方付运费（我司现一般不做第三方付费）。

2. BILL DUTIES AND TAXES TO（DUTIABLE SHIPMENTS ONLY）：关税/税款的支付。

（1）SHIPPER（S）：发件人付关税（一般情况下，需要单独确认关税预付，且会收取手续费用）。

（2）RECEIVER（R）收件人付关税。

（3）THIRD PARTY：第三方付关税（我司现一般不做第三方付费）。

（四）SERVICE LEVEL（服务方式）

1. EXPRESS/PLUS：UPS 全球特快加急服务（一般情况下，需要单独确认特快加急）。

2. EXPRESS：UPS 全球特快服务。

3. EXPRESS SAVER：UPS 全球速快服务；此种方式为当前 UPS 常用方式。

4. EXPEDITED：UPS 全球快捷服务。

（五）SHIPMENT INFORMATION：装运资料

1. NO. OF PACKAGES IN SHIPMENT：包裹件数。

2. TOTAL ACTUAL WEIGHT OF SHIPMENT：包裹总实际重量。

3. TOTAL DIMENSIONAL WEIGHT OF SHIPMENT：包裹总体积重量。

4. ZONE：目的地国家分区号（可参照 UPS 分区表）。

5. 包装方式（括号内为老 UPS 运单的内容）。

（1）ENV UPS（UPS EXPRESS ENVELOPE）：UPS 文件封。

（2）（UPS EXPRESS PAK）：UPS PAK 袋。

（3）10KG BOX：UPS 10KG 标准箱（一般不能勾此项，UPS 会按勾的收费）。

（4）25KG BOX：UPS 25KG 标准箱（一般不能勾此项，UPS 会按勾的收费）。

（5）OTHER————：其它包装。（一般选择项）。

6. DESCRIPTION OF GOODS：包裹描述（货物名称及数量）。

7. DECLARE VALUE：申报价值。

（1）DECLARE VALUEFOR CARRIAGE ONLY（SPECIFY CURRENCY）：此为是否购买保险（一般不填，如填写则为需要购买保险）。

（2）DECLARE VALUE FOR SHIPMENT FOR CUSTOMS ONLY：此为货物的申报价值，供海关清关时用。

8. REFERENCE NO. 1 &REFERENCE　NO. 2：货件参考编码1及货件参考编码2。

（六）COUNTRY OF ORIGIN（MANUFACTURE）OF GOODS 货物原产国（一般注明"MADE IN CHINA"或"CHINA"字样）

（七）DATE OF SHIPMENT/SHIPPER'S SIGNATURE 出货日期/发件人确认签名（勿填）

（八）SPECIAL INSTRUCTIONS（特殊说明）

此处可以填写包裹尺码，也可以填写特殊要求：SATURDAY DELIEVERY（周六派送）；如需 SATURDAY DELIEVERY，则需加收费用。

三、电子订单

1. 电子订单的概念。

电子订单是指以数字化方式在计算机中进行存放和传输的用以订购商品的数据或者合同，是传统纸介质订单的电子化形式。虽然电子订单从功能上与传统纸质订单几乎一致，但是由于电子订单存放的场所和传输所经过的信道均不同于传统纸质订单，因此电子订单与传统订单会有较大的不同。

2. 电子订单与传统订单的区别。

一般来说传统订单流程：

（1）客户要求购买商品，必须提出口头、书面、电子表格等形式的购买申请，只有该申请通过后，企业才能录入订单信息进而生成规范格式的订单。

（2）企业生成订单后，首先必须核查订单的有效性，以免发生不必要的错误，如果检查出错误，必须根据订单的修改需求对订单信息进行修改，这个过程可能使原有的订单作废，因为原则上的订单是不允许有涂改的，所以必须再重新填入另一份新的订单。

（3）订单的检查通过后，就可以通知客户并洽谈交货日期和付款日期，如果双方没有洽谈成功，那么订单就会被冻结；如果洽谈成功，则该企业的交易最终成功。

根据以上流程分析，我们不难看出传统订单存在几个显著问题：首先，客户在下订单前必须提交购买申请，申请通过后才能形成订单。这与传统的采购模式有关，在传统的管理模式下，供应商不容易查看自己的库存商品信息，要花很多人力和时间来查看自己是否能够满足采购商提出的申请，如果不能够满足申请，则该申请作废。其次，由于订单是纸质的，在订单的管理过程中就需要大量的人力物力来从事订单的修改、审核等工作。最后，订单的传输需要耗费很长的时间和较高的成本，这就很大程度上限制了企业运转的效率，甚至导致很多合作无法实现。

针对传统订单的几点缺陷，电子订单有着明显的优势：

第一：电子订单是以数字化方式存放在计算机及其附属存储设备中的，当然，企业的商品信息和客户信息也存储在计算机中。这样，供应商很容易查看自己的商品信息和客户信息，客户在订购商品时不需要再提交申请，可以直接下单，这就大大减少了供应商和采购商的工作量，缩短了采购时间。

第二：电子订单主要通过互联网、专用增值网等计算机网络进行传输。采购的相关信息在以太网上以光速传播，完全突破了距离的限制，从而大大提高了采购的效率。

第三：电子订单最典型的应用是基于计算机网络的电子数据交换，由于计算机的高智能性，订单的处理需要很少的人力，尤其是在完全电子化采购形式下，几乎不需要人员处理订单，只要有几名专业的计算机维护人员就可以。

一份完整的电子订单信息包括电子订单基本信息和电子订单商品信息，电子订单信息型见图 11－3。

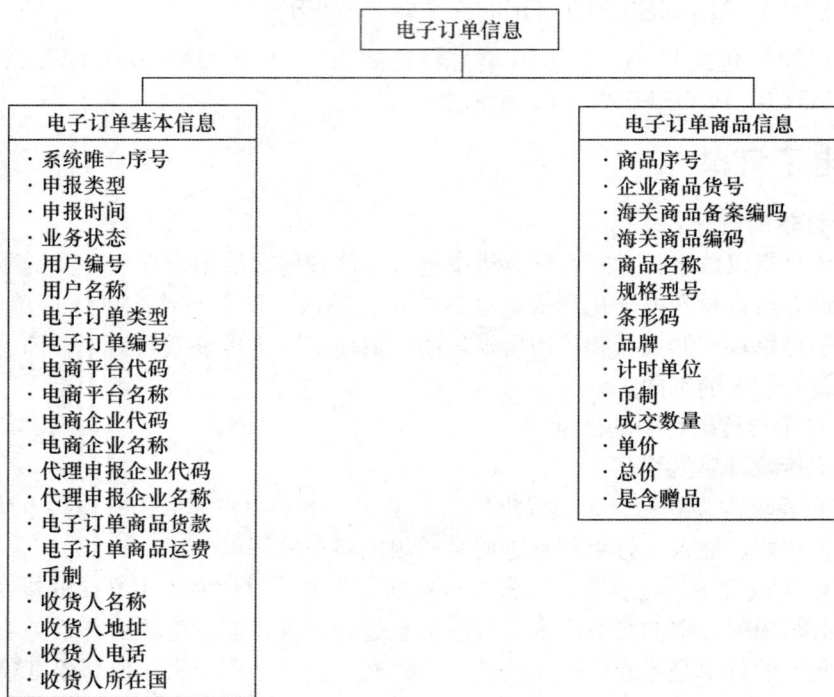

图 11－3　电子订单信息模型图

第三节　典型业务演示

根据业务需要，单证员李望应完成的跨境电商单证工作任务包括：

任务 1：认真审核电子订单，并填制电子报关单。

任务 2：使用跨境电商平台（以速卖通为例）进入到物流页面使用中国邮政小包或者国际快递途径填写电子运单。

1. 李望进入"我的速卖通"——"交易"，选择"等待您发货"状态的订单。他看到了所有等待发货的订单明细。李望选择了需要发货的订单，点击"发货"。

之后李望看到下方页面，他选择"线上发货"。

对于已部分发货的商品，李望看到了"填写发货通知""发货完毕确认"和"线上发货"三个按钮。李望选择了"线上发货"，进入到了选择物流方案的环节。

2. 选择物流方案。

在"选择物流方案"页面里，李望可以选择他所需要的物流服务。如果李望选择的物流服务与买家下单的服务不一致时，系统将提示他进行确认。李望选择完毕后，点击"下一步"，创建相应的物流订单。

选择物流方案　　　　　　　　　　　　　　　选择物流方案　创建物流订单　创建成功

通知：线上发货新增"燕文航空经济小包" 查看详情>>
通知：物流商端午节放假安排 查看详情>>
国际小包物流介绍：【AliExpress无忧物流】【中国邮政平常小包+】【4PX新邮挂号小包】【4PX新邮经济小包】【燕文航空挂号小包】【燕文航空经济小包】【速优宝芬邮挂号小包】【速优宝芬邮经济小包】【中俄航空Ruston】【中俄快递-SPSR】【中外运-西邮经济小包】【中外运-西邮标准小包】【中外运-英邮经济小包】
国际快递物流介绍：【EMS】【e-EMS】【FedEx】【DPEX】【UPS】【TNT】【HK DHL】

交易订单号　77158988075804　隐藏订单包裹信息▲

发货地址　安徽省　　　　收货国家　United States

包裹重量　1.0 KG　修改

服务名称	参考运输时效	试算运费⊘
● AliExpress 无忧物流-标准	15-45天	CN￥79.50

您选择使用的物流服务和买家下单时选择的不一致，可能导致买家拒收或提纠纷。

○ AliExpress 无忧物流-优先	8-15天	CN￥90.10
○ e邮宝	20-40天	CN￥89.00
○ EMS	20-40天	CN￥114.00
○ FedEx IE	7-15天	CN￥126.15
○ FedEx IP	7-15天	CN￥134.43
○ UPS全球速快	7-15天	CN￥95.31
○ UPS Expedited	7-15天	CN￥79.66
○ TNT	7-15天	CN￥291.48

⚠ 物流服务E特快，DPEX，顺丰国际经济小包不能送达United States.
若选择了Aliexpress无忧物流，您需要自物流订单创建起的5个工作日内，通过揽收或自寄的方式将包裹交接给物流商且确保成功展示揽收或签收成功信息(注：对于仓库揽收需预留2个工作日/自寄方式需要预留1个工作日，给仓库进行货物处理及信息上网展示时间)，若发货延迟，您将无法获得限时达赔付补偿，查看详情

下一步，创建物流订单

3. 创建物流订单。

李望选择"创建物流订单"之后，出现了下方页面。

如果李望需要修改买家收件信息，可以点击"修改收件信息"，会显示下方弹窗，他就可以在此编辑他的收件信息。

这里可以编辑您的发件信息

这里可以选择免费上门揽货或自送至中转仓库

这里会显示中转仓相关信息，如果您有关于
仓库相关问题，可以选择在线客服咨询。

如果李望的发件地址在物流商揽收范围内，系统会为他自动配置对应的仓库。如果他所在的地址没有推荐的揽收仓，系统会提示他"自寄至指定中转仓库"。

如果李望依旧选择"免费上门揽收"，他可以点击"申请仓库上门揽收"。但是如果他要申请揽收仓库，他必须先于仓库沟通能否上门揽收，否则仓库将会拒单。

在李望创建物流订单的时候，在页面底部有关于无法投递的包裹处理方案。他可以根据自己的需要，选择是否需要将包裹退回，或者在海外销毁。当李望选择"退回"时，每单会收取固定金额的退件服务费，对于选择退回的包裹，一旦发生目的国无法投递的情况，将不再收取退回运费。而当他选择"销毁"时，则不产生退件服务费，将会免费为他销毁包裹。

这里可以选择如果包裹在目的国无法投递，
是否需要退回，或者直接销毁
如果选择退回，需支付退回附加费，填写
退货地址

以上选择全部完毕之后，李望勾选了"我已阅读并同意《在线发货－阿里巴巴使用者协议》"，并选择"提交发货"。至此，物流订单创建完毕。

4. 查看国际物流单号，打印发货标签。

在物流订单创建完毕之后，会出现下方页面，提示"成功创建物流订单"。李望点击"物流订单详情"链接，看到了生成的国际物流单号，他可以打印发货标签。

5. 填写发货通知。

物流订单创建成功后，系统会生成运单号给李望。李望在卖家完成打包发货，交付物流商之后，即可填写发货通知。

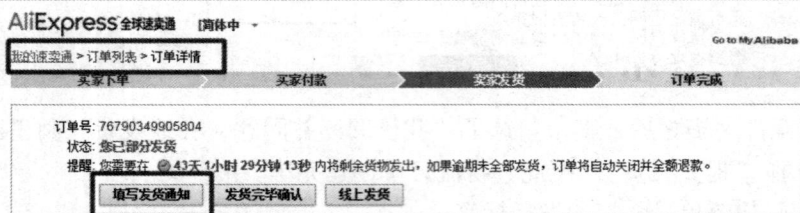

至此，跨境贸易的三个电子单证在跨境平台全部完成。

第四节　学习导航

一、参考资料

［1］鲁丹萍. 跨境电子商务［M］. 北京：中国商务出版社，2015.

［2］肖旭. 跨境电商实务［M］. 北京：中国人民大学出版社，2015.

［3］林清山. 跨境电子商务电子单证信息描述研究［J］. 质量技术监督研究，2016（2）.

二、自主学习平台

［1］https：//www. aliexpress. com 速卖通官网

［2］跨境电商操作课程国家教学资源库

《跟单信用证统一规则》（UCP600）

一、规则说明

第1~5条为总则部分，包括UCP的适用范围、定义条款、解释规则、信用证的独立性等；第6~13条明确了有关信用证的开立、修改、各当事人的关系与责任等问题；第14~16条是关于单据的审核标准、单证相符或不符的处理的规定；第17~28条属单据条款，包括商业发票、运输单据、保险单据等；第29~32条规定了有关款项支取的问题；第33~37条属银行的免责条款；第38条是关于可转让信用证的规定；第39条是关于款项让渡的规定。

二、中英文对照条款

Article 1　Application of UCP
第一条　统一惯例的适用范围

The Uniform Customs and Practice for Documentary Credits, 2007 Revision, ICC Publication no. 600 ("UCP") are rules that apply to any documentary credit ("credit") (including, to the extent to which they may be applicable, any standby letter of credit) when the text of the credit expressly indicates that it is subject to these rules. They are binding on all parties thereto unless expressly modified or excluded by the credit.

跟单信用证统一惯例，2007年修订本，国际商会第600号出版物，适用于所有在正文中标明按本惯例办理的跟单信用证（包括本惯例适用范围内的备用信用证）。除非信用证中另有规定，本惯例对一切有关当事人均具有约束力。

Article 2　Definitions
第二条　定义

For the purpose of these rules:

就本惯例而言：

Advising bank means the bank that advises the credit at the request of the issuing bank.

通知行意指应开证行要求通知信用证的银行。

Applicant means the party on whose request the credit is issued.

申请人意指发出开立信用证申请的一方。

Banking day means a day on which a bank is regularly open at the place at which an act subject to these rules is to be performed.

银行日意指银行在其营业地正常营业，按照本惯例行事的行为得以在银行履行的日子。

Beneficiary means the party in whose favour a credit is issued.

受益人意指信用证中受益的一方。

Complying presentation means a presentation that is in accordance with the terms and conditions of the credit, the applicable provisions of these rules and international standard banking practice.

相符提示意指与信用证中的条款及条件、本惯例中所适用的规定及国际标准银行实务相一致的提示。

Confirmation means a definite undertaking of the confirming bank, in addition to that of the issuing bank, to honour or negotiate a complying presentation.

保兑意指保兑行在开证行之外对于相符提示做出兑付或议付的确定承诺。

Confirming bank means the bank that adds its confirmation to a credit upon the issuing bank's authorization or request.

保兑行意指应开证行的授权或请求对信用证加具保兑的银行。

Credit means any arrangement, however named or described, that is irrevocable and thereby constitutes a definite undertaking of the issuing bank to honour a complying presentation.

信用证意指一项约定，无论其如何命名或描述，该约定不可撤销并因此构成开证行对于相符提示予以兑付的确定承诺。

Honour means:

a. to pay at sight if the credit is available by sight payment.

b. to incur a deferred payment undertaking and pay at maturity if the credit is available by deferred payment.

c. to accept a bill of exchange ("draft") drawn by the beneficiary and pay at maturity if the credit is available by acceptance.

兑付意指:

a. 对于即期付款信用证即期付款。

b. 对于延期付款信用证发出延期付款承诺并到期付款。

c. 对于承兑信用证承兑由受益人出具的汇票并到期付款。

Issuing bank means the bank that issues a credit at the request of an applicant or on its own behalf.

开证行意指应申请人要求或代表其自身开立信用证的银行。

Negotiation means the purchase by the nominated bank of drafts (drawn on a bank other than the nominated bank) and/or documents under a complying presentation, by advancing or agreeing to advance funds to the beneficiary on or before the banking day on which reimbursement is due to (to be paid the nominated bank.

议付意指被指定银行在其应获得偿付的银行日或在此之前，通过向受益人预付或者同意向受益人预付款项的方式购买相符提示项下的汇票（汇票付款人为被指定银行以外的银行）及/或单据。

Nominated bank means the bank with which the credit is available or any bank in the case of a credit available with any bank.

被指定银行意指有权使用信用证的银行，对于可供任何银行使用的信用证而言，任何银行均为被指定银行。

Presentation means either the delivery of documents under a credit to the issuing bank or nominated bank or the documents so delivered.

提示意指信用证项下单据被提交至开证行或被指定银行，抑或按此方式提交的单据。

Presenter means a beneficiary, bank or other party that makes a presentation.

提示人意指做出提示的受益人、银行或其他一方。

Article 3　Interpretations
第三条　释义

For the purpose of these rules:

就本惯例而言：

Where applicable, words in the singular include the plural and in the plural include the singular.

在适用的条款中，词汇的单复数同义。

A credit is irrevocable even if there is no indication to that effect.

信用证是不可撤销的，即使信用证中对此未作指示也是如此。

A document may be signed by handwriting, facsimile signature, perforated signature, stamp, symbol or any other mechanical or electronic method of authentication.

单据可以通过手签、签样印制、穿孔签字、盖章、符号表示的方式签署，也可以通过其它任何机械或电子证实的方法签署。

A requirement for a document to be legalized, visaed, certified or similar will be satisfied by any signature, mark, stamp or label on the document which appears to satisfy that requirement.

当信用证含有要求使单据合法、签证、证实或对单据有类似要求的条件时，这些条件可由在单据上签字、标注、盖章或标签来满足，只要单据表面已满足上述条件即可。

Branches of a bank in different countries are considered to be separate banks.

一家银行在不同国家设立的分支机构均视为另一家银行。

Terms such as "first class", "well known", "qualified", "independent", "official", "competent" or "local" used to describe the issuer of a document allow any issuer except the beneficiary to issue that document.

诸如"第一流""著名""合格""独立""正式""有资格""当地"等用语用于描述单据出单人的身份时，单据的出单人可以是除受益人以外的任何人。

Unless required to be used in a document, words such as "prompt", "immediately" or "as soon as possible" will be disregarded.

除非确需在单据中使用，银行对诸如"迅速""立即""尽快"之类词语将不予置理。

The expression "on or about" or similar will be interpreted as a stipulation that an event is to occur during a period of five calendar days before until five calendar days after the specified date, both start and end dates included.

"于或约于"或类似措辞将被理解为一项约定，按此约定，某项事件将在所述日期前后各五天内发生，起迄日均包括在内。

The words "to", "until", "till", "from" and "between" when used to determine a period of shipment include the date or dates mentioned, and the words "before" and "after" exclude the date mentioned.

词语"×月×日止"（to）、"至×月×日"（until）、"直至×月×日"（till）、"从×月×日"（from）及"在 X 月 X 日至 X 月 X 日之间"（between）用于确定装运期限时，包括所述日期。词语"X 月 X 日之前"（before）及"X 月 X 日之后"（after）不包括所述日期。

The words "from" and "after" when used to determine a maturity date exclude the date mentioned.

词语"从 X 月 X 日"（from）以及"X 月 X 日之后"（after）用于确定到期日时不包括所述日期。

The terms "first half" and "second half" of a month shall be construed respectively as the 1st to the 15th and the 16th to the last day of the month, all dates inclusive.

术语"上半月"和"下半月"应分别理解为自每月"1 日至 15 日"和"16 日至月末最后一天"，包括起迄日期。

The terms "beginning", "middle" and "end" of a month shall be construed respectively as the 1st to the 10th, the 11th to the 20th and the 21st to the last day of the month, all dates inclusive.

术语"月初""月中"和"月末"应分别理解为每月 1 日至 10 日、11 日至 20 日和 21 日至月末最后一天，包括起迄日期。

Article 4 Credits v. Contracts
第四条 信用证与合同

a. A credit by its nature is a separate transaction from the sale or other contract on which it may be based. Banks are in no way concerned with or bound by such contract, even if any reference whatsoever to it is included in the credit. Consequently, the undertaking of a bank to honour, to negotiate or to fulfil any other obligation under the credit is not subject to claims or defences by the applicant resulting from its relationships with the issuing bank or the beneficiary.

A beneficiary can in no case avail itself of the contractual relationships existing between banks or between the applicant and the issuing bank.

a. 就性质而言，信用证与可能作为其依据的销售合同或其他合同，是相互独立的交易。即使信用证中提及该合同，银行亦与该合同完全无关，且不受其约束。因此，一家银行作出兑付、议付或履行信用证项下其他义务的承诺，并不受申请人与开证行之间或与受益人之间在已有关系下产生的索偿或抗辩的制约。受益人在任何情况下，不得利用银行之间或申请人与开证行之间的契约关系。

b. An issuing bank should discourage any attempt by the applicant to include, as an integral part of the credit, copies of the underlying contract, proforma invoice and the like.

b. 开证行应劝阻申请人将基础合同、形式发票或其他类似文件的副本作为信用证整体组成部分的作法。

Article 5　Documents v. Goods, Services or Performance
第五条　单据与货物/服务/行为

Banks deal with documents and not with goods, services or performance to which the documents may relate.

银行处理的是单据，而不是单据所涉及的货物、服务或其他行为。

Article 6　Availability, Expiry Date and Place for Presentation
第六条　有效性、有效期限及提示地点

a. A credit must state the bank with which it is available or whether it is available with any bank. A credit available with a nominated bank is also available with the issuing bank.

a. 信用证必须规定可以有效使用信用证的银行，或者信用证是否对任何银行均为有效。对于被指定银行有效的信用证同样也对开证行有效。

b. A credit must state whether it is available by sight payment, deferred payment, acceptance or negotiation.

b. 信用证必须规定它是否适用于即期付款、延期付款、承兑抑或议付。

c. A credit must not be issued available by a draft drawn on the applicant.

c. 不得开立包含有以申请人为汇票付款人条款的信用证。

d.

i. A credit must state an expiry date for presentation. An expiry date stated for honour or negotiation will be deemed to be an expiry date for presentation.

d.

i 信用证必须规定提示单据的有效期限。规定的用于兑付或者议付的有效期限将被认为是提示单据的有效期限。

ii. The place of the bank with which the credit is available is the place for presentation. The place for presentation under a credit available with any bank is that of any bank. A place for presentation other than that of the issuing bank is in addition to the place of the issuing bank.

ii. 可以有效使用信用证的银行所在的地点是提示单据的地点。对任何银行均为有效的信用证项下单据提示的地点是任何银行所在的地点。不同于开证行地点的提示单据的地点是开证行地点之外提交单据的地点。

e. Except as provided in sub-article 29（a）, a presentation by or on behalf of the beneficiary must be made on or before the expiry date.

e. 除非如 29（a）中规定，由受益人或代表受益人提示的单据必须在到期日当日或在此之前提交。

Article 7   Issuing Bank Undertaking
第七条   开证行的承诺

a. Provided that the stipulated documents are presented to the nominated bank or to the issuing bank and that they constitute a complying presentation, the issuing bank must honour if the credit is available by：

倘若规定的单据被提交至被指定银行或开证行并构成相符提示，开证行必须按下述信用证所适用的情形予以兑付：

i. sight payment, deferred payment or acceptance with the issuing bank；

i. 由开证行即期付款、延期付款或者承兑；

ii. sight payment with a nominated bank and that nominated bank does not pay；

ii. 由被指定银行即期付款而该被指定银行未予付款；

iii. deferred payment with a nominated bank and that nominated bank does not incur its deferred payment undertaking or, having incurred its deferred payment undertaking, does not pay at maturity；

iii. 由被指定银行延期付款而该被指定银行未承担其延期付款承诺，或者虽已承担延期付款承诺但到期未予付款；

iv. acceptance with a nominated bank and that nominated bank does not accept a draft drawn on it or, having accepted a draft drawn on it, does not pay at maturity；

iv. 由被指定银行承兑而该被指定银行未予承兑以其为付款人的汇票，或者虽已承兑以其为付款人的汇票但到期未予付款；

v. negotiation with a nominated bank and that nominated bank does not negotiate.

v. 由被指定银行议付而该被指定银行未予议付。

b. An issuing bank is irrevocably bound to honour as of the time it issues the credit.

b. 自信用证开立之时起，开证行即不可撤销地受到兑付责任的约束。

c. An issuing bank undertakes to reimburse a nominated bank that has honoured or negotiated a complying presentation and forwarded the documents to the issuing bank. Reimbursement for the amount of a complying presentation under a credit available by acceptance or deferred payment is due at maturity, whether or not the nominated bank prepaid or purchased before maturity. An issuing bank's undertaking to reimburse a nominated bank is independent of the issuing bank's undertaking to the beneficiary.

c. 开证行保证向对于相符提示已经予以兑付或者议付并将单据寄往开证行的被指定银行进行偿付。无论被指定银行是否于到期日前已经对相符提示予以预付或者购买，对于承兑或延期付款信用证项下相符提示的金额的偿付于到期日进行。开证行偿付被指定银行的承诺独立于开证行对于受益人的承诺。

Article 8　Confirming Bank Undertaking
第八条　保兑行的承诺

a. Provided that the stipulated documents are presented to the confirming bank or to any other nominated bank and that they constitute a complying presentation, the confirming bank must:

a. 倘若规定的单据被提交至保兑行或者任何其他被指定银行并构成相符提示，保兑行必须：

i. honour, if the credit is available by:

i. 兑付，如果信用证适用于：

a. sight payment, deferred payment or acceptance with the confirming bank;

a. 由保兑行即期付款、延期付款或者承兑；

b. sight payment with another nominated bank and that nominated bank does not pay;

b. 由另一家被指定银行即期付款而该被指定银行未予付款；

c. deferred payment with another nominated bank and that nominated bank does not incur its deferred payment undertaking or, having incurred its deferred payment undertaking, does not pay at maturity;

c. 由另一家被指定银行延期付款而该被指定银行未承担其延期付款承诺，或者虽已承担延期付款承诺但到期未予付款；

d. acceptance with another nominated bank and that nominated bank does not accept a draft drawn on it or, having accepted a draft drawn on it, does not pay at maturity;

d. 由另一家被指定银行承兑而该被指定银行未予承兑以其为付款人的汇票，或者虽已承兑以其为付款人的汇票但到期未予付款；

e. negotiation with another nominated bank and that nominated bank does not negotiate.

e. 由另一家被指定银行议付而该被指定银行未予议付。

ii. negotiate, without recourse 无追索权, if the credit is available by negotiation with the confirming bank.

ii. 若信用证由保兑行议付，无追索权地议付。

b. A confirming bank is irrevocably bound to honour or negotiate as of the time it adds its confirmation to the credit.

b. 自为信用证加具保兑之时起，保兑行即不可撤销地受到兑付或者议付责任的约束。

c. A confirming bank undertakes to reimburse another nominated bank that has honoured or negotiated a complying presentation and forwarded the documents to the confirming bank. Reimbursement for the amount of a complying presentation under a credit available by acceptance or deferred payment is due at maturity, whether or not another nominated bank prepaid or purchased before maturity. A confirming bank's undertaking to reimburse another nominated bank is independent of the confirming bank's undertaking to the beneficiary.

c. 保兑行保证向对于相符提示已经予以兑付或者议付并将单据寄往开证行的另一家被指定银行进行偿付。无论另一家被指定银行是否到期日前已经对相符提示予以预付或者购买，对于承兑或延期付款信用证项下相符提示的金额的偿付于到期日进行。保兑行偿付另一家被指定银行的承诺独立于保兑行对于受益人的承诺。

d. If a bank is authorized or requested by the issuing bank to confirm a credit but is not prepared to do so, it must inform the issuing bank without delay and may advise the credit without confirmation.

d. 如开证行授权或要求另一家银行对信用证加具保兑，而该银行不准备照办时，它必须不延误地告知开证行并仍可通知此份未经加具保兑的信用证。

Article 9   Advising of Credits and Amendments
第九条   信用证及修改的通知

a. A credit and any amendment may be advised to a beneficiary through an advising bank. An advising bank that is not a confirming bank advises the credit and any amendment without any undertaking to honour or negotiate.

a. 信用证及其修改可以通过通知行通知受益人。除非已对信用证加具保兑，通知行通知信用证不构成兑付或议付的承诺。

b. By advising the credit or amendment, the advising bank signifies that it has satisfied itself as to the apparent authenticity of the credit or amendment and that the advice accurately reflects the terms and conditions of the credit or amendment received.

b. 通过通知信用证或修改，通知行即表明其认为信用证或修改的表面真实性得到满足，且通知准确地反映了所收到的信用证或修改的条款及条件。

c. An advising bank may utilize the services of another bank ("second advising bank") to advise the credit and any amendment to the beneficiary. By advising the credit or amendment, the second advising bank signifies that it has satisfied itself as to the apparent authenticity of the advice it has received and that the advice accurately reflects the terms and conditions of the credit or amendment received.

c. 通知行可以利用另一家银行的服务（"第二通知行"）向受益人通知信用证及其修改。通过通知信用证或修改，第二通知行即表明其认为所收到的通知的表面真实性得到满足，且通知准确地反映了所收到的信用证或修改的条款及条件。

d. A bank utilizing the services of an advising bank or second advising bank to advise a credit must use the same bank to advise any amendment thereto.

d. 如一家银行利用另一家通知行或第二通知行的服务将信用证通知给受益人，它也必须利用同一家银行的服务通知修改书。

e. If a bank is requested to advise a credit or amendment but elects not to do so, it must so inform, without delay, the bank from which the credit, amendment or advice has been received.

e. 如果一家银行被要求通知信用证或修改但决定不予通知，它必须不延误通知向其发送信用证、修改或通知的银行。

f. If a bank is requested to advise a credit or amendment but cannot satisfy itself as to the apparent authenticity of the credit, the amendment or the advice, it must so inform, without delay, the bank from which the instructions appear to have been received. If the advising bank or second advising bank elects nonetheless to advise the credit or amendment, it must inform the beneficiary or second advising bank that it has not been able to satisfy itself as to the apparent authenticity of the credit, the amendment or the advice.

f. 如果一家被要求通知信用证或修改，但不能确定信用证、修改或通知的表面真实性，就必须不延误地告知向其发出该指示的银行。如果通知行或第二通知行仍决定通知信用证或修改，则必须告知受益人或第二通知行其未能核实信用证、修改或通知的表面真实性。

Article 10　Amendments
第十条　修改

a. Except as otherwise provided by article 38, a credit can neither be amended nor cancelled without the agreement of the issuing bank, the confirming bank, if any, and the beneficiary.

a. 除本惯例第 38 条另有规定外，凡未经开证行、保兑行（如有）以及受益人同意，信用证既不能修改也不能撤销。

b. An issuing bank is irrevocably bound by an amendment as of the time it issues the amendment. A confirming bank may extend its confirmation to an amendment and will be irrevocably bound as of the time it advises the amendment. A confirming bank may, however, choose to advise an amendment without extending its confirmation and, if so, it must inform the issuing bank without delay and inform the beneficiary in its advice.

b. 自发出信用证修改书之时起，开证行就不可撤销地受其发出修改的约束。保兑行可将其保兑承诺扩展至修改内容，且自其通知该修改之时起，即不可撤销地受到该修改的约束。然而，保兑行可选择仅将修改通知受益人而不对其加具保兑，但必须不延误地将此情况通知开证行和受益人。

c. The terms and conditions of the original credit (or a credit incorporating previously accepted amendments) will remain in force for the beneficiary until the beneficiary communicates its acceptance of the amendment to the bank that advised such amendment. The beneficiary should give notification of acceptance or rejection of an amendment. If the beneficiary fails to give such notification, a presentation that complies with the credit and to any not yet accepted amendment will be deemed to be notification of acceptance by the beneficiary of such amendment. As of that moment the credit will be amended.

c. 在受益人向通知修改的银行表示接受该修改内容之前，原信用证（或包含先前已被接受修改的信用证）的条款和条件对受益人仍然有效。受益人应发出接受或拒绝接受修改的通知。如受益人未提供上述通知，当其提交至被指定银行或开证行的单据与信用证以及尚未表示接受的修改的要求一致时，则该事实即视为受益人已作出接受修改的通知，并从此时起，该信用证已被修改。

d. A bank that advises an amendment should inform the bank from which it received the amendment of any notification of acceptance or rejection.

d. 通知修改的银行应当通知向其发出修改书的银行任何有关接受或拒绝接受修改的

通知。

e. Partial acceptance of an amendment is not allowed and will be deemed to be notification of rejection of the amendment.

e. 不允许部分接受修改，部分接受修改将被视为拒绝接受修改的通知。

f. A provision in an amendment to the effect that the amendment shall enter into force unless rejected by the beneficiary within a certain time shall be disregarded.

f. 修改书中作出的除非受益人在某一时间内拒绝接受修改，否则修改将开始生效的条款将被不予置理。

Article 11　Teletransmitted and Pre-Advised Credits and Amendments
第十一条　电讯传递与预先通知的信用证和修改

a. An authenticated teletransmission of a credit or amendment will be deemed to be the operative credit or amendment, and any subsequent mail confirmation shall be disregarded.

If a teletransmission states "full details to follow" (or words of similar effect), or states that the mail confirmation is to be the operative credit or amendment, then the teletransmission will not be deemed to be the operative credit or amendment. The issuing bank must then issue the operative credit or amendment without delay in terms not inconsistent with the teletransmission.

a. 经证实的信用证或修改的电讯文件将被视为有效的信用证或修改，任何随后的邮寄证实书将被不予置理。若该电讯文件声明"详情后告"（或类似词语）或声明随后寄出的邮寄证实书将是有效的信用证或修改，则该电讯文件将被视为无效的信用证或修改。开证行必须随即不延误地开出有效的信用证或修改，且条款不能与与电讯文件相矛盾。

b. A preliminary advice of the issuance of a credit or amendment ("pre-advice") shall only be sent if the issuing bank is prepared to issue the operative credit or amendment. An issuing bank that sends a pre-advice is irrevocably committed to issue the operative credit or amendment, without delay, in terms not inconsistent with the pre-advice.

b. 只有准备开立有效信用证或修改的开证行，才可以发出开立信用证或修改预先通知书。发出预先通知的开证行应不可撤销地承诺将不延误地开出有效的信用证或修改，且条款不能与预先通知书相矛盾。

Article 12　Nomination
第十二条　指定

a. Unless a nominated bank is the confirming bank, an authorization to honour or negotiate does not impose any obligation on that nominated bank to honour or negotiate, except when expressly agreed to by that nominated bank and so communicated to the beneficiary.

a. 除非一家被指定银行是保兑行，对被指定银行进行兑付或议付的授权并不构成其必须兑付或议付的义务，被指定银行明确同意并照此通知受益人的情形除外。

b. By nominating a bank to accept a draft or incur a deferred payment undertaking, an issuing bank authorizes that nominated bank to prepay or purchase a draft accepted or a deferred payment undertaking incurred by that nominated bank.

b. 通过指定一家银行承兑汇票或承担延期付款承诺，开证行即授权该被指定银行预付或购买经其承兑的汇票或由其承担延期付款的承诺。

c. Receipt or examination and forwarding of documents by a nominated bank that is not a confirming bank does not make that nominated bank liable to honour or negotiate, nor does it constitute honour or negotiation.

c. 非保兑行身份的被指定银行接受、审核并寄送单据的行为既不使得该被指定银行具有兑付或议付的义务，也不构成兑付或议付。

Article 13　Bank-to-Bank Reimbursement Arrangements
第十三条　银行间偿付约定

a. If a credit states that reimbursement is to be obtained by a nominated bank （ "claiming bank" ） claiming on another party （ "reimbursing bank" ）, the credit must state if the reimbursement is subject to the ICC rules for bank-to-bank reimbursements in effect on the date of issuance of the credit.

a. 如果信用证规定被指定银行（"索偿行"）须通过向另一方银行（"偿付行"）索偿获得偿付，则信用证中必须声明是否按照信用证开立日正在生效的国际商会《银行间偿付规则》办理。

b. If a credit does not state that reimbursement is subject to the ICC rules for bank-to-bank reimbursements, the following apply:

b. 如果信用证中未声明是否按照国际商会《银行间偿付规则》办理，则适用于下列条款：

i. An issuing bank must provide a reimbursing bank with a reimbursement authorization that conforms with the availability stated in the credit. The reimbursement authorization should not be subject to an expiry date.

i. 开证行必须向偿付行提供偿付授权书，该授权书须与信用证中声明的有效性一致。偿付授权书不应规定有效日期。

ii. A claiming bank shall not be required to supply a reimbursing bank with a certificate of compliance with the terms and conditions of the credit.

ii. 不应要求索偿行向偿付行提供证实单据与信用证条款及条件相符的证明。

iii. An issuing bank will be responsible for any loss of interest, together with any expenses incurred, if reimbursement is not provided on first demand by a reimbursing bank in accordance with the terms and conditions of the credit.

iii. 如果偿付行未能按照信用证的条款及条件在首次索偿时即行偿付，则开证行应对索偿行的利息损失以及产生的费用负责。

iv. A reimbursing bank's charges are for the account of the issuing bank. However, if the charges are for the account of the beneficiary, it is the responsibility of an issuing bank to so indicate in the credit and in the reimbursement authorization. If a reimbursing bank's charges are for the account of the beneficiary, they shall be deducted from the amount due to a claiming bank when reimbursement is made. If no reimbursement is made, the reimbursing bank's charges remain the obligation of the issuing bank.

iv. 偿付行的费用应由开证行承担。然而，如果费用系由受益人承担，则开证行有责任在信用证和偿付授权书中予以注明。如偿付行的费用系由受益人承担，则该费用应在偿付时从支付索偿行的金额中扣除。如果未发生偿付，开证行仍有义务承担偿付行的费用。

c. An issuing bank is not relieved of any of its obligations to provide reimbursement if reimbursement is not made by a reimbursing bank on first demand.

c. 如果偿付行未能于首次索偿时即行偿付，则开证行不能解除其自身的偿付责任。

Article 14　Standard for Examination of Documents
第十四条　审核单据的标准

a. A nominated bank acting on its nomination, a confirming bank, if any, and the issuing bank must examine a presentation to determine, on the basis of the documents alone, whether or not the documents appear on their face to constitute a complying presentation.

a. 按照指定行事的被指定银行、保兑行（如有）以及开证行必须对提示的单据进行审核，并仅以单据为基础，以决定单据在表面上看来是否构成相符提示。

b. A nominated bank acting on its nomination, a confirming bank, if any, and the issuing bank shall each have a maximum of five banking days following the day of presentation to determine if a presentation is complying. This period is not curtailed or otherwise affected by the occurrence on or after the date of presentation of any expiry date or last day for presentation. 、

b. 按照指定行事的被指定银行、保兑行（如有）以及开证行，自其收到提示单据的翌日起算，应各自拥有最多不超过五个银行工作日的时间以决定提示是否相符。该期限不因单据提示日适逢信用证有效期或最迟提示期或在其之后而被缩减或受到其他影响。

c. A presentation including one or more original transport documents subject to articles 19, 20, 21, 22, 23, 24 or 25 must be made by or on behalf of the beneficiary not later than 21 calendar days after the date of shipment as described in these rules, but in any event not later than the expiry date of the credit.

c. 提示若包含一份或多份按照本惯例第 19 条、20 条、21 条、22 条、23 条、24 条或 25 条出具的正本运输单据，则必须由受益人或其代表按照相关条款在不迟于装运日后的二十一个公历日内提交，但无论如何不得迟于信用证的到期日。

d. Data in a document, when read in context with the credit, the document itself and international standard banking practice, need not be identical to, but must not conflict with, data in that document, any other stipulated document or the credit.

d. 单据中内容的描述不必与信用证、信用证对该项单据的描述以及国际标准银行实务完全一致，但不得与该项单据中的内容、其他规定的单据或信用证相冲突。

e. In documents other than the commercial invoice, the description of the goods, services or performance, if stated, may be in general terms not conflicting with their description in the credit.

e. 除商业发票外，其他单据中的货物、服务或行为描述若须规定，可使用统称，但不得与信用证规定的描述相矛盾。

f. If a credit requires presentation of a document other than a transport document, insurance document or commercial invoice, without stipulating by whom the document is to be issued or its data content, banks will accept the document as presented if its content appears to fulfil the function of the required document and otherwise complies with sub-article 14 (d).

f. 如果信用证要求提示运输单据、保险单据和商业发票以外的单据，但未规定该单据由何人出具或单据的内容。如信用证对此未做规定，只要所提交单据的内容看来满足其功能需要且其它方面与十四条（d）款相符，银行将对提示的单据予以接受。

g. A document presented but not required by the credit will be disregarded and may be returned to the presenter.

g. 提示信用证中未要求提交的单据，银行将不予置理。如果收到此类单据，可以退还提示人。

h. If a credit contains a condition without stipulating the document to indicate compliance with the condition, banks will deem such condition as not stated and will disregard it.

h. 如果信用证中包含某项条件而未规定需提交与之相符的单据，银行将认为未列明此条件，并对此不予置理。

i. A document may be dated prior to the issuance date of the credit, but must not be dated later than its date of presentation.

i. 单据的出单日期可以早于信用证开立日期，但不得迟于信用证规定的提示日期。

j. When the addresses of the beneficiary and the applicant appear in any stipulated document, they need not be the same as those stated in the credit or in any other stipulated document, but must be within the same country as the respective addresses mentioned in the credit. Contact details (telefax, telephone, email and the like) stated as part of the beneficiary's and the applicant's address will be disregarded. However, when the address and contact details of the applicant appear as part of the consignee or notify party details on a transport document subject to articles 19, 20, 21, 22, 23, 24 or 25, they must be as stated in the credit.

j. 当受益人和申请人的地址显示在任何规定的单据上时，不必与信用证或其他规定单据中显示的地址相同，但必须与信用证中述及的各自地址处于同一国家内。用于联系的资料（电传、电话、电子邮箱及类似方式）如作为受益人和申请人地址的组成部分将被不予置理。然而，当申请人的地址及联系信息作为按照19条、20条、21条、22条、23条、24条或25条出具的运输单据中收货人或通知方详址的组成部分时，则必须按照信用证规定予以显示。

k. The shipper or consignor of the goods indicated on any document need not be the beneficiary of the credit.

k. 显示在任何单据中的货物的托运人或发货人不必是信用证的受益人。

l. A transport document may be issued by any party other than a carrier, owner, master or charterer provided that the transport document meets the requirements of articles 19, 20, 21,

22，23 or 24 of these rules.

l. 假如运输单据能够满足本惯例第 19 条、20 条、21 条、22 条、23 条或 24 条的要求，则运输单据可以由承运人、船东、船长或租船人以外的任何一方出具。

Article 15　Complying Presentation
第十五　条相符提示

a. When an issuing bank determines that a presentation is complying, it must honour.

a. 当开证行确定提示相符时，就必须予以兑付。

b. When a confirming bank determines that a presentation is complying, it must honour or negotiate and forward the documents to the issuing bank.

b. 当保兑行确定提示相符时，就必须予以兑付或议付并将单据寄往开证行。

c. When a nominated bank determines that a presentation is complying and honours or negotiates, it must forward the documents to the confirming bank or issuing bank.

c. 当被指定银行确定提示相符并予以兑付或议付时，必须将单据寄往保兑行或开证行。

Article 16　Discrepant Documents, Waiver and Notice
第十六条　不符单据及不符点的放弃与通知

a. When a nominated bank acting on its nomination, a confirming bank, if any, or the issuing bank determines that a presentation does not comply, it may refuse to honour or negotiate.

a. 当按照指定行事的被指定银行、保兑行（如有）或开证行确定提示不符时，可以拒绝兑付或议付。

b. hen an issuing bank determines that a presentation does not comply, it may in its sole judgement approach the applicant for a waiver of the discrepancies. This does not, however, extend the period mentioned in sub-article 14 (b).

b. 证行确定提示不符时，可以依据其独立的判断联系申请人放弃有关不符点。然而，这并不因此延长 14 条（b）款中述及的期限。

c. cting on its nomination, a confirming bank, if any, or the issuing bank decides to refuse to honour or negotiate, it must give a single notice to that effect to the presenter.

c. 按照指定行事的被指定银行、保兑行（如有）或开证行决定拒绝兑付或议付时，必须一次性通知提示人。

d. The notice must state:

d. 通知必须声明：

i. that the bank is refusing to honour or negotiate; and

i. 银行拒绝兑付或议付；及

ii. each discrepancy in respect of which the bank refuses to honour or negotiate; and

ii. 银行凭以拒绝兑付或议付的各个不符点；及

iii.

a）that the bank is holding the documents pending further instructions from the presenter; or
iii.

a）银行持有单据等候提示人进一步指示；或

b）that the issuing bank is holding the documents until it receives a waiver from the applicant and agrees to accept it, or receives further instructions from the presenter prior to agreeing to accept a waiver; or

b）开证行持有单据直至收到申请人通知弃权并同意接受该弃权，或在同意接受弃权前从提示人处收到进一步指示；或

c）that the bank is returning the documents; or

c）银行退回单据；或

d）that the bank is acting in accordance with instructions previously received from the presenter.

d）银行按照先前从提示人处收到的指示行事。

d. The notice required in sub-article 16（c）must be given by telecommunication or, if that is not possible, by other expeditious means no later than the close of the fifth banking day following the day of presentation.

d. 第十六条（c）款中要求的通知必须以电讯方式发出，或者，如果不可能以电讯方式通知时，则以其他快捷方式通知，但不得迟于提示单据日期翌日起第五个银行工作日终了。

e. A nominated bank acting on its nomination, a confirming bank, if any, or the issuing bank may, after providing notice required by sub-article 16（c）（iii）（a）or（b）, return the documents to the presenter at any time.

e. 按照指定行事的被指定银行、保兑行（如有）或开证行可以在提供第十六条（c）款（iii）、（a）款或（b）款要求提供的通知后，于任何时间将单据退还提示人。

f. If an issuing bank or a confirming bank fails to act in accordance with the provisions of this article, it shall be precluded from claiming that the documents do not constitute a complying presentation.

f. 如果开证行或保兑行未能按照本条款的规定行事，将无权宣称单据未能构成相符提示。

g. When an issuing bank refuses to honour or a confirming bank refuses to honour or negotiate and has given notice to that effect in accordance with this article, it shall then be entitled to claim a refund, with interest, of any reimbursement made.

g. 当开证行拒绝兑付或保兑行拒绝兑付或议付，并已经按照本条款发出通知时，该银行将有权就已经履行的偿付索取退款及其利息。

Article 17 Original Documents and Copies
第十七条 正本单据和副本单据

a. At least one original of each document stipulated in the credit must be presented.

a. 信用证中规定的各种单据必须至少提供一份正本。

b. A bank shall treat as an original any document bearing an apparently original signature, mark, stamp, or label of the issuer of the document, unless the document itself indicates that it is not an original.

b. 除非单据本身表明其不是正本，银行将视任何单据表面上具有单据出具人正本签字、标志、图章或标签的单据为正本单据。

c. Unless a document indicates otherwise 另外的, a bank will also accept a document as original if it:

c. 除非单据另有显示，银行将接受单据作为正本单据如果该单据：

i. appears to be written, typed, perforated or stamped by the document issuer's hand; or

i. 表面看来由单据出具人手工书写、打字、穿孔签字或盖章；或

ii. appears to be on the document issuer's original stationery; or

ii. 表面看来使用单据出具人的正本信笺；或

iii. states that it is original, unless the statement appears not to apply to the document presented.

iii. 声明单据为正本，除非该项声明表面看来与所提示的单据不符。

d. If a credit requires presentation of copies of documents, presentation of either originals or copies is permitted.

d. 如果信用证要求提交副本单据，则提交正本单据或副本单据均可。

e. If a credit requires presentation of multiple documents by using terms such as "in duplicate", "in two fold" or "in two copies", this will be satisfied by the presentation of at least one original and the remaining number in copies, except when the document itself indicates otherwise.

e. 如果信用证使用诸如"一式两份""两张""两份"等术语要求提交多份单据，则可以提交至少一份正本，其余份数以副本来满足。但单据本身另有相反指示者除外。

Article 18 Commercial Invoice
第十八条　商业发票

a. A commercial invoice:

a. 商业发票：

i. must appear to have been issued by the beneficiary (except as provided in article 38);

i. 必须在表面上看来系由受益人出具（第三十八条另有规定者除外）；

ii. must be made out in the name of the applicant (except as provided in sub-article 38 (g));

ii. 必须做成以申请人的名称为抬头（第三十八条（g）款另有规定者除外）；

iii. must be made out in the same currency as the credit; and

iii. 必须将发票币别作成与信用证相同币种。

iv. need not be signed.

iv. 无须签字。

b. A nominated bank acting on its nomination, a confirming bank, if any, or the issuing bank may accept a commercial invoice issued for an amount in excess of the amount permitted by the credit, and its decision will be binding upon all parties, provided the bank in question has not honoured or negotiated for an amount in excess of that permitted by the credit.

b. 按照指定行事的被指定银行、保兑行（如有）或开证行可以接受金额超过信用证所允许金额的商业发票，倘若有关银行已兑付或已议付的金额没有超过信用证所允许的金额，则该银行的决定对各有关方均具有约束力。

c. The description of the goods, services or performance in a commercial invoice must correspond with that appearing in the credit.

c. 商业发票中货物、服务或行为的描述必须与信用证中显示的内容相符。

Article 19 Transport Document Covering at Least Two Different Modes of Transport
第十九条 至少包括两种不同运输方式的运输单据

a. A transport document covering at least two different modes of transport (multimodal or combined transport document), however named, must appear to:

a. 至少包括两种不同运输方式的运输单据（即多式运输单据或联合运输单据），不论其称谓如何，必须在表明上看来：

i. indicate the name of the carrier and be signed by:

i. 显示承运人名称并由下列人员签署：

● the carrier or a named agent for or on behalf of the carrier, or
承运人或承运人的具名代理或代表，或

● the master or a named agent for or on behalf of the master.
船长或船长的具名代理或代表。

Any signature by the carrier, master or agent must be identified as that of the carrier, master or agent.

承运人、船长或代理的任何签字必须分别表明承运人、船长或代理的身份。

Any signature by an agent must indicate whether the agent has signed for or on behalf of the carrier or for or on behalf of the master.

代理的签字必须显示其是否作为承运人或船长的代理或代表签署提单。

ii. indicate that the goods have been dispatched, taken in charge or shipped on board at the place stated in the credit, by:

ii. 通过下述方式表明货物已在信用证规定的地点发运、接受监管或装载：

● pre-printed wording, or
预先印就的措词，或

● a stamp or notation indicating the date on which the goods have been dispatched, taken in charge or shipped on board.
注明货物已发运、接受监管或装载日期的图章或批注。

The date of issuance of the transport document will be deemed to be the date of dispatch, taking in charge or shipped on board, and the date of shipment. However, if the transport docu-

223

ment indicates, by stamp or notation, a date of dispatch, taking in charge or shipped on board, this date will be deemed to be the date of shipment.

运输单据的出具日期将被视为发运、接受监管或装载以及装运日期。然而，如果运输单据以盖章或批注方式标明发运、接受监管或装载日期，则此日期将被视为装运日期。

iii. indicate the place of dispatch, taking in charge or shipment and the place of final destination stated in the credit, even if:

iii. 显示信用证中规定的发运、接受监管或装载地点以及最终目的地的地点，即使：

a. the transport document states, in addition, a different place of dispatch, taking in charge or shipment or place of final destination,

or

a. 运输单据另外显示了不同的发运、接受监管或装载地点或最终目的地的地点，

或

b. the transport document contains the indication "intended" or similar qualification in relation to the vessel, port of loading or port of discharge.

b. 运输单据包含"预期"或类似限定有关船只、装货港或卸货港的指示。

iv. be the sole original transport document or, if issued in more than one original, be the full set as indicated on the transport document.

iv. 系仅有的一份正本运输单据，或者，如果出具了多份正本运输单据，应是运输单据中显示的全套正本份数。

v. contain terms and conditions of carriage or make reference to another source containing the terms and conditions of carriage (short form or blank back transport document). Contents of terms and conditions of carriage will not be examined.

v. 包含承运条件须参阅包含承运条件条款及条件的某一出处（简式或背面空白的运输单据）者，银行对此类承运条件的条款及条件内容不予审核。

vi. contain no indication that it is subject to a charter party.

vi. 未注明运输单据受租船合约约束。

b. For the purpose of this article, transhipment means unloading from one means of conveyance and reloading to another means of conveyance (whether or not in different modes of transport) during the carriage from the place of dispatch, taking in charge or shipment to the place of final destination stated in the credit.

b. 就本条款而言，转运意指货物在信用证中规定的发运、接受监管或装载地点到最终目的地的运输过程中，从一个运输工具卸下并重新装载到另一个运输工具上（无论是否为不同运输方式）的运输。

c.

i. A transport document may indicate that the goods will or may be transhipped provided that the entire carriage is covered by one and the same transport document.

c.

i. 只要同一运输单据包括运输全程，则运输单据可以注明货物将被转运或可被转运。

ii. A transport document indicating that transhipment will or may take place is acceptable, even if the credit prohibits transhipment.

ii. 即使信用证禁止转运，银行也将接受注明转运将发生或可能发生的运输单据。

Article 20 Bill of Lading
第二十条 提单

a. A bill of lading, however named, must appear to：

a. 无论其称谓如何，提单必须表面上看来：

i. indicate the name of the carrier and be signed by：

i. 显示承运人名称并由下列人员签署：

• the carrier or a named agent for or on behalf of the carrier, or

承运人或承运人的具名代理或代表，或

• the master or a named agent for or on behalf of the master.

船长或船长的具名代理或代表。

Any signature by the carrier, master or agent must be identified as that of the carrier, master or agent.

承运人、船长或代理的任何签字必须分别表明其承运人、船长或代理的身份。

Any signature by an agent must indicate whether the agent has signed for or on behalf of the carrier or for or on behalf of the master.

代理的签字必须显示其是否作为承运人或船长的代理或代表签署提单。

ii. indicate that the goods have been shipped on board a named vessel at the port of loading stated in the credit by：

ii. 通过下述方式表明货物已在信用证规定的装运港装载上具名船只：

• pre-printed wording, or

预先印就的措词，或

• an on board notation indicating the date on which the goods have been shipped on board.

注明货物已装船日期的装船批注。

The date of issuance of the bill of lading will be deemed to be the date of shipment unless the bill of lading contains an on board notation indicating the date of shipment, in which case the date stated in the on board notation will be deemed to be the date of shipment.

提单的出具日期将被视为装运日期，除非提单包含注明装运日期的装船批注。在此情况下，装船批注中显示的日期将被视为装运日期。

If the bill of lading contains the indication "intended vessel" or similar qualification in relation to the name of the vessel, an on board notation indicating the date of shipment and the name of the actual vessel is required.

如果提单包含"预期船"字样或类似有关限定船只的词语时，装上具名船只必须由注明装运日期以及实际装运船只名称的装船批注来证实。

iii. indicate shipment from the port of loading to the port of discharge stated in the credit.

iii. 注明装运从信用证中规定的装货港至卸货港。

If the bill of lading does not indicate the port of loading stated in the credit as the port of loading, or if it contains the indication "intended" or similar qualification in relation to the port of loading, an on board notation indicating the port of loading as stated in the credit, the date of shipment and the name of the vessel is required. This provision applies even when loading on board or shipment on a named vessel is indicated by pre-printed wording on the bill of lading.

如果提单未注明以信用证中规定的装货港作为装货港，或包含"预期"或类似有关限定装货港的标注者，则需要提供注明信用证中规定的装货港、装运日期以及船名的装船批注。即使提单上已注明印就的"已装船"或"已装具名船只"措词，本规定仍然适用。

iv. be the sole original bill of lading or, if issued in more than one original, be the full set as indicated on the bill of lading.

iv. 系仅有的一份正本提单，或者，如果出具了多份正本，应是提单中显示的全套正本份数。

v. contain terms and conditions of carriage or make reference to another source containing the terms and conditions of carriage (short form or blank back bill of lading). Contents of terms and conditions of carriage will not be examined.

v. 包含承运条件须参阅包含承运条件条款及条件的某一出处（简式或背面空白的提单）者，银行对此类承运条件的条款及条件内容不予审核。

vi. contain no indication that it is subject to a charter party.

vi. 未注明运输单据受租船合约约束。

b. For the purpose of this article, transhipment means unloading from one vessel and reloading to another vessel during the carriage from the port of loading to the port of discharge stated in the credit.

b. 就本条款而言，转运意指在信用证规定的装货港到卸货港之间的海运过程中，将货物由一艘船卸下再装上另一艘船的运输。

c.

i. A bill of lading may indicate that the goods will or may be transhipped provided that the entire carriage is covered by one and the same bill of lading.

c.

i. 只要同一提单包括运输全程，则提单可以注明货物将被转运或可被转运。

ii. A bill of lading indicating that transhipment will or may take place is acceptable, even if the credit prohibits transhipment, if the goods have been shipped in a container, trailer or LASH barge as evidenced by the bill of lading.

ii. 银行可以接受注明将要发生或可能发生转运的提单。即使信用证禁止转运，只要提单上证实有关货物已由集装箱、拖车或子母船运输，银行仍可接受注明将要发生或可能发生转运的提单。

d. Clauses in a bill of lading stating that the carrier reserves the right to tranship will be disregarded.

d. 对于提单中包含的声明承运人保留转运权利的条款，银行将不予置理。

Article 21　Non-Negotiable Sea Waybill
第二十一条　非转让海运单

a. A non-negotiable sea waybill, however named, must appear to:

a. 无论其称谓如何，非转让海运单必须表面上看来：

i. indicate the name of the carrier and be signed by:

i. 显示承运人名称并由下列人员签署：

- the carrier or a named agent for or on behalf of the carrier, or

承运人或承运人的具名代理或代表，或

- the master or a named agent for or on behalf of the master.

船长或船长的具名代理或代表。

Any signature by the carrier, master or agent must be identified as that of the carrier, master or agent.

承运人、船长或代理的任何签字必须分别表明其承运人、船长或代理的身份。

Any signature by an agent must indicate whether the agent has signed for or on behalf of the carrier or for or on behalf of the master.

代理的签字必须显示其是否作为承运人或船长的代理或代表签署提单。

ii. indicate that the goods have been shipped on board a named vessel at the port of loading stated in the credit by:

ii. 通过下述方式表明货物已在信用证规定的装运港装载上具名船只：

- pre-printed wording, or

预先印就的措词，或

- an on board notation indicating the date on which the goods have been shipped on board.

注明货物已装船日期的装船批注。

The date of issuance of the non-negotiable sea waybill will be deemed to be the date of shipment unless the non-negotiable sea waybill contains an on board notation indicating the date of shipment, in which case the date stated in the on board notation will be deemed to be the date of shipment.

非转让海运单的出具日期将被视为装运日期，除非非转让海运单包含注明装运日期的装船批注，在此情况下，装船批注中显示的日期将被视为装运日期。

If the non-negotiable sea waybill contains the indication "intended vessel" or similar qualification in relation to the name of the vessel, an on board notation indicating the date of shipment and the name of the actual vessel is required.

如果非转让海运单包含"预期船"字样或类似有关限定船只的词语时，装上具名船只必须由注明装运日期以及实际装运船只名称的装船批注来证实。

iii. indicate shipment from the port of loading to the port of discharge stated in the credit.

iii. 注明装运从信用证中规定的装货港至卸货港。

If the non-negotiable sea waybill does not indicate the port of loading stated in the credit as the port of loading, or if it contains the indication "intended" or similar qualification in relation to the port of loading, an on board notation indicating the port of loading as stated in the credit, the date of shipment and the name of the vessel is required. This provision applies even when loading on board or shipment on a named vessel is indicated by pre-printed wording on the non-negotiable sea waybill.

如果非转让海运单未注明以信用证中规定的装货港作为装货港，或包含"预期"或类似有关限定装货港的标注者，则需要提供注明信用证中规定的装货港、装运日期以及船名的装船批注。即使非转让海运单上已注明印就的"已装船"或"已装具名船只"措词，本规定仍然适用。

iv. be the sole original non-negotiable sea waybill or, if issued in more than one original, be the full set as indicated on the non-negotiable sea waybill.

iv. 系仅有的一份正本非转让海运单，或者，如果出具了多份正本，应是非转让海运单中显示的全套正本份数。

v. contain terms and conditions of carriage or make reference to another source containing the terms and conditions of carriage (short form or blank back non-negotiable sea waybill). Contents of terms and conditions of carriage will not be examined.

v. 包含承运条件须参阅包含承运条件条款及条件的某一出处（简式或背面空白的提单）者，银行对此类承运条件的条款及条件内容不予审核。

vi. contain no indication that it is subject to a charter party.

vi. 未注明运输单据受租船合约约束。

b. For the purpose of this article, transhipment means unloading from one vessel and reloading to another vessel during the carriage from the port of loading to the port of discharge stated in the credit.

b. 就本条款而言，转运意指在信用证规定的装货港到卸货港之间的海运过程中，将货物由一艘船卸下再装上另一艘船的运输。

c.

i. A non-negotiable sea waybill may indicate that the goods will or may be transhipped provided that the entire carriage is covered by one and the same non-negotiable sea waybill.

c.

i. 只要同一非转让海运单包括运输全程，则非转让海运单可以注明货物将被转运或可被转运。

ii. A non-negotiable sea waybill indicating that transhipment will or may take place is acceptable, even if the credit prohibits transhipment, if the goods have been shipped in a container, trailer or LASH barge 子母船 as evidenced by the non-negotiable sea waybill.

ii. 银行可以接受注明将要发生或可能发生转运的非转让海运单。即使信用证禁止转运，只要非转让海运单上证实有关货物已由集装箱、拖车或子母船运输，银行仍可接受注明将要发生或可能发生转运的非转让海运单。

d. Clauses in a non-negotiable sea waybill stating that the carrier reserves the right to tranship will be disregarded.

d. 对于非转让海运单中包含的声明承运人保留转运权利的条款，银行将不予置理。

Article 22　Charter Party Bill of Lading
第二十二条　租船合约提单

a. A bill of lading, however named, containing an indication that it is subject to a charter party (charter party bill of lading), must appear to：

a. 无论其称谓如何，倘若提单包含有提单受租船合约约束的指示（即租船合约提单），则必须在表面上看来：

i. be signed by：

i. 由下列当事方签署：

- the master or a named agent for or on behalf of the master, or

船长或船长的具名代理或代表，或

- the owner or a named agent for or on behalf of the owner, or

船东或船东的具名代理或代表，或

- the charterer or a named agent for or on behalf of the charterer.

租船主或租船主的具名代理或代表。

Any signature by the master, owner, charterer or agent must be identified as that of the master, owner, charterer or agent.

船长、船东、租船主或代理的任何签字必须分别表明其船长、船东、租船主或代理的身份。

Any signature by an agent must indicate whether the agent has signed for or on behalf of the master, owner or charterer.

代理的签字必须显示其是否作为船长、船东或租船主的代理或代表签署提单。

An agent signing for or on behalf of the owner or charterer must indicate the name of the owner or charterer.

代理人代理或代表船东或租船主签署提单时必须注明船东或租船主的名称。

ii. indicate that the goods have been shipped on board a named vessel at the port of loading stated in the credit by：

ii. 通过下述方式表明货物已在信用证规定的装运港装载上具名船只：

- pre-printed wording, or

预先印就的措词，或

- an on board notation indicating the date on which the goods have been shipped on board.

注明货物已装船日期的装船批注。

The date of issuance of the charter party bill of lading will be deemed to be the date of shipment unless the charter party bill of lading contains an on board notation indicating the date of shipment, in which case the date stated in the on board notation will be deemed to be the date of shipment.

租船合约提单的出具日期将被视为装运日期，除非租船合约提单包含注明装运日期的装船批注，在此情况下，装船批注中显示的日期将被视为装运日期。

iii. indicate shipment from the port of loading to the port of discharge stated in the credit. The port of discharge may also be shown as a range of ports or a geographical area, as stated in the credit.

iii. 注明货物由信用证中规定的装货港运输至卸货港。卸货港可以按信用证中的规定显示为一组港口或某个地理区域。

iv. be the sole original charter party bill of lading or, if issued in more than one original, be the full set as indicated on the charter party bill of lading.

iv. 系仅有的一份正本租船合约提单，或者，如果出具了多份正本，应是租船合约提单中显示的全套正本份数。

b. A bank will not examine charter party contracts, even if they are required to be presented by the terms of the credit.

b. 即使信用证中的条款要求提交租船合约，银行也将对该租船合约不予审核。

Article 23 Air Transport Document
第二十三条 空运单据

a. An air transport document, however named, must appear to:

a. 无论其称谓如何，空运单据必须在表面上看来：

i. indicate the name of the carrier and be signed by:

i. 注明承运人名称并由下列当事方签署：

• the carrier, or

承运人，或

• a named agent for or on behalf of the carrier.

承运人的具名代理或代表。

Any signature by the carrier or agent must be identified as that of the carrier or agent.

承运人或代理的任何签字必须分别表明其承运人或代理的身份。

Any signature by an agent must indicate that the agent has signed for or on behalf of the carrier.

代理的签字必须显示其是否作为承运人的代理或代表签署空运单据。

ii. indicate that the goods have been accepted for carriage.

ii. 注明货物已收妥待运。

iii. indicate the date of issuance. This date will be deemed to be the date of shipment unless the air transport document contains a specific notation of the actual date of shipment, in which case the date stated in the notation will be deemed to be the date of shipment.

iii. 注明出具日期。这一日期将被视为装运日期，除非空运单据包含注有实际装运日期的专项批注，在此种情况下，批注中显示的日期将被视为装运日期。

Any other information appearing on the air transport document relative to the flight number and date will not be considered in determining the date of shipment.

空运单据显示的其它任何与航班号和起飞日期有关的信息不能被视为装运日期。

iv. indicate the airport of departure and the airport of destination stated in the credit.

iv. 表明信用证规定的起飞机场和目的地机场。

v. be the original for consignor or shipper, even if the credit stipulates a full set of originals.

v. 为开给发货人或拖运人的正本，即使信用证规定提交全套正本。

vi. contain terms and conditions of carriage or make reference to another source containing the terms and conditions of carriage. Contents of terms and conditions of carriage will not be examined.

vi. 载有承运条款和条件，或提示条款和条件参见别处。银行将不审核承运条款和条件的内容。

b. For the purpose of this article, transhipment means unloading from one aircraft and reloading to another aircraft during the carriage from the airport of departure to the airport of destination stated in the credit.

b. 就本条而言，转运是指在信用证规定的起飞机场到目的地机场的运输过程中，将货物从一飞机卸下再装上另一飞机的行为。

c.

i. An air transport document may indicate that the goods will or may be transhipped, provided that the entire carriage is covered by one and the same air transport document.

c.

i. 空运单据可以注明货物将要或可能转运，只要全程运输由同一空运单据涵盖。

ii. An air transport document indicating that transhipment will or may take place is acceptable, even if the credit prohibits transhipment.

ii. 即使信用证禁止转运，注明将要或可能发生转运的空运单据仍可接受。

Article 24 Road, Rail or Inland Waterway Transport Documents
第二十四条 公路、铁路或内陆水运单据

a. A road, rail or inland waterway transport document, however named, must appear to:

a. 公路、铁路或内陆水运单据，无论名称如何，必须看似：

i. indicate the name of the carrier and:

i. 表明承运人名称，并且

• be signed by the carrier or a named agent for or on behalf of the carrier, or

•由承运人或其具名代理人签署，或者

• indicate receipt of the goods by signature, stamp or notation by the carrier or a named agent for or on behalf of the carrier.

•由承运人或其具名代理人以签字、印戳或批注表明货物收讫。

Any signature, stamp or notation of receipt of the goods by the carrier or agent must be identified as that of the carrier or agent.

承运人或其具名代理人的售货签字、印戳或批注必须标明其承运人或代理人的身份。

Any signature, stamp or notation of receipt of the goods by the agent must indicate that the agent has signed or acted for or on behalf of the carrier.

代理人的收获签字、印戳或批注必须标明代理人系代表承运人签字或行事。

If a rail transport document does not identify the carrier, any signature or stamp of the railway company will be accepted as evidence of the document being signed by the carrier.

如果铁路运输单据没有指明承运人，可以接受铁路运输公司的任何签字或印戳作为承运人签署单据的证据。

ii. indicate the date of shipment or the date the goods have been received for shipment, dispatch or carriage at the place stated in the credit. Unless the transport document contains a dated reception、stamp, an indication of the date of receipt or a date of shipment, the date of issuance of the transport document will be deemed to be the date of shipment.

ii. 表明货物在信用证规定地点的发运日期，或者收讫代运或代发送的日期。运输单据的出具日期将被视为发运日期，除非运输单据上盖有带日期的收货印戳，或注明了收货日期或发运日期。

ii. indicate the place of shipment and the place of destination stated in the credit.

iii. 表明信用证规定的发运地及目的地。

b.

i. A road transport document must appear to be the original for consignor or shipper or bear no marking indicating for whom the document has been prepared.

b.

i. 公路运输单据必须看似为开给发货人或托运人的正本，或没有认可标记表明单据开给何人。

ii. A rail transport document marked "duplicate" will be accepted as an original.

ii. 注明"第二联"的铁路运输单据将被作为正本接受。

iii. A rail or inland waterway transport document will be accepted as an original whether marked as an original or not.

iii. 无论是否注明正本字样，铁路或内陆水运单据都被作为正本接受。

c. In the absence of an indication on the transport document as to the number of originals issued, the number presented will be deemed to constitute a full set.

c. 如运输单据上未注明出具的正本数量，提交的分数即视为全套正本。

d. For the purpose of this article, transhipment means unloading from one means of conveyance and reloading to another means of conveyance, within the same mode of transport, during the carriage from the place of shipment, dispatch or carriage to the place of destination stated in the credit.

d. 就本条而言，转运是指在信用证规定的发运、发送或运送的地点到目的地之间的运输过程中，在同一运输方式中从一运输工具卸下再装上另一运输工具的行为。

e.

i. A road, rail or inland waterway transport document may indicate that the goods will or may be transhipped provided that the entire carriage is covered by one and the same transport document.

e.

i. 只要全程运输由同一运输单据涵盖，公路、铁路或内陆水运单据可以注明货物将要或可能被转运。

ii. A road, rail or inland waterway transport document indicating that transhipment will or may take place is acceptable, even if the credit prohibits transhipment.

ii. 即使信用证禁止转运，注明将要或可能发生转运的公路、铁路或内陆水运单据仍可接受。

Article 25   Courier Receipt, Post Receipt or Certificate of Posting
第二十五条   快递收据、邮政收据或投邮证明

a. A courier receipt, however named, evidencing receipt of goods for transport, must appear to：

a. 证明货物收讫待运的快递收据，无论名称如何，必须看似：

i. indicate the name of the courier service and be stamped or signed by the named courier service at the place from which the credit states the goods are to be shipped；and

i. 表明快递机构的名称，并在信用证规定的货物发运地点由该具名快递机构盖章或签字；并且

ii. indicate a date of pick-up or of receipt or wording to this effect. This date will be deemed to be the date of shipment.

ii. 表明取件或收件的日期或类似词语。该日期将被视为发运日期。

b. A requirement that courier charges are to be paid or prepaid may be satisfied by a transport document issued by a courier service evidencing that courier charges are for the account of a party other than the consignee.

b. 如果要求显示快递费用付讫或预付，快递机构出具的表明快递费由收货人以外的一方支付的运输单据可以满足该项要求。

c. A post receipt or certificate of posting, however named, evidencing receipt of goods for transport, must appear to be stamped or signed and dated at the place from which the credit states the goods are to be shipped. This date will be deemed to be the date of shipment.

c. 证明货物收讫待运的邮政收据或投邮证明，无论名称如何，必须看似在信用证规定的货物发运地点盖章或签署并注明日期。该日期将被视为发运日期。

Article 26   "On Deck", "Shipper's Load and Count", "Said by Shipper to Contain" and Charges Additional to Freight
第二十六条   "货装舱面"、"托运人装载和计数"、"内容据托运人报称" 及运费之外的费用

a. A transport document must not indicate that the goods are or will be loaded on deck. A clause on a transport document stating that the goods may be loaded on deck is acceptable.

a. 运输单据不得表明货物装于或者将装于舱面。声明货物可能被装于舱面的运输单据条款可以接受。

b. A transport document bearing a clause such as "shipper's load and count" and "said by shipper to contain" is acceptable.

b. 载有诸如"托运人装载和计数"或"内容据托运人报称"条款的运输单据可以接受。

c. A transport document may bear a reference, by stamp or otherwise, to charges additional to the freight.

c. 运输单据上可以以印戳或其他方式提及运费之外的费用。

Article 27　Clean Transport Document
第二十七条　清洁运输单据

A bank will only accept a clean transport document. A clean transport document is one bearing no clause or notation expressly declaring a defective condition of the goods or their packaging. The word "clean" need not appear on a transport document, even if a credit has a requirement for that transport document to be "clean on board".

银行只接受清洁运输单据。清洁运输单据指未载有明确宣称货物或包装有缺陷的条款或批注的运输单据。"清洁"一词并不需要在运输单据上出现，即使信用证要求运输单据为"清洁已装船"的。

Article 28　Insurance Document and Coverage
第二十八条　保险单据及保险范围

a. An insurance document, such as an insurance policy, an insurance certificate or a declaration under an open cover, must appear to be issued and signed by an insurance company, an underwriter or their agents or their proxies.

a. 保险单据，例如保险单或预约保险项下的保险证明书或者声明书，必须看似由保险公司或承保人或其代理人或代表出具并签署。

Any signature by an agent or proxy must indicate whether the agent or proxy has signed for or on behalf of the insurance company or underwriter.

代理人或代表的签字必须标明其系代表保险公司或承保人签字。

b. When the insurance document indicates that it has been issued in more than one original, all originals must be presented.

b. 如果保险单据表明其以多份正本出具，所有正本均须提交。

c. Cover notes will not be accepted.

c. 暂保单将不被接受。

d. An insurance policy is acceptable in lieu of an insurance certificate or a declaration under an open cover.

d. 可以接受保险单代替预约保险项下的保险证明书或声明书。

e. The date of the insurance document must be no later than the date of shipment, unless it appears from the insurance document that the cover is effective from a date not later than the date of shipment.

e. 保险单据日期不得晚于发运日期，除非保险单据表明保险责任不迟于发运日生效。

f.

i. The insurance document must indicate the amount of insurance coverage and be in the same currency as the credit.

f.

i. 保险单据必须表明投保金额并以与信用证相同的货币表示。

ii. A requirement in the credit for insurance coverage to be for a percentage of the value of the goods, of the invoice value or similar is deemed to be the minimum amount of coverage required.

ii. 信用证对于投保金额为货物价值、发票金额或类似金额的某一比例的要求，将被视为对最低保额的要求。

If there is no indication in the credit of the insurance coverage required, the amount of insurance coverage must be at least 110% of the CIF or CIP value of the goods.

如果信用证对投保金额未作规定，投保金额须至少为货物的 CIF 或 CIP 价格的 110%。

When the CIF or CIP value cannot be determined from the documents, the amount of insurance coverage must be calculated on the basis of the amount for which honour or negotiation is requested or the gross value of the goods as shown on the invoice, whichever is greater.

如果从单据中不能确定 CIF 或者 CIP 价格，投保金额必须基于要求承付或议付的金额，或者基于发票上显示的货物总值来计算，两者之中取金额较高者。

iii. The insurance document must indicate that risks are covered at least between the place of taking in charge or shipment and the place of discharge or final destination as stated in the credit.

iii. 保险单据须标明承包的风险区间至少涵盖从信用证规定的货物监管地或发运地开始到卸货地或最终目的地为止。

g. A credit should state the type of insurance required and, if any, the additional risks to be covered. An insurance document will be accepted without regard to any risks that are not covered if the credit uses imprecise terms such as "usual risks" or "customary risks".

g. 信用证应规定所需投保的险别及附加险（如有的话）。如果信用证使用诸如"通常风险"或"惯常风险"等含义不确切的用语，则无论是否有漏保之风险，保险单据将被照样接受。

h. When a credit requires insurance against "all risks" and an insurance document is presented containing any "all risks" notation or clause, whether or not bearing the heading "all risks", the insurance document will be accepted without regard to any risks stated to be excluded.

h. 当信用证规定投保"一切险"时，如保险单据载有任何"一切险"批注或条款，

235

无论是否有"一切险"标题，均将被接受，即使其声明任何风险除外。

i. An insurance document may contain reference to any exclusion clause.

i. 保险单据可以援引任何除外责任条款。

j. An insurance document may indicate that the cover is subject to a franchise or excess (deductible).

j. 保险单据可以注明受免赔率或免赔额（减除额）约束。

Article 29 Extension of Expiry Date or Last Day for Presentation
第二十九条 截止日或最迟交单日的顺延

a. If the expiry date of a credit or the last day for presentation falls on a day when the bank to which presentation is to be made is closed for reasons other than those referred to in article 36, the expiry date or the last day for presentation, as the case may be, will be extended to the first following banking day.

a. 如果信用证的截至日或最迟交单日适逢接受交单的银行非因第三十六条所述原因而歇业，则截止日或最迟交单日，视何者适用，将顺延至其重新开业的第一个银行工作日。

b. If presentation is made on the first following banking day, a nominated bank must provide the issuing bank or confirming bank with a statement on its covering schedule that the presentation was made within the time limits extended in accordance with sub-article 29 (a).

b. 如果在顺延后的第一个银行工作日交单，指定银行必须在其致开证行或保兑行的面涵中声明交单是在根据第二十九条 a 款顺延的期限内提交的。

c. The latest date for shipment will not be extended as a result of sub-article 29 (a).

c. 最迟发运日不因第二十九条 a 款规定的原因而顺延。

Article 30 Tolerance in Credit Amount, Quantity and Unit Prices
第三十条 信用证金额、数量与单价的增减幅度

a. The words "about" or "approximately" used in connection with the amount of the credit or the quantity or the unit price stated in the credit are to be construed as allowing a tolerance not to exceed 10% more or 10% less than the amount, the quantity or the unit price to which they refer.

a. "约"或"大约"用语信用证金额或信用证规定的数量或单价时，应解释为允许有关金额或数量或单价有不超过 10% 的增减幅度。

b. A tolerance not to exceed 5% more or 5% less than the quantity of the goods is allowed, provided the credit does not state the quantity in terms of a stipulated number of packing units or individual items and the total amount of the drawings does not exceed the amount of the credit.

b. 在信用证未以包装单位件数或货物自身件数的方式规定货物数量时，货物数量允许有 5% 的增减幅度，只要总支取金额不超过信用证金额。

c. Even when partial shipments are not allowed, a tolerance not to exceed 5% less than the amount of the credit is allowed, provided that the quantity of the goods, if stated in the credit, is shipped in full and a unit price, if stated in the credit, is not reduced or that sub-article 30（b）is not applicable. This tolerance does not apply when the credit stipulates a specific tolerance or uses the expressions referred to in sub-article 30（a）.

c. 如果信用证规定了货物数量，而该数量已全部发运，及如果信用证规定了单价，而该单价又未降低，或当第三十条 b 款不适用时，则即使不允许部分装运，也允许支取的金额有 5% 的减幅。若信用证规定有特定的增减幅度或使用第三十条 a 款提到的用语限定数量，则该减幅不适用。

Article 31 Partial Drawings or Shipments
第三十一条 分批支款或分批装运

a. Partial drawings or shipments are allowed.

a. 允许分批支款或分批装运

b. A presentation consisting of more than one set of transport documents evidencing shipment commencing on the same means of conveyance and for the same journey, provided they indicate the same destination, will not be regarded as covering a partial shipment, even if they indicate different dates of shipment or different ports of loading, places of taking in charge or dispatch. If the presentation consists of more than one set of transport documents, the latest date of shipment as evidenced on any of the sets of transport documents will be regarded as the date of shipment.

b. 表明使用同一运输工具并经由同次航程运输的数套运输单据在同一次提交时，只要显示相同目的地，将不视为部分发运，即使运输单据上标明的发运日期不通或装卸港、接管地或发送地点不同。如果交单由数套运输单据构成，其中最晚的一个发运日将被视为发运日。

A presentation consisting of one or more sets of transport documents evidencing shipment on more than one means of conveyance within the same mode of transport will be regarded as covering a partial shipment, even if the means of conveyance leave on the same day for the same destination.

含有一套或数套运输单据的交单，如果表明在同一种运输方式下经由数件运输工具运输，即使运输工具在同一天出发运往同一目的地，仍将被视为部分发运。

c. A presentation consisting of more than one courier receipt, post receipt or certificate of posting will not be regarded as a partial shipment if the courier receipts, post receipts or certificates of posting appear to have been stamped or signed by the same courier or postal service at the same place and date and for the same destination.

c. 含有一份以上快递收据、邮政收据或投邮证明的交单，如果单据看似由同一块地或邮政机构在同一地点和日期加盖印戳或签字并且表明同一目的地，将不视为部分发运。

Article 32 Instalment Drawings or Shipments
第三十二条 分期支款或分期装运

If a drawing or shipment by instalments within given periods is stipulated in the credit and any instalment is not drawn or shipped within the period allowed for that instalment, the credit ceases to be available for that and any subsequent instalment.

如信用证规定在指定的时间段内分期支款或分期发运，任何一期未按信用证规定期限支取或发运时，信用证对该期及以后各期均告失效。

Article 33　Hours of Presentation
第三十三条　交单时间

A bank has no obligation to accept a presentation outside of its banking hours.

银行在其营业时间外无接受交单的义务。

Article 34　Disclaimer on Effectiveness of Documents
第三十四条　关于单据有效性的免责

A bank assumes no liability or responsibility for the form, sufficiency, accuracy, genuineness, falsification or legal effect of any document, or for the general or particular conditions stipulated in a document or superimposed thereon; nor does it assume any liability or responsibility for the description, quantity, weight, quality, condition, packing, delivery, value or existence of the goods, services or other performance represented by any document, or for the good faith or acts or omissions, solvency, performance or standing of the consignor, the carrier, the forwarder, the consignee or the insurer of the goods or any other person.

银行对任何单据的形式、充分性、准确性、内容真实性、虚假性或法律效力，或对单据中规定或添加的一般或特殊条件，概不负责；银行对任何单据所代表的货物、服务或其他履约行为的描述、数量、重量、品质、状况、包装、交付、价值或其存在与否，或对发货人、承运人、货运代理人、收货人、货物的保险人或其他任何人的诚信与否，作为或不作为、清偿能力、履约或资信状况，也概不负责。

Article 35　Disclaimer on Transmission and Translation
第三十五条　关于信息传递和翻译的免责

A bank assumes no liability or responsibility for the consequences arising out of delay, loss in transit, mutilation or other errors arising in the transmission of any messages or delivery of letters or documents, when such messages, letters or documents are transmitted or sent according to the requirements stated in the credit, or when the bank may have taken the initiative in the choice of the delivery service in the absence of such instructions in the credit.

当报文、信件或单据按照信用证的要求传输或发送时，或当信用证未作指示，银行自行选择传送服务时，银行对报文传输或信件或单据的递送过程中发生的延误、中途遗失、残缺或其他错误产生的后果，概不负责。

If a nominated bank determines that a presentation is complying and forwards the documents to the issuing bank or confirming bank, whether or not the nominated bank has honoured or negotiated, an issuing bank or confirming bank must honour or negotiate, or reimburse that nominated bank, even when the documents have been lost in transit between the nominated bank and the issuing bank or confirming bank, or between the confirming bank and the issuing bank.

如果指定银行确定交单相符并将单据发往开证行或保兑行。无论指定的银行是否已经承付或议付，开证行或保兑行必须承付或议付，或偿付指定银行，即使单据在指定银行送往开证行或保兑行的途中，或保兑行送往开证行的途中丢失。

A bank assumes no liability or responsibility for errors in translation or interpretation of technical terms and may transmit credit terms without translating them.

银行对技术术语的翻译或解释上的错误，不负责任，并可不加翻译地传送信用证条款。

Article 36　Force Majeure
第三十六条　不可抗力

A bank assumes no liability or responsibility for the consequences arising out of the interruption of its business by Acts of God, riots, civil commotions, insurrections, wars, acts of terrorism, or by any strikes or lockouts or any other causes beyond its control.

银行对由于天灾、暴动、骚乱、叛乱、战争、恐怖主义行为或任何罢工、停工或其无法控制的任何其他原因导致的营业中断的后果，概不负责。

A bank will not, upon resumption of its business, honour or negotiate under a credit that expired during such interruption of its business.

银行恢复营业时，对于在营业中断期间已逾期的信用证，不再进行承付或议付。

Article 37　Disclaimer for Acts of an Instructed Party
第三十七条　关于被指示方行为的免责

a.　A bank utilizing the services of another bank for the purpose of giving effect to the instructions of the applicant does so for the account and at the risk of the applicant.

a.　为了执行申请人的指示，银行利用其他银行的服务，其费用和风险由申请人承担。

b.　An issuing bank or advising bank assumes no liability or responsibility should the instructions it transmits to another bank not be carried out, even if it has taken the initiative in the choice of that other bank.

b.　即使银行自行选择了其他银行，如果发出指示未被执行，开证行或通知行对此亦不负责。

c.　A bank instructing another bank to perform services is liable for any commissions, fees, costs or expenses ("charges") incurred by that bank in connection with its instructions.

c.　指示另一银行提供服务的银行有责任负担被执释放因执行指示而发生的任何佣金、手续费、成本或开支（"费用"）。

If a credit states that charges are for the account of the beneficiary and charges cannot be collected or deducted from proceeds, the issuing bank remains liable for payment of charges.

如果信用证规定费用由受益人负担，而该费用未能收取或从信用证款项中扣除，开证行依然承担支付此费用的责任。

A credit or amendment should not stipulate that the advising to a beneficiary is conditional upon the receipt by the advising bank or second advising bank of its charges.

信用证或其修改不应规定向受益人的通知以通知行或第二通知行收到其费用为条件。

d. The applicant shall be bound by and liable to indemnify a bank against all obligations and responsibilities imposed by foreign laws and usages.

d. 外国法律和惯例加诸于银行的一切义务和责任，申请人应受其约束，并就此对银行负补偿之责。

Article 38　Transferable Credits
第三十八条　可转让信用证

a. A bank is under no obligation to transfer a credit except to the extent and in the manner expressly consented to by that bank.

a. 银行无办理转让信用证的义务，除非该银行明确同意其转让范围和转让方式。

b. For the purpose of this article：

b. 就本条款而言：

Transferable credit means a credit that specifically states it is "transferable". A transferable credit may be made available in whole or in part to another beneficiary ("second beneficiary") at the request of the beneficiary ("first beneficiary").

转让信用证意指明确表明其"可以转让"的信用证。根据受益人（"第一受益人"）的请求，转让信用证可以被全部或部分地转让给其他受益人（"第二受益人"）。

Transferring bank means a nominated bank that transfers the credit or, in a credit available with any bank, a bank that is specifically authorized by the issuing bank to transfer and that transfers the credit. An issuing bank may be a transferring bank.

转让银行意指办理信用证转让的被指定银行，或者，在适用于任何银行的信用证中，转让银行是由开证行特别授权并办理转让信用证的银行。开证行也可担任转让银行。

Transferred credit means a credit that has been made available by the transferring bank to a second beneficiary.

转让信用证意指经转让银行办理转让后可供第二受益人使用的信用证。

c. Unless otherwise agreed at the time of transfer, all charges (such as commissions, fees, costs or expenses) incurred in respect of a transfer must be paid by the first beneficiary.

c. 除非转让时另有约定，所有因办理转让而产生的费用（诸如佣金、手续费、成本或开支）必须由第一受益人支付。

d. A credit may be transferred in part to more than one second beneficiary provided partial drawings or shipments are allowed.

d. 倘若信用证允许分批支款或分批装运，信用证可以被部分地转让给一个以上的第二受益人。

A transferred credit cannot be transferred at the request of a second beneficiary to any subsequent beneficiary. The first beneficiary is not considered to be a subsequent beneficiary.

第二受益人不得要求将信用证转让给任何次序位居其后的其他受益人。第一受益人不属于此类其他受益人之列。

e. Any request for transfer must indicate if and under what conditions amendments may be advised to the second beneficiary. The transferred credit must clearly indicate those conditions.

e. 任何有关转让的申请必须者明是否以及在何种条件下可以将修改通知第二受益人。转让信用证必须明确指明这些条件。

f. If a credit is transferred to more than one second beneficiary, rejection of an amendment by one or more second beneficiary does not invalidate the acceptance by any other second beneficiary, with respect to which the transferred credit will be amended accordingly. For any second beneficiary that rejected the amendment, the transferred credit will remain unamended.

f. 如果信用证被转让给一个以上的第二受益人，其中一个或多个第二受益人拒绝接受某个信用证修改并不影响其他第二受益人接受修改。对于接受修改的第二受益人而言，信用证已做相应的修改；对于拒绝接受修改的第二受益人而言，该转让信用证仍未被修改。

g. The transferred credit must accurately reflect the terms and conditions of the credit, including confirmation, if any, with the exception of:

g. 转让信用证必须准确转载原证的条款及条件，包括保兑（如有），但下列项目除外：

——the amount of the credit,

——信用证金额，

——any unit price stated therein,

——信用证规定的任何单价，

——the expiry date,

——到期日，

——the period for presentation, or

——单据提示期限

——the latest shipment date or given period for shipment,

——最迟装运日期或规定的装运期间。

any or all of which may be reduced or curtailed.

以上任何一项或全部均可减少或缩短。

The percentage for which insurance cover must be effected may be increased to provide the amount of cover stipulated in the credit or these articles.

必须投保的保险金额的投保比例可以增加，以满足原信用证或本惯例规定的投保金额。

The name of the first beneficiary may be substituted for that of the applicant in the credit.

可以用第一受益人的名称替换原信用证中申请人的名称。

If the name of the applicant is specifically required by the credit to appear in any document other than the invoice, such requirement must be reflected in the transferred credit.

如果原信用证特别要求开证申请人名称应在除发票以外的任何单据中出现时，则转让信用证必须反映出该项要求。

h. The first beneficiary has the right to substitute its own invoice and draft, if any, for those of a second beneficiary for an amount not in excess of that stipulated in the credit, and upon such substitution the first beneficiary can draw under the credit for the difference, if any, between its invoice and the invoice of a second beneficiary.

h. 第一受益人有权以自己的发票和汇票（如有），替换第二受益人的发票和汇票（如有），其金额不得超过原信用证的金额。在如此办理单据替换时，第一受益人可在原信用证项下支取自己发票与第二受益人发票之间产生的差额（如有）。

i. If the first beneficiary is to present its own invoice and draft, if any, but fails to do so on first demand, or if the invoices presented by the first beneficiary create discrepancies that did not exist in the presentation made by the second beneficiary and the first beneficiary fails to correct them on first demand, the transferring bank has the right to present the documents as received from the second beneficiary to the issuing bank, without further responsibility to the first beneficiary.

i. 如果第一受益人应当提交其自己的发票和汇票（如有），但却未能在收到第一次要求时照办；或第一受益人提交的发票导致了第二受益人提示的单据中本不存在的不符点，而其未能在收到第一次要求时予以修正，则转让银行有权将其从第二受益人处收到的单据向开证行提示，并不再对第一受益人负责。

j. The first beneficiary may, in its request for transfer, indicate that honour or negotiation is to be effected to a second beneficiary at the place to which the credit has been transferred, up to and including the expiry date of the credit. This is without prejudice to the right of the first beneficiary in accordance with sub-article 38 (h).

j. 第一受益人可以在其提出转让申请时，表明可在信用证被转让的地点，在原信用证的到期日之前（包括到期日）向第二受益人予以兑付或议付。本条款并不损害第一受益人在第三十八条（h）款下的权利。

k. Presentation of documents by or on behalf of a second beneficiary must be made to the transferring bank.

k. 由第二受益人或代表第二受益人提交的单据必须向转让银行提示。

Article 39　Assignment of Proceeds
第三十九条　款项让渡

The fact that a credit is not stated to be transferable shall not affect the right of the beneficiary to assign any proceeds to which it may be or may become entitled under the credit, in accordance with the provisions of applicable law. This article relates only to the assignment of proceeds and not to the assignment of the right to perform under the credit.

信用证未表明可转让，并不影响受益人根据所适用的法律规定，将其在该信用证项下有权获得的款项让渡与他人的权利。本条款所涉及的仅是款项的让渡，而不是信用证项下执行权力的让渡。